Северный Ледовитый океан

Берингово море

КАМЧАТКА

Маґадан •

Охотское море

СИБИРЬ

Лена

О. САХАЛИН

ФЕДЕРАЦИЯ

АЯ

Хабаровск •

озеро Байкал

ск

Иркутск

Владивосток •

ДАЛЬНИЙ ВОСТОК

Голоса

A Basic Course in Russian

BOOK 1

RICHARD ROBIN

The George Washington University

JOANNA ROBIN

The George Washington University

KATHRYN HENRY

University of Iowa

Prentice Hall
Englewood Cliffs, New Jersey 07632

Library of Congress Cataloging-in-Publication Data

ROBIN, RICHARD M.
     Golosa: a beginning Russian course. Book 1 and 2 / Richard
Robin, Kathryn Henry, Joanna Robin.
     ISBN 0-13-257429-2
1. Russian language--Textbooks for foreign speakers --English.
I. Henry, Kathryn. II. Robin, Joanna. III. Title.
PG2129.E5R63   1993
491.782'421--dc20

93-22993
CIP

Executive Editor: Steve Debow
Director of Development: Marian Wassner
Development and Project Editor: Tünde A. Dewey
Managing Editor, Production: Jan Stephan
Production Coordinator: Herb Klein
Editorial Assistant: Maria F. Garcia
Design Supervisor: Christine Gehring-Wolf
Cover Design: Nikita G. Pristouris
Illustrators: Mikhail Gipsov and Yelena Gipsov
Cover Photo: By Larry Fried/ Image Bank

 © 1994 by Prentice-Hall, Inc.
A Paramount Communications Company
Englewood Cliffs, New Jersey 07632

Printed in the United States of America
10 9 8 7 6 5 4 3 2 1

ISBN 0-13-257429-2

Prentice-Hall International (UK) Limited, *London*
Prentice-Hall of Australia Pty. Limited, *Sydney*
Prentice-Hall Canada Inc., *Toronto*
Prentice-Hall Hispanoamericana, S. A., *Mexico*
Prentice-Hall of India Private Limited, *New Delhi*
Prentice-Hall of Japan, Inc., *Tokyo*
Simon & Schuster Asia Pte. Ltd., *Singapore*
Editora Prentice-Hall do Brasil, Ltda., *Rio de Janeiro*

Быть—значит общаться диалогически.
Два голоса—минимум жизни, минимум бытия...

М. М. Бахтин

СОДЕРЖАНИЕ

SCOPE AND SEQUENCE

PREFACE

Голоса A Basic Course in Russian is a completely new introductory Russian-language program that strikes a true balance between communication and structure. It takes a contemporary approach to language learning by focusing on the development of functional competence in the four skills (listening, speaking, reading, and writing), as well as the expansion of cultural knowledge. It also provides a comprehensive explanation of Russian grammar along with the structural practice students need to build accuracy.

Голоса is divided into two books of ten units each. Each book is accompanied by a fully integrated Student Workbook and Laboratory Cassettes. The units are organized thematically, and each unit contains dialogs, texts, exercises, and other material designed to guide students to read, speak, and write about the topic, as well as to understand simple conversations. The systematic grammar explanations and exercises in *Голоса* enable students to develop a conceptual understanding and partial control of all basic Russian structures, including the declensions of nouns, adjectives, and pronouns; verb conjugations; and verbal aspect. This strong structural base enables students to accomplish the linguistic tasks in *Голоса* and prepares them for further study of the language.

Students successfully completing Books 1 and 2 of *Голоса* will be able to perform the following skill-related tasks.

Listening

- Understand simple face-to-face conversations about daily routine, home, family, school and work.

- Understand simple airport announcements, radio and television advertisements, and brief news items such as weather forecasts.

Speaking

- Use complete sentences to express immediate needs and interests.

- Hold a simple face-to-face conversation consisting of questions and answers with a Russian interlocutor about daily routine, home, family, school, and work. Discuss basic likes and dislikes in literature and the arts.

- Manage simple transactions in stores, post offices, hotels, dormitories, libraries, and so on.

Reading

- Read signs and public notices.

- Understand common printed advertisements and announcements.

- Understand simple personal and business correspondence.

- Get the gist and important details in brief articles of topical interest such as news reports on familiar topics, weather forecasts, and entries in reference books.

- Understand significant parts of longer articles on familiar topics and brief literary texts.

Writing

- Write short notes to Russian acquaintances, including invitations, thank-you notes, and simple directions.

- Write longer letters providing basic biographical information.

- Write simple compositions about daily routine, home, family, school, and work.

Culture

- Grasp the essentials of small-c culture necessary to behave appropriately in most everyday situations in Russian-speaking society.

- Control sociolinguistic aspects of Russian necessary for basic interaction, such as forms of address, greeting and leave-taking, giving and accepting compliments and invitations, and telephone etiquette.

- Become familiar with some of Russia's cultural heritage: famous writers and their works, as well as other figures in the arts.

Features of the *Голоса* program

- **Goals**
  Objectives are stated explicitly for each book and unit in terms of language tools (grammar and lexicon), skills, and cultural knowledge.

- **Focused attention to skill development**
  Each language skill (speaking, reading, writing, listening) is addressed in its own right. Abundant activities are provided to promote the development of competence and confidence in each skill area.

- **Flexibility**
  Голоса incorporates the best aspects of a variety of methods, as appropriate to the material. All skills are presented on an equal footing, but instructors may choose to focus on those that best serve their students' needs without violating the structural integrity of individual units or the program as a whole.

- **Authenticity**
  Each unit contains authentic materials and realistic communicative activities for all skills.

- **Spiraling approach**
  Students are exposed repeatedly to similar functions and structures at an increasing level of complexity. Vocabulary and structures are consistently and carefully recycled.

- **Cultural relevance**
  All texts and conversations are embedded within cultural content relevant to Russia and other states of the former Soviet Union today.

- **Learner-centered approach**
  Each unit places students into communicative settings to practice the four skills. In addition to core lexicon, students acquire personalized vocabulary to express individual needs.

- **Abundance and variety of exercise material**
  Oral drills and written exercises progress from mechanical to contextualized to personalized, open-ended activities. The wide variety in exercises and activities ensures that a range of learning styles is served.

- **Learning strategies**
  Students acquire strategies that help them develop both the productive and receptive skills. This problem-solving approach leads students to become independent and confident in using the language.

- **Phonetics and intonation**
  Pronunciation is fully integrated and practiced with the material in each unit rather than covered in isolation. Intonation training includes requests, commands, nouns of address, exclamations, and non-final pauses, in addition to declaratives and interrogatives.

Organization of the Student Texts

The *Голоса* package consists of three components: Textbooks, Student Workbooks, and Laboratory Cassettes. The course is divided into two books of ten units each. Every unit maintains the following organization.

Overview. The opening page of each unit provides a clear list of the communicative tasks the unit contains, of the grammatical material it introduces, and of the cultural knowledge it conveys.

ТОЧКА ОТСЧЁТА

О чём идёт речь? This warm-up section uses illustrations and simple contexts to introduce the unit vocabulary. A few simple activities provide practice of the new material, thereby preparing students for the taped **Разговоры,** which introduce the unit topics. Simple questions in English help students understand these introductory conversations. Students learn to grasp the gist of what they hear, rather than focus on every word.

Диалоги. Also recorded on cassette, these shorter versions of the preceding **Разговоры** provide the basic speech models for the new vocabulary and grammar of the unit. The accompanying exercises provide contextualized and personalized practice to activate the new material.

ЯЗЫК В ДЕЙСТВИИ

Давайте поговорим. This section is devoted to developing the conversational skills based on the **Диалоги.** Among these are the following:

- **Подготовка к разговору.** Students use lexical items from the **Диалоги** in short sentences with meaningful context.

- **Игровые ситуации.** Students perform role plays in which they use new vocabulary and structures in simple conversational situations.

- **Устный перевод.** Students provide face-to-face oral interpretation in situations based on the **Диалоги.**

Давайте почитаем. Authentic reading texts are supplemented with activities that direct students' attention to global content. Students learn strategies for guessing unfamiliar vocabulary from context and for getting information they might consider too difficult. The variety of text types included in **Давайте почитаем** ensures that students gain extensive practice with many kinds of reading material: official forms and documents; daily schedules; menus; shopping directories; maps; newspaper advertisements; TV and movie schedules; weather reports; classified ads; brief messages; newspaper articles; poetry; short stories. Verbal adjectives and adverbs are introduced and practiced in this section in Book 2.

Давайте послушаем. Guided activities teach students strategies for developing global listening skills. Questions in the Textbook accompany texts on the Laboratory Cassettes (scripts appear in the Instructor's Manual). Students learn to get the gist of and extract important information from what they hear, rather than trying to understand every word. They are exposed to a great variety of aural materials, including messages recorded on telephone answering machines; public announcements; weather reports; radio and TV advertisements; letters on cassette; brief speeches; conversations; interviews; news features and reports, poems.

В ПОМОЩЬ УЧАЩИМСЯ

This section contains grammatical presentations designed to encourage students to study the material at home. They feature clear, succint explanations, charts and tables for easy reference, and numerous examples. Important rules and tricky points are highlighted in special boxes. Simple exercises follow each grammar explanation, for use in class. Additional practice is provided by taped oral pattern drills and written exercises in the Student Workbook, for homework.

ОБЗОРНЫЕ УПРАЖНЕНИЯ

Located at the end of each unit, these activities present situations that call for students to integrate several skills. For example, students scan part of a newspaper to find out what weather to expect. Based on the weather report they then call to invite a friend to either a movie or a picnic. When they cannot get hold of the friend on the phone, they leave a note. Many writing exercises that fulfill real communicative needs are included in this section.

НОВЫЕ СЛОВА И ВЫРАЖЕНИЯ

The vocabulary list includes all new active words and expressions presented in the unit, and provides space for students to write in additional personalized vocabulary items.

ADDITIONAL COMPONENTS OF THE *ГОЛОСА* PROGRAM

Student Workbook

The fully integrated Student Workbook includes exercises on listening to numbers (**Числительные**) and pronunciation (**Фонетика и интонация**) with taped exercises involving imitation and cognitive activities such as marking intonation patterns, reduced vowels, and so on. **Устные упражнения** are oral pattern drills, recorded on tape. They are keyed numerically to the grammar presentations in the Textbook. **Письменные упражнения** are written exercises designed to be turned in as homework. They are numerically keyed to the grammar presentations in the Textbook. Mechanical, meaningful, communicative, and personalized exercises are included.

Laboratory Cassettes

Recorded on cassettes are the **Разговоры** (at normal conversational tempo for listening practice), **Диалоги** (at a slightly slower tempo to allow for easier perception and repetition), **Давайте послушаем** (authentic tempo), audio portions of the **Обзорные упражнения**, as well as activities from the Student Workbook: Practice listening to numbers, **Фонетика и интонация,** and **Устные упражнения** (oral pattern practice).

Acknowledgments

The authors would like especially to thank Irene Thompson of the George Washington University. It was her pioneering work in the methodology of teaching Russian that paved the way for this endeavor. But more than that, Professor Thompson has been a mentor to the three of us. Over the many years that she has known us, she has watched each of us grow. As work on this project progressed, she guided, challenged, cajoled, and inspired us. For the personal encouragement and the vision she provided, our debt to her is unrepayable, and our gratitude immense.

We would like to thank our reviewers, who helped in the initial stages of the manuscript.

David Andrews, Georgetown University
James Augerot, University of Wisconsin
Thomas R. Beyer, Jr., Middlebury Collge
Arna Bronstein, University of New Hampshire
Linda Bruce, University of Southern California
Patricia Chaput, Harvard University
Rasio Donatov, University of Illinois
Deborah Garretson, Dartmouth College
Robert Howerton, University of Illinois
Olga Kagan, University of California, Los Angeles
Michael Katz, University of Texas
Halimur Khan, Wayne State University
Maria Lunk, Emory University
Frank Miller, Columbia University
George Mitrevski, Auburn University
Natasha Pervukhin, University of Illinois
Marc Robinson, St. Olaf College
Karen Roblee, The Pennsylvania State University
Barry Scherr, Dartmouth College
Dorothy Soudakoff, Indiana University
Alice Speh, West Chester University
Carol Ueland, Rutgers University
Edward Vajda, Western Washington University
Fred Van Doren, Dickinson College
Anthony Vanchu, University of Texas
Ludmila Vergunova-Longan, University of Michigan

We are indebted to the following colleagues who diligently consulted with us throughout the development of the project:

William Comer, University of Kansas
Joseph Denny, University of Cincinnati
Olga Kagan, University of California, Los Angeles
Nathan Longan, Oakland University
Ben Rifkin, University of Wisconsin

We thank the following colleagues who read *Голоса* for linguistic accuracy:

Ludmila Guslistova, Marina Lukanov, Sergei Mikhailov, Yuri Olkhovsky, Valentina Umanets.

One of the key ingredients in the success of *Голоса* is the company of authentic voices on cassette. We gratefully acknowledge

Irina Bazer, Asya Feldman, Tatyana Gritsevich, Aleksandr Guslistov, Ludmila Guslistova, Isaac Kokotov, Anna Litman, Igor Litman, Sergei Petukhov, Viktor Ponomarev, Klara Shrayber, and Emily Urevich.

We would like to thank the staff at the Media Group in Washington, D.C.: Andrea Stelter, Gregor Hoffman, and Les Crandell.

We thank the Middlebury College Russian School for supporting this project by providing release time from teaching for Kathryn Henry during the summer of 1991.

We are grateful to our students at The George Washington University, the University of Iowa, the Middlebury College Russian School, and the University of Vermont, who used *Голоса* during its developmental stages and encouraged us with their enthusiastic responses.

We gratefully acknowledge the cooperation of our colleagues at The George Washington University, the University of Iowa, and the Middlebury College Russian School in field testing *Голоса:* Ludmila Guslistova, Virginia Javurek, Terry Krugman, Yuri Olkhovsky, Irene Thompson, and Justine Cotsoradis.

Finally, we would like to thank the Prentice Hall staff: Tünde Dewey (Development and Project Editor), who took the project from a raw manuscript until its final printed form; Maria Garcia (Project Assistant), who coordinated reviews, handled correspondence, and was always there when we needed her; Jan Stephan (Production Supervisor); Chris Wolf (Art Director, Interior Design, Cover Design); Herb Klein (Manufacturing); Marian Wassner (Director of Development, Foreign Languages); Roland Hernandez (Marketing); and Steve Debow (Acquisitions Editor), who brought us all together, pulled us all along, and without whose unflinching faith in the project and its authors, these materials would never have appeared.

CREDITS

Photos

Page 74   George Harrison/ Ron Galella; Whitney Houston/Globe Photos;
            Boris Becker/Ron Galella; Princess Diana/Ron Galella; Boris
            Yeltsin by Richard Open/Camera Press, Globe photos; Sophia
            Loren/Ron Galella; Midori by Satoru Ishikawa, Courtesy of the
            Midori Foundation

Page 215   GUM's Department Store, Russia/M. DiGiacomo/ The Image
            Bank

Pages 30   (The Czar's Bell), 43 (The Bronze Horseman), and
            283 (A. P. Chekhov) by Meg Van Arsdale

Pages 21, 93, 151, 157, 164, 179, 225, 255 (Market place), 265 by
            Richard Robin

Pages 1, 69, 121, 220 by Tünde A. Dewey

АЛФАВИТ

Точка отсчёта

---

1. Read the text silently as you listen to your teacher or the speaker on the tape. The sound of the Russian words and their context should help you understand their meaning. Looking at the words as you hear them pronounced will help you begin to associate the Russian letters and their sounds.

In 1990 **Эрик** became a **студент** at the University of Wisconsin in **Мадисон**. **Мадисон** is an interesting city in the **штат** of **Висконсин**. During winter break **Эрик** visited his **мама** and **папа** in the city of **Даллас** in the **штат** of **Техас**.

Almost every day during the first year when **Эрик** was in college, the news on **телевизор** and **радио** included at least one story on the **СССР**. **Горбачёв** had introduced new policies known as **гласность** and **перестройка**. The words **гласность** and **перестройка** were used so often on the news on **американский телевизор** and **радио** that they became part of the **английский** language. In school **Эрик** learned about previous Soviet leaders: **Ленин, Сталин, Хрущёв, Брежнев, Черненко, Андропов**.

Because of his interest in the **СССР**, **Эрик** travelled there in the summer of 1991. He went to three of the fifteen republics: **Россия, Эстония,** and **Грузия**. To prepare for his trip, he had to get a **паспорт** and **виза**. He flew from **Нью-Йорк** to **Москва**. While he was in **Москва** he met a woman named **Анна**. **Анна** spoke **английский язык** very well, which was good, because **Эрик** knew very little **русский язык**. **Анна** told **Эрик** that she was hoping to visit **Америка** the next year. She hoped to see **Нью-Йорк, Вашингтон, Филадельфия, Сан-Франциско, Лос-Анджелес,** and **Чикаго**. **Эрик** told her she should also try to visit his two favorite states: **Техас** and **Висконсин**. **Анна** asked **Эрик** many questions about **Америка** and answered his questions about the **СССР**.

The second day **Эрик** was in **Москва,** he and **Анна** went to the **университет.** They discussed some of the subjects that both American and Soviet **студенты** study: **математика, биология, химия, история, русский язык, английский язык, французский язык, русская литература,** and **английская литература. Эрик** was surprised to learn that Soviet university **студенты** decide their major before they begin the **университет.** He decided he would learn more about the **СССР** when he returned to **Мадисон.**

Эрик returned to the **США** in late **июль.** In **август** there was a **путч** in the **СССР**—some hardline **коммунисты** tried to oust **Горбачёв** from office. **Эрик** along with many other **американцы** and people from all over the world watched **телевизор** for reports of the actions in **Москва** and other Soviet cities.

When **Эрик** returned to **Висконсинский университет** in **Мадисон** he rearranged his schedule so he could take a class on **русский язык.** By the end of the semester, the **СССР** had disintegrated. The Baltic **республики (Эстония, Латвия, Литва)** had become independent. Eleven of the twelve other **республики** of the former **СССР (Армения, Азербайджан, Беларусь, Казахстан, Кыргистан, Молдова, Россия, Таджикистан, Туркменистан, Узбекистан, Украина)** declared themselves the Commonwealth of Independent States **(СНГ). Эрик** decided to focus his studies on **Россия.** In the spring semester he continued his study of **русский язык** and signed up for courses on **русская история, русская литература,** and **политология** in order to learn more about Russian culture and politics. He began to consider a career as a **профессор** or a **журналист.**

2. Go over the text one or two more times. Can you say some of the Russian words *before* they are pronounced by your teacher or the speaker on the tape?

3. The text contains some basic information on Soviet history and politics and on the Russian educational system. In a small group, list 5 things about Russian culture and Russian history that prompted you to study the Russian language. Compare your list with the lists made by other groups.

4. With your teacher, discuss the changes that have taken place in Russian culture and politics since the putsch of 1991.

В ПОМОЩЬ УЧАЩИМСЯ

THE RUSSIAN ALPHABET IN ITS PRINTED FORM

After reading the text on pages 2-3 several times, you have already begun to recognize some Russian words and to note the correspondence between Russian letters and their sounds. Once you learn the alphabet and a few pronunciation rules, you will be able to recognize many familiar words.

The Russian alphabet contains 33 characters: 10 vowel letters, 21 consonant letters, and 2 signs. Most Russian letters represent only one or two sounds. And in their printed form, the capital and the lower case of most Russian letters look alike.

Some Russian letters look and sound somewhat like their English counterparts:

Consonants

Letter		*Approximate pronunciation*
K	к	like **k** in skit
M	м	like **m** in mother
C	c	like **s** in sail—(*never like **k***)
T	т	like **t** in stay, but tongue against upper teeth

Vowels

Letter		*Approximate pronunciation*
A	a	when stressed, like **a** in father
O	o	when stressed, between the **o** in mole and the vowel sound in talk

Imitate the speaker's pronunciation of the following words.

маска	(something you might wear to a costume party)
мама	(even adult Russians use this word)
тост	(something you might propose at a party)
кот	(=*cat*)
Том	(a man's first name)
Кто?	(=*Who?*)

Some Russian letters look like Greek letters, which you may recognize from their use in mathematics or by some student organizations:

Letter		*Approximate pronunciation*
Г	г	like **g** in gamma
Д	д	like **d** in delta, but with tongue against upper teeth
Л	л	like **l** in lambda, but tongue against upper teeth
П	п	like **p** in spot (looks like Greek pi)
Р	р	flap **r**, similar to trilled **r** in Spanish; similar to **tt** in better and butter (looks like Greek *rho*)
Ф	ф	like **f** in fun (looks like Greek *phi)*
Х	х	like **ch** in Loch Ness (looks like Greek *chi*)

Imitate the speaker's pronunciation of the following words:

глаго́л	(=*verb*)
го́лос	(=*voice*)
голоса́	(=*voices*)
да	(what Russians say to agree)
Да́ллас	(a U.S. city)
дом	(=*building, house*)
ла́мпа	(you turn this on to read at night)
па́па	(even adult Russians use this word)
па́спорт	(a document to travel to another country)
фо́то	(=*photo*)
фотоаппара́т	(the instrument you use to take pictures)
фото́граф	(=*photographer*)
ха́ос	(=*chaos*)
ха-ха-ха	(the noise made when one laughs)
хор	(=*choir*)
Оклахо́ма	(a U.S. state)

Here are four Russian letters that look but do not sound like English letters:

Consonants

Letter		Approximate pronunciation
В	в	like **v** in volcano
Н	н	like **n** in no, but tongue against upper teeth

Vowels

Letter		Approximate pronunciation
Е	е	when stressed, like **ye** in yesterday
У	у	like **oo** in shoot, but with extreme lip rounding

Imitate the speaker's pronunciation of the following words:

вода́	(=*water*)
вор	(=*thief*)
Москва́	(a large city)
Ве́ра	(a woman's name)
Анна	(a woman's name)
но́та	(=*a musical note*)
до́нор	(someone who gives blood)
нога́	(=*leg*)
нет	(what Russians say to disagree)
Где?	(=*Where?*)
кларне́т	(a musical instrument)
профе́ссор	(a profession)
студе́нт	(someone who studies at a college, university, or institute)
Ура́!	(a cheer)
а́вгуст	(the name of a month)

A Note on Stress Marks

Stress marks are not written on capital letters, such as the first letter in the name **Анна** in the list above. If a word begins with a capital letter and no other vowel in the word has a stress mark, the stress is on the initial, capital letter.

When the letter **е** is not stressed, it is pronounced like the **i** in trick, as in the Russian name of *Texas*–**Теха́с.** More information on vowel reduction is given on pp. 13-15.

Four more Russian consonants are introduced below. Note that **Б б** has a different shape for its upper and lower case forms.

Letter		*Approximate pronunciation*
З	з	like **z** in zebra
Б	б	like **b** in boy
Й	й	like **y** in boy or grey
Ж	ж	like **s** in measure, but with tongue further back

Imitate the speaker's pronunciation of the following words:

Канза́с	(a U.S. state)
Арканза́с	(a U.S. state)
Бо́стон	(a U.S. city)
Небра́ска	(a U.S. state)
бана́н	(a type of fruit)
зе́бра	(an animal)
тромбо́н	(a musical instrument)
перестро́йка	(a policy introduced by Gorbachev)
фле́йта	(a musical instrument)
Толсто́й	(a 19th-century Russian author)
Ога́йо	(a U.S. state)
Айдахо	(a U.S. state)
Айо́ва	(a U.S. state)
Род-Айленд	(a U.S. state)
журна́л	(=*magazine, journal*)
Бре́жнев	(a former leader of the USSR)
Лос-Анджелес	(a U.S. city)

Here are two more vowel letters and the last four Russian consonants:

Consonants

Letter		*Approximate pronunciation*
Ц	ц	like **ts** in cats
Ч	ч	like **ch** in cheer
Ш	ш	like **sh** sound in sure, but with tongue further back
Щ	щ	like long **sh** sound in fresh sherbet, but with tongue further forward

Vowels

Letter		*Approximate pronunciation*
И	и	usually like **i** in machine after letters **ж, ш, ц,** like **ы** (see p. 9)
Ё	ё	like **yo** in New York; always stressed

 Imitate the speaker's pronunciation of the following words:

Цинцинна́ти	(a U.S. city)
Сан-Франци́ско	(a U.S. city)
Цвета́ева	(a Russian poet)
Достое́вский	(a 19th-century Russian author)
Тро́цкий	(a Russian political figure)
Чика́го	(a U.S. city)
Черне́нко	(a former Soviet leader)
Горбачёв	(the last president of the USSR)
Чёрное мо́ре	(= *The Black Sea*)
путч	(=*putsch, coup*)
штат	(the U.S. has 50 of these)
Вашингто́н	(the capital of the following country)
США	(the country of which the previous city is the capital)
Пу́шкин	(the father of Russian literature)
маши́на	(=*car*)
шокола́д	(something to eat for dessert)
Хрущёв	(a former Soviet leader)
щено́к	(=*puppy*)

A Note on Stress

Since the letter ё is *always* stressed, no stress mark is written on words containing it. Authentic Russian texts (those prepared by and for native speakers) normally omit the two dots over this letter, making it indistinguishable from e. In this textbook the ё is written ё in all words that you may be asked to pronounce (e.g., dialogs, word lists, and tables); it is written e in texts that are included strictly for reading purposes (e.g., copies of Russian maps, calendars, newspaper articles).

The last four Russian vowel letters are given below:

Letter		**Approximate pronunciation**
	ы	between the **a** in about and the **ee** in see
Э	э	like **e** in set
Ю	ю	like **yu** in yule
Я	я	when stressed, like **ya** in yacht

Imitate the speaker's pronunciation of the following words:

америка́нцы	(=*Americans*)
студе́нты	(people who study at a college, university, or institute)
Соединённые	(the full Russian name of the **США**)
Шта́ты Аме́рики	
сын	(=*son*)
Э́рик	(a man's name)
Кто э́то?	(=*Who is that?*)
Что э́то?	(=*What is that?*)
Ю́та	(a U.S. state)
ю́бка	(=*skirt*)
Ю́жная Кароли́на	(a U.S. state: South …)
юри́ст	(=*lawyer*)
я	(=*I*)
я́блоко	(=*apple*)
я́года	(=*berry*)
я́щик	(=*drawer*)

The Russian alphabet also includes the following two symbols, which represent no sound in and of themselves:

ь	(мя́гкий знак)	soft sign—indicates that the preceding consonant is palatalized; before a vowel it also indicates a full [y] sound between the consonant and vowel.
ъ	(твёрдый знак)	hard sign—rarely used in contemporary language—indicates [y] sound between consonant and vowel.

The soft sign and hard sign are discussed in the next section, "Palatalization."

➤ Complete the reading exercise on the next page and Exercises 1–8 in the Workbook.

Упражнение

Read the text to find answers to the questions. You will not know all the words, but try to answer the questions anyway.

> Здравствуйте! Меня зовут Вадим Иванович Петров. Я русский, из Санкт-Петербурга. Теперь живу в Москве, работаю профессором в Московском Государственном Университете.

1. What is the person's first name?
   ___ Boris ___ Vadim ___ Peter

2. What is his nationality?
   ___ Russian ___ American ___ Peruvian

3. Where is he from?
   ___ Yalta ___ St. Petersburg ___ Petrov

4. What is his profession?
   ___ Professor ___ Engineer ___ Chemist

5. Where does he work?
   ___ Institute ___ Laboratory ___ University

PALATALIZATION: "HARD" vs. "SOFT" CONSONANTS

The Russian Sound System

Most of the Russian consonant letters represent two different sounds each: one sound that is pronounced with the tongue raised high and forward in the mouth, and another that is pronounced with the tongue low and back in the mouth. Those consonant sounds produced with the tongue close to the roof of the mouth, or palate, are called "palatalized" or "soft." The consonant sounds made with the tongue low in the mouth are called "nonpalatalized" or "hard." The difference between hard and soft consonants plays a fundamental role in the structure of the Russian language.

The pronunciation of four English words will help to illustrate the difference between **palatalized** (soft) and **nonpalatalized** (hard) consonants:

NONPALATALIZED (HARD) CONSONANT (tongue low and back in mouth)	PALATALIZED (SOFT) CONSONANT (tongue high and forward in mouth)
moo **n**ut	**m**usic o**n**ion

In the English words *music* and *onion* there is a **y** sound immediately following the **m** and (first) **n**. The Russian palatalized **м** and **н** are similar to the English sounds noted in the words *music* and *onion*, except that in Russian the **y** is produced together with, rather than after, the base consonant sound.

If you are a native speaker of English, it will probably take some time before you are able to distinguish between hard and soft consonant sounds the way native speakers of Russian do, and before you are able to produce these sounds accurately. The following units will give you many opportunities to work on this, and other, aspects of the Russian sound system, so do not be too concerned if you do not hear the differences now.

It is, however, very important that you understand the following concepts of hard and soft consonants.

The Russian Writing System

In the writing system the letter written *after* a consonant indicates whether the consonant is hard or soft, as shown in the following chart:

Ø*	а	э	о	у	ы	indicate that the preceding consonant is hard.
ь	я	е	ё	ю	и	indicate that the preceding consonant is soft.

* In grammar tables in this book, the sign Ø indicates that no vowel follows the consonant; it is the last letter in the word.

The soft sign **ь** (**мягкий знак** in Russian) is used to indicate that the preceding consonant is soft (palatalized). You know one Russian word with **ь**: **гла́сность.**

Imitate the pronunciation of the following Russian words with **ь**:

гла́сность	(policy of openness introduced by Gorbachev)
Филаде́льфия	(a U.S. city)
Тайва́нь	(an Asian country)
фильм	(you can watch these at a theater or on television)
Ольга Ко́рбут	(a famous gymnast)

You have learned that the Russian vowel letters **я, е, ё,** and **ю** represent the sounds **ya, ye, yo,** and **yu,** respectively. When these letters are written after a consonant, the **y** sound becomes embedded in the consonant, that is, the consonant becomes soft. The Russian vowel letter **и**, although it does not begin with a **y** sound when it is pronounced alone, also makes a preceding consonant soft.

The Russian vowel letters **а, э, о, у** and **ы** represent the same vowel sounds as their counterparts but without the initial **y** sound.

Imitate the pronunciation of the following words:

Hard Consonants

ма́ма	(you know this word)
Кэ́трин	(a woman's name)
по́сле	(=*after*)
му́зыка	(something to listen to)
журна́лы	(=*magazines*)

Soft Consonants

мя́со	(=*meat*)
кекс	(=*fruitcake*)
пёс	(=*dog, hound*)
мю́зик-хо́лл	(a place to listen to **му́зыка**)
портфе́ли	(=*briefcases*)

Summary

- Soft consonants are pronounced with the tongue close to the roof of the mouth, as if a **y** were embedded in the consonant.

- When a consonant letter is followed by **ь, я, е, ё, ю,** or **и**, it is pronounced soft. Otherwise it is pronounced hard.

When **ь** is followed by a soft-series vowel letter (for example: **Нью-Йо́рк**), there is a **y** sound between the soft consonant and the vowel sound. The same thing is true of words with **ъ**.

➤ Complete Exercise 9 in the Workbook.

VOWEL REDUCTION

You have seen and heard several examples of Russian vowel reduction, the regular changes in certain vowel sounds depending on whether the vowel is stressed. The basic rules for the pronunciation of the vowel letters **о, а, я,** and **е** are presented below. There is no need to discuss vowel reduction for the other Russian vowel letters, because **ё** is always stressed, and the pronunciation of the vowel letters **э, у, ю, ы,** and **и** changes only very slightly when these vowels are unstressed.

The pronunciation of the letter о

IN STRESSED SYLLABLE	IN UNSTRESSED SYLLABLES
[o]	[a] if first letter in word [a] in syllable immediately before stress [ə] elsewhere

The letter **о** is pronounced as [o] *only when it is stressed*.

When it is not stressed, the letter **о** is "reduced" and pronounced like the **a** in *mama* or the **a** in *about,* depending on the position in the word.

Imitate the pronunciation of the following words:

о ➡ [o] *only if stressed*

перестро́йка   **Нью-Йо́рк**   **Ольга**   **Эсто́ния**

о ➡ [a] *in syllable just before stress*

Росси́я   **Москва́**

о ➡ [ə] *in any other unstressed position*

гла́сность   **телеви́зор** (*after stress*)
Горбачёв   **конститу́ция** (*more than one syllable before stress*)

The following words have **о** in more than one position. Imitate their pronunciation:

политоло́гия   **шокола́д**
профе́ссор   **хорошо́** (=*good, well*)
го́лос (= *voice*)   **голоса́** (=*voices*)

Pronunciation of the letter a

IN STRESSED SYLLABLE	IN UNSTRESSED SYLLABLES
[a]	[a] in syllable immediately before stress [ə] elsewhere

The letter **a** is pronounced [a] like the **a** in *father* only in the stressed syllable and in the syllable immediately preceding the stress (although the pronunciation is a bit more lax in the unstressed syllable). In other unstressed syllables it is pronounced [ə], like the **a** in *about*.

Imitate the pronunciation of the following words:

a ➡ [a] *in stressed syllable and in syllable immediately preceding stress*

штат	Англия
маши́на	Андро́пов

a ➡ [ə] *elsewhere*

ю́бка (=*skirt*)
Ю́жная Кароли́на (a U.S. state)

The following words have **a** in more than one position. Imitate their pronunciation:

ма́ма   па́па   Анна   америка́нцы

Pronunciation of the letter я

IN STRESSED SYLLABLE	IN UNSTRESSED SYLLABLES
[ya]	[yə] if last letter in a word [yɪ] elsewhere

The letter **я** is pronounced [ya] *only when stressed*. If an unstressed **я** is the last letter in a word, it is pronounced [yə]. In all other unstressed syllables, **я** is pronounced [yɪ].

If the **я** is written after a consonant, the [y] sound will be embedded in the consonant. See the discussion of palatalization.

🔊 Imitate the pronunciation of the following words:

я ➡ [ya] *in stressed syllable*
я (=*I*)
я́блоко (= *an apple*)

я ➡ [yə] *if unstressed and last letter in word*

исто́рия	хи́мия	политоло́гия	биоло́гия
А́нглия	Фра́нция	Испа́ния	Португа́лия

я ➡ [yɪ] *elsewhere*
язы́к (=*language*)
мясно́й (=*meat*)

Pronunciation of the letter e

IN STRESSED SYLLABLE	IN UNSTRESSED SYLLABLES
[ye]	[yɪ]

The letter **e** is pronounced [ye] only when stressed. In unstressed syllables, **e** is pronounced [yɪ].

If the **e** is written after a consonant, the **y** sound will be embedded in the consonant. See the discussion of palatalization.

🔊 Imitate the pronunciation of the following words:

e ➡ [ye] *in stressed syllable*
профе́ссор
кларне́т

e ➡ [yɪ] *in unstressed syllable*
респу́блики
литерату́ра

The following words have **e** in more than one position. Imitate their pronunciation.

Черне́нко
Бре́жнев

ONE STRESS PER WORD

A Russian word normally has only one stressed syllable, no matter how long the word is. Imitate the Russian pronunciation of the following words, paying particular attention to the stress in the Russian word and trying to avoid the secondary stress that is common in English.

🔊 Imitate the pronunciation of the following words:

коммуни́сты	Вашингто́н	америка́нцы
журнали́ст	Филаде́льфия	университе́т

VOICED vs. VOICELESS CONSONANTS

Consonant sounds that involve movement of the vocal chords are called voiced. Those which do not involve movement of the vocal chords are called voiceless. The same distinction exists in Engish. For example: bat–pat where **b** is voiced and **p** is voiceless. Twelve of the Russian consonants can be arranged in voiced-voiceless pairs, as indicated in the table.

VOICED CONSONANTS	VOICELESS CONSONANTS
Б б	П п
В в	Ф ф
Г г	К к
Д д	Т т
Ж ж	Ш ш
З з	С с

DEVOICING OF CONSONANTS AT THE END OF WORDS

Voiced consonants that have voiceless partners are not pronounced at the end of Russian words. When one of these voiced consonants is written at the end of a word, it is *pronounced* like its voiceless partner.

🔊 Imitate the pronunciation of the following words:

We see:	We say:
зуб (=*tooth*)	зу(п)
Горбачёв	Горбачё(ф)
Санкт-Петербу́рг	Санкт-Петербу́р(к)
шокола́д	шокола́(т)
гара́ж	гара́(ш)
газ	га(с)

CONSONANT ASSIMILATION

When two paired consonant letters are next to each other, they will usually both be pronounced voiced or voiceless, depending on the quality of the second consonant letter. ("When two consonants go walking, the second one does the talking.")

Imitate the pronunciation of the following words:

We see:	We say:
Достое́вский	Достое́(ф)ский
во́дка	во́(т)ка
францу́зский	францу́(с)ский

ITALIC LETTERS

Although most italicized Russian letters look like their printed counterparts, some are quite different. They are given in this chart.

PRINTED LETTERS	ITALIC LETTERS
В в	*В в*
Г г	*Г г*
Д д	*Д д*
П п	*П п*
Т т	*Т т*

➤ Complete Exercise 10 in the Workbook.

CURSIVE LETTERS

1. The letters *л, м,* and *я* begin with hooks!
2. There are only two tall lower case script letters: *б* (б) and *в* (в).
3. **Мягкий знак (ь)** looks like a *small* six. **Твёрдый знак (ъ)** looks like a *small* six with a tail. Neither letter has anything in common with a script *ы*.
4. The letter **ы**, like **мягкий знак (ь)**, doesn't extend above the midline.
5. Do not confuse *м* (м) with *т* (т) or *з* (з) with *э* (э).
6. The letters *ш, и,* and *й* all terminate on the base line. Don't confuse these letters with the Engish *w* or *v*. The Russian letters connect from the bottom.
7. The letters connect as follows:

абвгдеёжзийклмнопрстуфхцчшщъыьэюя

➤ Complete Exercises 11–19 in the Workbook.

PRINTED LETTER	ITALIC LETTER	CURSIVE LETTER	COMMENTS
А а	*А а*	*А а*	
Б б	*Б б*	*Б б*	
В в	*В в*	*В в*	Note formation of lower case italic and cursive letters.
Г г	*Г г*	*Г г*	The lower case cursive letter must be rounded.
Д д	*Д д*	*Д д*	Note formation of lower case italic and cursive letters. Do not confuse lower case italic *д* with *б*.
Е е	*Е е*	*Е е*	
Ё ё	*Ё ё*	*Ё ё*	Authentic Russian texts often omit the two dots, making this letter indistinguishable from the one above.

PRINTED LETTER	ITALIC LETTER	CURSIVE LETTER	COMMENTS
Ж ж	*Ж ж*	*Ж ж*	
З з	*З з*	*З з*	Note indented back, to differentiate from **Э, э**.
И и	*И и*	*И и*	
Й й	*Й й*	*Й й*	This letter is a consonant; do not confuse it with **И, и**.
К к	*К к*	*К к*	Lower case cursive *к* does not extend above midline.
Л л	*Л л*	*Л л*	In cursive this letter always begins with a HOOK.
М м	*М м*	*М м*	In cursive this letter always begins with a HOOK.
Н н	*Н н*	*Н н*	
О о	*О о*	*О о*	
П п	*П п*	*П п*	Note the formation of the upper case cursive *П*.
Р р	*Р р*	*Р р*	Cursive letter not closed.
С с	*С с*	*С с*	
Т т	*Т т*	*Т т*	Note the formation of the upper case cursive *Т*. Lower case cursive *т* often has a line drawn over it.
У у	*У у*	*У у*	
Ф ф	*Ф ф*	*Ф ф*	
Х х	*Х х*	*Х х*	

PRINTED LETTER	ITALIC LETTER	CURSIVE LETTER	COMMENTS
Ц ц	*Ц ц*	*Ц ц*	Tail on *Ц ц* very short. Do not confuse *Ц ц* with *И и*.
Ч ч	*Ч ч*	*Ч ч*	Do not confuse *Ч* with *У* or *ч* with *г*.
Ш ш	*Ш ш*	*Ш ш*	Unlike English *W w*, this cursive letter cannot end on midline, but must end on baseline: *Ш ш*. Often a line is drawn under the lower case *ш*.
Щ щ	*Щ щ*	*Щ щ*	Tail on *Щ щ* very short.
ъ	*ъ*	*ъ*	Never begins a word.
ы	*ы*	*ы*	Never begins a word.
ь	*ь*	*ь*	Never begins a word.
Э э	*Э э*	*Э э*	Be sure to differentiate cursive *Э э* from cursive *З з*.
Ю ю	*Ю ю*	*Ю ю*	
Я я	*Я я*	*Я я*	In cursive this letter always begins with a HOOK.

УРОК 1

НЕМНОГО О СЕБЕ

▼ **КОММУНИКАТИВНЫЕ ЗАДАНИЯ**

Greeting people
Introducing and giving
    information about yourself
Asking for information about some-
    one else

▼ **В ПОМОЩЬ УЧАЩИМСЯ**

The pronouns **ты** and **вы**
Introduction to gender and case
в + prepositional case for location
Absence of the verb *to be* in
    Russian present tense sentences

Workbook: Numbers 1–10
            Intonation contour (IC–1)
            Unstressed **o** and **e**

▼ **МЕЖДУ ПРОЧИМ**

Russian names
Russian greeting habits
Changes in the former Soviet Union

ТОЧКА ОТСЧЁТА

О ЧЁМ ИДЁТ РЕЧЬ?

When greeting each other, Russians say:

Other greetings include:

Между прочим

Saying "Hello"? Russians greet each other only the first time they meet on a particular day. During subsequent encounters that day they usually just nod or make eye contact.

Physical contact. Russian men tend to shake hands each time they meet. If they haven't seen each other for a long time, they may embrace and kiss. Russian women often kiss and hug when they meet, and they frequently stroll along arm in arm.

A. How would you greet people at the following times of day?

9:00 am	3:00 pm	2:00 pm
10:00 am	7:00 pm	9:00 pm

B. Imagine that you want to get acquainted with someone. What is the first thing you would say in English? How would you introduce yourself? What would you say as you parted?

> Russians often initiate an introduction by saying **Дава́йте познако́мимся / Дава́й познако́мимся** (*Let's get acquainted*). Then they give their names and conclude by saying **Очень прия́тно** (*Nice to meet you*).

— Дава́йте познако́мимся.
— Ли́за.
— Алексе́й.
— Очень прия́тно.

Use the model above to practice getting acquainted with your classmates.

C. Match the noun referring to a man with the corresponding noun referring to a woman.

америка́нец	студе́нтка
кана́дец	бизнесме́нка
студе́нт	кана́дка
бизнесме́н	америка́нка

Which words would you use to describe yourself?

Я _____ .

Я _____ .

D. Разговóры. Read the following sets of questions. Then listen to the conversations, keeping these questions in mind. Listen as many times as you need.

> You will probably always be able to *understand* more Russian than you are able to speak. So, one part of each unit will be devoted to listening to conversations that practice the unit's topic. In the following conversations you will hear the way Russians greet each other and introduce themselves. You will not be able to understand everything you hear. In fact, you shouldn't even try. As soon as you have understood enough information to answer the questions, you have completed the assignment.

Разговóр 1: Давáйте познакóмимся!

1. What is the name of the male speaker?
2. What is the name of the female speaker?
3. What nationality is the woman?
4. Where is she from?
5. Where does the man go to school?

You will now hear two more conversations that resemble the one you just heard. Here are some suggestions on how to proceed:

- Read the questions first.
- Listen to the whole conversation to get the gist of it.
- Keeping the questions in mind, listen to the conversation again for more detail.
- If necessary, listen one more time to confirm your understanding of what is going on. Don't worry if you don't understand everything. (This cannot be overemphasized!)

Разговóр 2: Разрешúте предстáвиться.

1. What is the American's name?
2. What is the Russian's name?
3. What does she teach?
4. What American cities has the young man lived in?
5. Where does he go to school?

Разговóр 3: Вы канáдец?

1. What is the name of the male speaker?
2. What is the name of the female speaker?
3. What is the man's nationality?
4. Where is he from?
5. Where does the woman go to school?

ДИАЛОГИ

1 Здравствуйте! Давайте познакомимся!

— Здравствуйте! Давайте познакомимся. Меня зовут Ольга Александровна. А как вас зовут?
— Меня зовут Джейн. Очень приятно.
— Вы студентка, Джейн?
— Да, студентка. Я учусь в университете здесь, в Москве.
— А в Англии где вы учитесь?
— В Англии? Я живу и учусь в Лондоне.

2 Доброе утро!

— Доброе утро! Давай познакомимся. Меня зовут Вера. А как тебя зовут?
— Меня? Эван.
— Как ты сказал? Эванс?
— Эван. Это имя. А фамилия—Джонсон. Я американец.
— Очень приятно познакомиться!

3 Добрый день!

— Добрый день! Меня зовут Джейн Паркер. Я американка.
— Здравствуйте. Краснова Ольга Петровна. Вы студентка, Джейн?
— Да, студентка. Простите, как ваше отчество?
— Петровна.
— Очень приятно с вами познакомиться, Ольга Петровна.

4 Добрый вечер!

— Добрый вечер! Давай познакомимся. Валерий.
— Джим. Очень приятно.
— Ты канадец, да? Где ты живёшь в Канаде?
— Я живу и учусь в Квебеке.
— Значит, ты студент. Я тоже.
— Правда? А где ты учишься?
— Я живу и учусь здесь, в Иркутске.

A. Review the second dialog. What do you think the words **и́мя** and **фами́лия** mean? Go through the rest of the dialogs and determine which names qualify as **и́мя** and which as **фами́лия.**

B. Review the dialogs again. Then read through the following introduction sequences and fill in the blanks with the appropriate words and phrases.

1. An older member of a Russian delegation visiting your university wants to get acquainted with you:

— Здра́вствуйте. Дава́йте _____ . Меня́ _____
Белоу́сова Анна Никола́евна. А _____ _____ зову́т?

— Меня́? _____ .

— Очень _____ познако́миться.

2. A fellow student wants to get acquainted with you:

— До́брое _____ ! Дава́й _____ .
_____ зову́т Ма́ша. А как _____ зову́т?

— _____ зову́т _____ .

— Очень _____ _____ .

C. **Немно́го о себе́.** Prepare a short statement about yourself. First fill in the blanks with words that are relevant to you. Then introduce yourself to your classmates. Ask your teacher for any words you need that are not given. Refer to the *Alphabet* unit in the Workbook for names of cities and states.

Меня́ зову́т _____ . Моя́ фами́лия _____ .

Я _____ . Я _____ .
  студе́нт, студе́нтка,   америка́нец, америка́нка,
  бизнесме́н, бизнесме́нка   кана́дец, кана́дка, англича́нин,
                                 англича́нка

Я живу́ в _____ .
  Бо́стоне, Вашингто́не, Нью-Йо́рке, Чика́го, Лос-Анджелесе,
  Сан-Франци́ско, Торо́нто, Квебе́ке, Монреа́ле

Я живу́ в _____ .
  Миссу́ри, Иллино́йсе, Ога́йо, Нью-Йо́рке,
  Монта́не, Торо́нто, Квебе́ке, Монреа́ле

Я учу́сь в _____ .
  шко́ле, университе́те

Язык в действии

ДАВАЙТЕ ПОГОВОРИМ

A. **Подготóвка к разговóру**. Review the dialogs. How would you do the following?

- initiate an introduction
- say what your name is
- ask a person with whom you are on formal terms what his/her name is
- ask a person with whom you are on informal terms what his/her name is
- give your first and last name
- state your nationality
- indicate how pleased you are to meet someone
- tell where you live
- tell where you go to school
- ask for a person's patronymic (first name, last name)

B. Look at the pictures below. What do you think these people are saying? Working in pairs, develop a short dialog for each picture and present them in class.

1.

2.

3.

4.

C. **Игровы́е ситуа́ции.**

> This part of the unit gives you the opportunity to use the language you have learned. Read the role-play situations and consider what language and strategies you would use to deal with each one. Do not write out dialogs. Get together with a partner and practice the situations. Then act them out in class.

You are in Moscow:

1. Get acquainted with the following people. Tell them as much as you can about yourself and find out as much as you can about them.

   a. your new Russian teacher
   b. a student sitting next to you in the cafeteria
   c. a Russian friend's parents
   d. a young Russian at a party

2. It is your first day of class in Russia. Introduce yourself to the class. Say as much about yourself as you can.

3. Working with a partner, prepare and act out an introduction situation of your own design. Use what you know, not what you don't know.

D. **Устный перево́д.**

> Here is your chance to act as an interpreter for an English speaker and a Russian. The purpose is to give additional practice using the linguistic material you are learning. Try to express your client's ideas rather than translating every word.
>
> One student will play the role of the English speaker who knows no Russian. This person's script is given. Your instructor will play the role of the Russian. All students should prepare the interpreter's role by planning how they will express the English speaker's comments in Russian. If you play the interpreter, you will have to give the English version of the Russian's comments as well as the Russian version of the English speaker's comments; those playing the English and Russian speakers must pretend not to know the other language. If the interpreter runs into difficulty, he/she may ask a classmate to help out.

You are in Moscow. A friend who does not know Russian has asked you to help her get acquainted with someone at a party.

English speaker's part

1. Hello. I'd like to meet you. What's your name?
2. I didn't catch that. What did you say?
3. It's nice to meet you. My name is …
4. My last name is …
5. Is that so! I'm a student too.
6. Yes, I am an American.

ДАВАЙТЕ ПОЧИТАЕМ

In each unit you will read Russian documents and other texts to develop specific strategies for reading in Russian. Do not be surprised or frustrated if you do not know many of the words. First, read the initial questions in English, and then look through the Russian text trying to find answers to the questions. Read the Russian texts silently for the specific information asked for.

A. **Визи́тные ка́рточки.** Look through these cards and decide whom you would consult if you:

- need to find out about a video copyright. _____
- need a visa to Russia. _____
- want to do research on Russian literature. _____
- want to study Russian in Moscow. _____
- are interested in Russian research on the U.S. _____

1.
Колпаков Леонид Федорович
старший научный сотрудник
Институт русской литературы
им. А.М. Горького (ИМЛИ) АН СССР
г. Москва
ул. Воровского, 25
Тел.: 290-50-30

2.
СОКОЛОВ ВАДИМ МАКСИМОВИЧ
старший научный сотрудник
Института США и Канады
г. Москва.
Тел.: 290-58-75

3.
РОЗАНОВА АЛЕКСАНДРА
БОРИСОВНА
главный редактор
Гостелерадио СССР
г. Москва

4.
ЗИНЧУК ПАВЕЛ ИГНАТЬЕВИЧ
заведующий паспортно-визовой
группой Министерства иностранных дел
Российской Федерации
г. Москва
Мира, 49а   Тел.: 281-10-14

5.
НОВИКОВА НАДЕЖДА
СТЕПАНОВНА
заведующая учебной частью
Педагогический институт
иностранных языков
им. Мориса Тореза
г. Москва
Метростроевская, 38   Тел.: 245-02-10

Which of these cardholders are women? _____

CHANGES IN THE FORMER SOVIET UNION

You may notice some "old" names in the reading materials. **CCCP (Сою́з Сове́тских Социалисти́ческих Респу́блик)** disappeared from the map at the end of 1991. The disintegration of the USSR engendered scores of changes in nomenclature, both geographic and bureaucratic. Within a few months, cities, streets, universities, ministries, even entire republics had their names changed.

For example, **Ленингра́д,** cited in the visa application, has had its historic name returned; it's now called **Санкт-Петербу́рг**. The **Педагоги́ческий институ́т иностра́нных языко́в им. Мори́са Торе́за** is now the **Университе́т иностра́нных языко́в.** The abbreviation **РСФСР (Росси́йская Сове́тская Федерати́вная Социалисти́ческая Респу́блика)** was the official name for the Russian Republic when it was one of the fifteen Soviet republics. As an independent country it is now **Росси́йская Федера́ция** or just plain **Росси́я.** You will find texts from both the Soviet and post-Soviet eras in this book.

In fact, most of the street signs in Russia still carry the old names, and many people find it hard to break old habits and switch to the new names.

B. **Визова́я анке́та.** Read through the visa application. Find out the following information.

1. What is the person's name?
2. When was she born?
3. Why is she going to Russia?
4. What cities does she want to visit?
5. When will she arrive in Russia?
6. When will she leave?
7. What does she do for a living?
8. Where does she work?
9. Where does she live?
10. How long will she be in Russia?
11. What is the date of this visa application?
12. How do Russians write dates?

Страна _____ Консульство Российской Федерации в США

ВИЗОВАЯ АНКЕТА

Национальность _Русская_ _Американец_

Гражданство _США_ _США_

Фамилия _Сорокина_ _Пруэтт_

Имя, отчество _Наталья Николаевна_ _Андрей_

Дата и место рождения _14. 03. 51 Ленинград_ _17.08.76 Колумбус_

Цель поездки _туризм_

Маршрут следования _Москва, С.-Петербург, Москва_

Дата въезда _10. 03. 93_ Дата выезда _30. 03. 93_

Профессия _преподаватель русского языка_

Место работы _Нью-Йоркский университет_

Паспорт №·- _1534762_

Дата _23. 07. 92_

Личная подпись _Н. Сорокина_

В ПОМОЩЬ УЧАЩИМСЯ

1.1 FORMAL AND INFORMAL SPEECH SITUATIONS

Family members and friends use informal forms of address with each other: they call each other by first name and use the informal forms of the pronoun *you*—**ты.** Adults are normally on formal speech terms when they first meet: they may call each other by name and patronymic, and they use the formal forms of the pronoun *you*—**вы.**

Вы is also used whenever one addresses more than one person. You would say **Здра́вствуй!** to your close friend, and **Здра́вствуйте!** to two or more friends.

INFORMAL FORMS	FORMAL (AND PLURAL) FORMS
Здра́вствуй!	Здра́вствуй**те**!
Дава́й познако́мимся!	Дава́й**те** познако́мимся!
Ты америка́нец (америка́нка)?	**Вы** америка́нец (америка́нка)?
Как **тебя́** зову́т?	Как **вас** зову́т?
Как **ты** сказа́л(а)?	Как **вы** сказа́ли?
Где **ты** у́чишься?	Где **вы** у́читесь?
Где **ты** живёшь?	Где **вы** живёте?

Упражнения

1. How would you say hello to the following people?
   a. your new Russian teacher
   b. a four-year-old boy
   c. three little girls
   d. your next door neighbor

2. How would you ask the above people their names?

3. Working in pairs, decide whether you would address the people below with **ты** or with **вы.** Discuss your decision in class.

4. The following dialog takes place between people on formal terms (**вы**). Change it to one between people whose relationship is informal.

— Здра́вствуйте! Дава́йте познако́мимся. Меня́ зову́т Ольга. А как вас зову́т?
— Меня́ зову́т Джейн. Очень прия́тно.
— Вы студе́нтка, Джейн?
— Да, студе́нтка. Я учу́сь в университе́те здесь, в Москве́.
— А в Аме́рике где вы у́читесь?
— В Аме́рике? Я живу́ и учу́сь в Лос-Анджелесе.

1.2 RUSSIAN NAMES

Russians have three names: a first name (**и́мя**), a patronymic (**о́тчество**) and a last name (**фами́лия**).

1. ИМЯ. This is the given name, the name the parents select when a baby is born. Examples are **Михаи́л, Серге́й, Екатери́на,** and **Ната́лья.** Most names have one or more commonly used nicknames. **Екатери́на** for example, may be called **Ка́тя, Ка́тенька,** or **Катю́ша** by close friends and relatives.

2. ОТЧЕСТВО. The **о́тчество** is derived from the father's first name by adding a suffix to it (**-овна** for daughters, **-ович** for sons). It means "daughter of …" or "son of …" It is part of a Russian's full name as it appears in all documents.

When Russians reach their twenties, usually when they acquire some degree of status at work, they begin to be addressed by their **и́мя-о́тчество** in formal situations. Russians do not use titles such as Mr., Mrs., or Ms. The use of **и́мя-о́тчество** is the nearest equivalent. The **о́тчество** is used only with the full form of the **и́мя,** never with a nickname.

Foreigners do not have an **о́тчество.** Unless you are Russian, it is culturally inappropriate for you to introduce yourself using **и́мя-о́тчество.**

3. ФАМИЛИЯ. Russian last names are slightly different for males and females: the female form of the last name ends in **-а.** He is **Каре́нин;** she is **Каре́нина;** he is **Петро́в;** she is **Петро́ва.** Women may or may not take their husband's **фами́лия** when they get married.

Между прочим

Address your Russian friends by their first name (**и́мя**) or nickname. Address all other adults, especially your teacher, by their name and patronymic (**и́мя-о́тчество**). Find out their patronymics and use them.

Упражнение

5. Match the people on the left to their fathers on the right. Which part of the name helped you?

CHILD'S FULL NAME	FATHER'S FIRST NAME
Еле́на Ви́кторовна Гусли́стова	Ива́н
И́горь Петро́вич Ка́спин	Серге́й
Алексе́й Миха́йлович Ма́рков	Пётр
Мари́на Андре́евна Соловьёва	Андре́й
Ива́н Серге́евич Канды́бин	Михаи́л
Ната́лья Ива́новна Петро́ва	Ви́ктор

1.3   GENDER—INTRODUCTION

Я студе́нтка.
Зо́я Ива́новна Петро́ва.

Я студе́нт.
Евге́ний Ива́нович Петро́в.

You have already seen that Russian women's last names end in **-а**, whereas men's last names end in a consonant. The same is true of first names and patronymics, and of many words referring to profession and nationality. Sometimes the **a** sound at the end of the word is spelled **я**. All Russian nouns, including names, show gender. You'll learn more about this in Unit 2.

Между прочим

Although the full form of Russian first names for males ends in a consonant, many male nicknames end in **-а** or **-я**: **Михаи́л-Ми́ша; Дми́трий-Ди́ма; Пётр-Пе́тя; Па́вел-Па́ша; Бори́с-Бо́ря.**

Упражнения

6. Which of the following are men?
   - а. Григо́рий Анто́нович Бо́ский
   - б. Мари́я Петро́вна Петро́ва
   - в. Ната́лья Петро́вна Ивано́ва
   - г. Фёдор Ива́нович Гага́рин

7. Parts of the following list were smeared when it was carried through the rain. Help restore the names by filling in the missing letters. Note that in official Russian, the **фами́лия** comes first, followed by the **и́мя** and **о́тчество.** They are not separated by commas.

   Аста́фьев____ Мари́я Ива́новна

   За́йцев____ Ольга Макси́мовна

   Мона́хов____ Серге́й Миха́йлович

   Три́шин____ Вале́рий Петро́вич

   Усти́нов____ Алекса́ндра Андре́евна

8. Russian nicknames often resemble the corresponding full name. Match each full name in the left column with its appropriate nickname in the right column. One nickname can be used twice.

____ Алекса́ндра		а.	Са́ша
____ Мари́я		б.	Бо́ря
____ Екатери́на		в.	Ле́на
____ Бори́с		г.	Пе́тя
____ Еле́на		д.	Ка́тя
____ Алекса́ндр		е.	Ма́ша
____ Пётр			

   Which of the above are women's names?

➤ Complete Oral Drills 3–5 in the Workbook.

1.4 CASE

One way in which Russian differs from English is that Russian nouns, adjectives, and pronouns have endings that indicate their function in a sentence. Consider these two English sentences.

Mother loves Maria.   and   Maria loves Mother.

How can you tell which is the subject and which is the object in these sentences? The answer is quite obvious. In English, word order tells you which is which. In Russian, however, endings on nouns and adjectives identify their syntactic roles in sentences. For instance, the Russian sentences

Máма лю́бит Мари́ю.   and   **Мари́ю лю́бит ма́ма.**

both mean "Mother loves Maria."

This system of putting endings on nouns, adjectives, and pronouns is called the case system. Russian has six cases: nominative, accusative, genitive, prepositional, dative, and instrumental. In this lesson you will learn the forms and uses of two of these cases.

1.5 THE NOMINATIVE CASE

The nominative case is used for naming. Nouns and adjectives given in the dictionary are in the nominative case. The nominative case is used for:

1. The subject of the sentence.

   Джон—америка́нец.   *John* is an American.

2. The predicate complement in an equational sentence (any word that "is" the subject).

   Джон—**америка́нец.**   John is an *American*.

1.6 THE PREPOSITIONAL CASE—INTRODUCTION

Я живу́ **в** Аме́рик**е**.	I live in America.
Я живу́ **в** Нью-Йо́рк**е**.	I live in New York.
Я живу́ **в** Мичига́н**е**.	I live in Michigan.
Я живу́ **в** Калифо́рн**ии**.	I live in California.

When used with the preposition **в**, the prepositional case indicates location. A singular noun in the prepositional case has the ending **-е** or **-и**.

The chart below shows the forms of the prepositional case that you will need for the exercises in this unit.

NOMINATIVE CASE		PREPOSITIONAL CASE	
Вашингто́н	-Ø	в Вашингто́не	-е
Аме́рика	-a	в Аме́рике	
Калифо́рния	-ия	в Калифо́рнии	-ии
Сан-Франци́ско Цинцинна́ти *foreign word ending in* **-o** *or* **-и**		в Сан-Франци́ско в Цинцинна́ти *no change*	

To say "in an American state," you may put the word **штат** in the prepositional case and then keep the state name in the nominative:

Я живу́ **в** Нью-Йо́рк**е.**   Я живу́ **в** шта́т**е** Нью-Йо́рк.
Я живу́ **в** Мичига́н**е.**   Я живу́ **в** шта́т**е** Мичига́н.
Я живу́ **в** Калифо́рн**ии.**   Я живу́ **в** шта́т**е** Калифо́рния.

Упражнения

9. In the sentences below, indicate which words are in the nominative case (N) and which ones are in the prepositional case (P).

   Джон (…) — студе́нт. (…)
   Джон (…) — америка́нец. (…)
   Джон (…) у́чится в университе́те (…) в Бо́стоне. (…)
   Джон (…) живёт в Массачу́сетсе. (…)
   Бо́стон (…) в Массачу́сетсе. (…)

10. How would you say where the following people live (**живёт**) in Russian?

    John lives in Illinois. (Иллино́йс)
    Susan lives in Indiana. (Индиа́на)
    Mary lives in California. (Калифо́рния)
    Dennis lives in Colorado. (Колора́до)

11. If asked where they live, how would people from the following cities answer?

Вашингто́н, Квебе́к, Ло́ндон, Та́мпа, Сан-Дие́го, Филаде́льфия

12. Answer these questions with your own information.

Где вы живёте?
Где вы у́читесь?

➤ Complete Oral Drills 6–9 and Written Exercises 3-4 in the Workbook.

1.7 THE VERB *TO BE* IN RUSSIAN PRESENT TENSE SENTENCES

As you may have noticed, the verb *to be* and its forms *am, are, is* are absent in Russian in the present tense. In writing, a dash is often used in present tense sentences in which both the subject and the predicate are nouns.

Джон—студе́нт.   Я студе́нт.
Джейн—студе́нтка.   Я студе́нтка.

ОБЗОРНЫЕ УПРАЖНЕНИЯ

A. **Расписа́ние.** You just arrived in Moscow to study Russian. You have a list of names of the Russian teachers, but you don't know who is teaching what. On the first day of class, the program director reads the schedule to you. Write down the names of the teachers in longhand next to the subjects they teach. The list of teachers is given below.

Па́влова Ири́на Семёновна   Авваку́мов Ива́н Алексе́евич
Купри́н Никола́й Влади́мирович   Каза́нцева Мари́на Васи́льевна
Али́ева Мари́на Никола́евна

Занятия	*Фамилия, имя, отчество преподавателя*
1. Грамма́тика	_____
2. Ле́ксика	_____
3. Фоне́тика	_____
4. Литерату́ра	_____
5. Пра́ктика	_____

B. **Игрова́я ситуа́ция.** Act out a situation in which you introduce yourself to one of the teachers in exercise A.

C. **Пресс-конфере́нция.** You are an American reporter in Moscow attending a press conference at the Ministry of Foreign Affairs. A government spokesperson is announcing the names of a delegation to an important meeting in Washington. Check them against the list you were given earlier. There are more names on your list than in the announcement.

1. Арбатова Татьяна Алексеевна
2. Борисов Кирилл Петрович
3. Герулайтис Герман Карлович
4. Константинов Евгений Павлович
5. Крапивкина Зоя Дмитриевна
6. Кужуева Нина Георгиевна
7. Курский Евгений Ильич
8. Муратов Ахмед Ашиевич
9. Туруханов Сергей Николаевич
10. Шестко Тарас Иванович
11. Чайкин Максим Павлович

D. **Приглаше́ние на ве́чер.** Listen to the announcer on the tape read the names of the people invited to a party. Check off the names you hear.

Бо́ский Григо́рий Анто́нович
Више́вский Анто́н Никола́евич
Влади́мирова Зинаи́да Серге́евна
Гага́рин Фёдор Игна́тьевич
Литви́нова Ната́лья Петро́вна
Ивано́ва Алекса́ндра Ива́новна
Ивано́в Макси́м Ильи́ч
Па́влов Пётр Петро́вич
Петро́ва Мари́я Петро́вна
Шукши́н Михаи́л Петро́вич

Could any of the people on the list be brother and sister? Who? How do you know?

E. Read the following descriptions. Then check the people you would like to meet.

- Меня́ зову́т Джон. Моя́ фами́лия Эванс. Я студе́нт. Я живу́
  в Лос-Анджелесе в шта́те Калифо́рния. Я учу́сь там в университе́те.

- Меня́ зову́т Боб. Моя́ фами́лия Го́рдон. Я живу́ в шта́те Пенсильва́ния в
  го́роде Филаде́льфия. Я учу́сь в шко́ле.

- Меня́ зову́т Луи́са. Моя́ фами́лия Ферна́ндез. Я студе́нтка. Я живу́ в го́роде
  Колу́мбус в шта́те Ога́йо. Я учу́сь в университе́те шта́та Ога́йо.

- Меня́ зову́т Сю́зен До́нальдсон. Я журнали́ст. Я живу́ в Ло́ндоне.

- Меня́ зову́т Кри́стофер. Моя́ фами́лия Макка́рти. Я из Англии. Там я живу́
  в Ло́ндоне. Сейча́с я учу́сь в Аме́рике. Я учу́сь в университе́те в Бо́стоне,
  в шта́те Массачу́сетс.

- Меня́ зову́т Элизабе́т. Моя́ фами́лия Мэйпл. Я живу́ в Бо́стоне. Я учу́сь
  в университе́те в го́роде Спри́нгфильд, штат Массачу́сетс.

- Меня́ зову́т Пи́тер. Моя́ фами́лия Кларк. Я кана́дец. Я живу́ и учу́сь
  в го́роде Торо́нто.

- Меня́ зову́т Сти́вен. Моя́ фами́лия Те́йлор. Я учу́сь в университе́те
  в Калифо́рнии. Я из Детро́йта, штат Мичига́н.

- Меня́ зову́т Па́мела. Моя́ фами́лия Шмидт. Я из Сиэ́тла, штат Вашингто́н.
  Я студе́нтка. Я учу́сь в университе́те во Флори́де.

НОВЫЕ СЛОВА И ВЫРАЖЕНИЯ

NOUNS

Аме́рика	America (the U.S.)
америка́нец/америка́нка	American
англича́нин/англича́нка	English
А́нглия	England
бизнесме́н/бизнесме́нка	businessperson
и́мя	first name
институ́т	institute (*institution of post-secondary education*)
Ирку́тск	Irkutsk (*city in Siberia*)
Кана́да	Canada
кана́дец/кана́дка	Canadian
Квебе́к	Quebec
Ло́ндон	London
Лос-Анджелес	Los Angeles
Москва́	Moscow
Нью-Йо́рк	New York
о́тчество	patronymic
студе́нт/студе́нтка	student
университе́т	university
фами́лия	last name
шко́ла	school (*primary or secondary; not post-secondary*)
штат	state

PRONOUNS

я	I
ты	you (*informal*)
вы	you (*formal and plural*)

VERBS

Я живу́ …	I live …
Я учу́сь …	I study …
Ты живёшь/вы живёте …	You live …
Ты у́чишься/вы у́читесь …	You study …

ADVERBS

здесь	here
то́же	also

QUESTION WORDS

где	where
кто	who

CONJUNCTIONS

а	and (*often used to begin questions or statements in continuing conversation*)

PREPOSITION

в (+ *prepositional case*)	in

PHRASES

да	yes
Давáй(те) познакóмимся!	Let's get acquainted.
Дóброе ýтро!	Good morning.
Дóбрый день!	Good afternoon.
Дóбрый вéчер!	Good evening.
Здрáвствуй(те)!	Hello.
Знáчит …	So …
Как вас (тебя́) зовýт?	What's your name?
Как вáше óтчество?	What's your patronymic?
Как ты сказáл?	What did you say? (*to a man*)
Как ты сказáла?	What did you say? (*to a woman*)
Меня́ зовýт …	My name is …
Немнóго о себé	a bit about myself (yourself)
Óчень прия́тно (с вáми, с тобóй) (познакóмиться)	Pleased to meet you.
Прáвда?	Really?
Прости́те.	Excuse me.

NUMBERS

1–10 (*for understanding*)

PERSONALIZED VOCABULARY

_____

_____

_____

_____

ЧТО У МЕНЯ ЕСТЬ?

▼ КОММУНИКАТИВНЫЕ ЗАДАНИЯ

Naming common objects
Passing through customs
Greeting friends at the airport
Reading and listening to ads

▼ В ПОМОЩЬ УЧАЩИМСЯ

Grammatical gender
Nominative plural of nouns
The 5- and 7-letter spelling rules
Pronouns **он, она́, оно́,** and **они́**
Possessive pronouns **чей, мой, твой,
    наш, ваш, его́, её,** and **их**
Nominative case of adjectives
Что vs. **Како́й**
э́то vs. **э́тот (э́то, э́та, э́ти)**
Having: **У меня́ (тебя́, вас) есть**

Workbook: Numbers 11–20
            Intonation of questions
              with question words
              (IC–2)

▼ МЕЖДУ ПРОЧИМ

Passing through Russian customs

ТОЧКА ОТСЧЁТА

О ЧЁМ ИДЁТ РЕЧЬ?

A. **Оде́жда.**

пла́вки

га́лстук

пиджа́к

руба́шка

футбо́лка

ю́бка

купа́льник

пла́тье

колго́тки

блу́зка

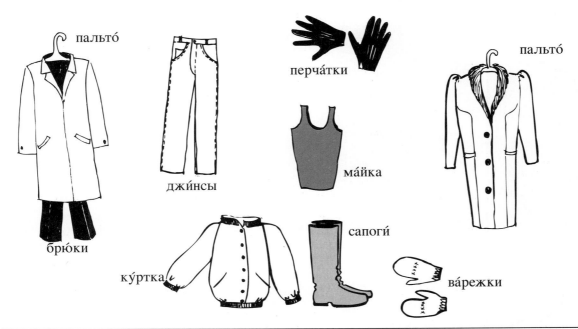

пальто́

перча́тки

пальто́

джи́нсы

ма́йка

брю́ки

ку́ртка

сапоги́

ва́режки

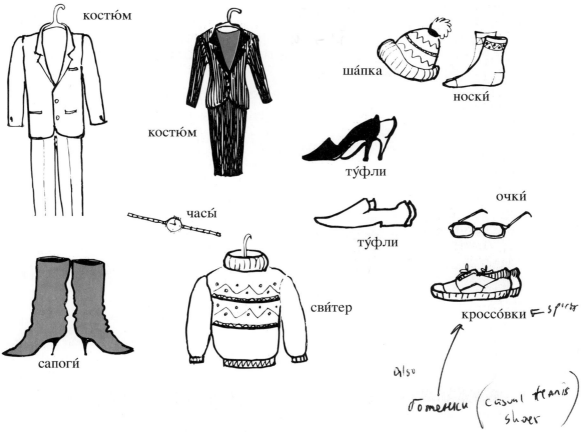

костюм

костюм

шáпка

носкú

тýфли

часы́

тýфли

очкú

свúтер

кроссóвки ⊨ sports

also

ботенки (casual feanis shoes)

сапогú

1. Classify the clothing into related groups such as casual-formal, top-bottom, winter-summer, etc.

2. You are going to visit a friend for three days. Name as many things as you can that you will have to take with you.

_____

_____

_____

_____

Андрей Пруэтт

B. **Техника.**

1. A lot of Russian technical terminology is borrowed from English. Match the pictures with the words. Are there any words you do not recognize?

___ 1. ра́дио (радиоприёмник)   ___ 5. кассе́тный магнитофо́н (кассе́тник)

___ 2. телеви́зор   ___ 6. маши́на

___ 3. компью́тер   ___ 7. видеомагнитофо́н

___ 4. фотоаппара́т   ___ 8. при́нтер

а.

б.

в.

г.

д.

е.

ж.

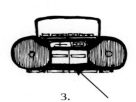

з.

2. Which items do you own? Write them down.

3. Which words go together?

____ 1. компью́тер   а. видеокассе́та

____ 2. фотоаппара́т   б. диске́тка

____ 3. видеомагнитофо́н   в. аудиокассе́та

____ 4. магнитофо́н   г. слайд

____ 5. радиоприёмник   д. анте́нна

C. **Печа́ть.** Here are some things that people read. What other things do people read?

кни́га   докуме́нты   газе́та   письмо́   журна́л   слова́рь

D. Here are some useful adjectives. Organize them into pairs of opposites. It will be easier to remember them that way.

но́вый	new	хоро́ший	good
большо́й	large	ма́ленький	small
ста́рый	old	плохо́й	bad
краси́вый	beautiful	некраси́вый	ugly

E. **Разгово́ры.** Keep the questions in mind as you listen to these conversations. Don't worry if you don't understand everything. Just get enough information to answer as many of the questions as you can.

Разгово́р 1: На тамо́жне
(Разгова́ривают америка́нец и рабо́тник тамо́жни)

1. What documents is the customs official interested in?
2. What is the American bringing in?

Разгово́р 2: По́сле тамо́жни
(Рагова́ривают Мэ́ри и Ка́тя)

1. What is Katya commenting on?
2. What does Mary have in the suitcase?
3. What is Katya's surprise?

Разгово́р 3: На тамо́жне
(Разгова́ривают Джим и рабо́тник тамо́жни.)

1. What document does the customs official want to see?
2. Which personal items is he particularly interested in?
3. What do we know about these items?

ДИАЛОГИ

1 На тамо́жне

— Ва́шу деклара́цию.
— Вот, пожа́луйста.
— Чей э́то чемода́н? Ваш?
— Мой.
— Откро́йте, пожа́луйста. Пода́рки есть?
— Нет.
— А э́то что?
— Магнитофо́н и кассе́ты.
— Поня́тно. Всё. Проходи́те.

2 Что в чемода́не?

— Ва́шу деклара́цию.
— Вот, пожа́луйста.
— Чей э́то чемода́н?
— Э́тот большо́й? Мой.
— Что в чемода́не?
— Кни́ги, журна́лы, оде́жда: ма́йки, джи́нсы, пла́тья, ту́фли.
— А те́хника? У вас есть фотоаппара́т, магнитофо́н?
— То́лько ма́ленький фотоаппара́т.
— А э́то что?
— Видеокассе́та.
— Хорошо́. Это всё. Проходи́те.

> **Э́тот большо́й?**
> *This big one?*

3 С прие́здом!

— С прие́здом, Джим! Ну, как ты? Где твой чемода́н?
— Вот он.
— Како́й большо́й! Что у тебя́ в чемода́не? Те́хника?
— Да. Магнитофо́н, фотоаппара́т, кассе́ты, пода́рки.
— Пода́рки! Каки́е?
— Это сюрпри́з.
— А у меня́ то́же сюрпри́з.
— Како́й?
— Но́вая маши́на.
— «Жигули́»?
— Нет, «Москви́ч».

> **С прие́здом!** Use this phrase only to greet someone who has arrived from another city or country.

Это вам карандаш

---

4 **Ты молодец!**

— Ли́нда! С прие́здом! Как ты?
— Хорошо́, спаси́бо. Здра́вствуй, Ка́тя!
— Это твой чемода́н? Ой, како́й большо́й!
— И э́тот—то́же мой. Тут у меня́ то́лько оде́жда, а там—кассе́ты, фотоаппара́т, пода́рки.
— Пода́рки?! Интере́сно, каки́е?
— Америка́нские журна́лы и кни́ги.
— Ну, Ли́нда, ты молоде́ц!

> **Молоде́ц!**
> Use this form of praise only with friends. It is not appropriate to praise a teacher or a business colleague like this.

A. **У вас есть …?** Working with a partner, ask and answer questions as in the models.

Образец: — У вас есть те́хника?
— Да, у меня́ есть магнитофо́н.

и́ли

— Нет, у меня́ не́ту.

Questions:

— У вас есть …?
— У тебя́ есть … ?

ра́дио, компью́тер, видеомагнитофо́н, телеви́зор, фотоаппара́т, маши́на, газе́та, а́нгло-ру́сский слова́рь, чемода́н, часы́, очки́

Answers:

— Да, (у меня́) есть.
— Нет, у меня́ не́ту.

B. Your luggage got lost. You have been asked to list at least ten items you had in your suitcase.

C. What would you wear if you were to go to the places mentioned below?

    a. theatre
    b. beach
    c. job interview
    d. class at the university
    e. ski resort

D. You have invited a Russian friend to visit you in your home town. List a few things your friend should bring.

E. Take turns telling your group that you have a gift, but don't tell them what it is. Others in the group will ask questions in Russian to find out what the gift is.

Possible questions:

Пода́рок большо́й и́ли ма́ленький?
Это оде́жда? Это блу́зка?
Это те́хника? Это кассе́та?

Язык в действии

A. **Подготóвка к разговóру.** Review the dialogs. How does the customs official ask the questions below? Practice answering these questions, using the American's responses in the conversations to help you.

- Whose suitcase is this?
- Do you have any gifts?
- What is this?

Review the dialogs again. How would you do the following?

- indicate that you have understood something
- welcome someone at the airport
- praise someone
- thank someone

B. **В аэропортý.** Working with a partner, pretend you are at the airport. Practice responding to the following situations. Then switch roles.

1. With Customs Official

— Вáшу декларáцию.
— Ваш пáспорт.
— Где вúза?
— Где пáспорт?
— Где докумéнты?
— Это ваш чемодáн?
— Это вáша декларáция?
— Что в чемодáне?
— Магнитофóн есть?
— Фотоаппарáт есть?

2. With Friend

— С приéздом!
— Как ты?
— Большóе спасúбо!
— Это подáрок.
— У меня нóвая машúна.

C. **Игровы́е ситуáции.**

1. You have just arrived in Russia. Go through customs with the following items to declare:

   a. tape recorder and cassettes
   b. computer and printer
   c. American newspapers and magazines
   d. VCR and tapes
   e. cameras, radio, and books

2. You have just arrived in Russia for a home-stay. Get acquainted with your host.
3. Working with a partner, prepare and act out a situation that deals with the topics of this unit.

D. **Устный перевод.** You have been asked to interpret for a tourist who is going through customs at Moscow's **Шереме́тьево-2** airport. The Russian customs official has the first line.

English speaker's part

1. Here it is.
2. Visa? Here it is.
3. This is my suitcase.
4. The big suitcase is mine too.
5. Okay.
6. Clothes, gadgets . . .
7. Computer, tape recorder, camera.
8. Ten.
9. Rock. Jazz.
10. Only a Russian-English dictionary.

ДАВАЙТЕ ПОЧИТАЕМ

A. **Продаю.** Look through this "for sale" column. What number would you call if you wanted to buy the items listed?

a. a stereo
b. a VCR
c. a car
d. a TV set
e. musical instruments

ПРОДАЮ

4016-540. Музыкальный стереоцентр «Шарп». Тел. 149-74-98.

4038-360. Пианино «Строуд» (США, не новое). Тел. 335-90-60.

4065-840. Контактные линзы (04, -5,5). Тел. 963-98-12.

4096-340. Автомашину «Вольво» (1986 г.). Тел. 388-09-38.

4227-1080. Новый японский видеомагнитофон «Санио-3100ЕЕ», телевизор «Рекорд ВЦ-311». Тел. 145-00-76.

4475-540. Компьютер «БК0010» (Бейсик, Фокал). Тел. 443-25-19.

4506-541. Видеомагнитофон «Джи-Ви-Си-120». Тел. 405-09-87.

456-260. Электрогитару, банджо. Тел. 285-41-57.

4189-360. Мотоцикл «К-58» недорого Тел. 534-98-67. Борис.

B. **Химчи́стка.**

1. This is a receipt from a dry cleaner. What articles were cleaned?

2. Was the customer more likely a man or a woman? Why do you think so?

Форма № 117 пр. Д

Предприятие __628__

Заказчик __Рольбина__

Заказ №. __703__

РАСЧЁТ ЗА ЗАСЛУГИ

Наименование одежды	Цена за шт.	Всего шт.	Сумма руб.	коп.
юбка	20	2	40	
свитер	25	1	25	
брюки	35	4	140	
платье	30	2	60	
пиджак	100	1	100	
			365	

Сумма всего

Руб. __триста шестьдесят пять__
　　　　(прописью)

Одежду из химчистки получил __Я. Рольбина__
　　　　　　　　　　　　　　Подпись

« __27__ » __ноября__ 19 __92__ г.

A. **Магази́н-сало́н.** Listen to the announcement with the following questions in mind.

1. Circle the items the store offers.

a.

б.

в.

> A **магази́н-сало́н** is a privately owned store that specializes in second-hand goods and goods produced by small businesses.

г.

д.

е.

ж.

2. What is the store's address?
3. What is its phone number?

B. **Кооперати́в «Мо́да».** Listen to the announcement and determine what is being advertised. Pick out at least four key words that lead you to your conclusion and jot them down in English or in Russian.

C. **Тамо́жня.** You call customs at the airport and get a recording of items that cannot be taken out of Russia. Listen and check off the things that can't be taken out of the country.

2.1 GRAMMATICAL GENDER

Russian nouns are made up of **stems** and **endings.** The stem carries the lexical meaning and the ending gives information about the grammatical nature of the word (for example, what gender it is, whether it is singular or plural, and what function it plays in the sentence). As you look at the endings of nominative singular nouns to determine their gender, you will note that the stems may be either nonpalatalized ("hard") or palatalized ("soft").

Russian nouns belong to one of three genders: **masculine, feminine,** or **neuter.** It is usually possible to identify the gender of a noun by looking at its ending (the last letter) in the nominative singular (the dictionary form). The following table shows the endings for singular nouns in the nominative case.

Gender of Russian Nouns: Schematic View

	MASCULINE	FEMININE	NEUTER
Hard stem	чемода́н - Ø	газе́т - **а**	о́тчеств - **о**
Soft stem	музе́ - **й** словар - **ь**	деклара́ци - **я** за́пис - **ь**	пла́ть - **е**

Masculine nouns. In the nominative case most masculine nouns have no explicit ending—they consist of the stem plus a zero vowel ending. In other words, masculine nouns usually end in a hard or soft consonant. Zero endings for hard-stem nouns are indicated in the tables by the symbol Ø. Zero endings for soft-stems nouns are reflected in writing by the letters **-ь** and **-й.** Although technically these letters are not endings, they are dropped before other endings are added, and therefore they are separated from the rest of the word in the grammar tables.

A few nouns referring to men and boys (for example, **па́па**-*dad*, **дя́дя**-*uncle,* **де́душка**-*grandfather,* and a large number of nicknames for males, **Ва́ня, Ви́тя, То́ля, Са́ша, …**) have the ending **-а** or **-я** rather than a zero ending. These nouns are of course masculine. They are modified by masculine adjectives, and they are replaced by masculine pronouns. However, the endings on the nouns themselves always look like the endings on feminine nouns. These nouns are not given a separate column in the charts.

Feminine nouns. Hard-stem feminine nouns end in **-a**. Soft-stem feminine nouns end in **-я**. Some feminine nouns end in a soft consonant (consonant + **ь**) just like some soft-stem masculine nouns. The vocabulary lists and glossaries in this textbook will indicate (*fem.*) next to the feminine nouns ending in **-ь**. You can assume that all other nouns ending in **-ь** are masculine.

Neuter nouns. Hard-stem neuter nouns end in **-o**. Soft-stem neuter nouns end in **-e**. Some soft-stem neuter nouns end in **-ё**.

Note: Nouns ending in **-мя** are also neuter. You know one such noun (**и́мя**–*first name*) and will learn only one more during this course (**вре́мя**–*time*). You will learn the declension of these nouns in a later course.

Упражнение

1. Indicate whether the following nouns are masculine, feminine, or neuter, and whether the stem is hard or soft.

   а. институ́т
   б. руба́шка
   в. слова́рь

   г. магази́н
   д. письмо́ (*letter*)
   е. за́пись (*recording*)

   ж. шко́ла
   з. маши́на
   и. Калифо́рния

2.2 NOMINATIVE PLURAL OF NOUNS

The nominative plural ending for most hard-stem masculine and feminine nouns is **-ы**. For soft-stem masculine and feminine nouns this ending is **-и**. The nominative plural ending for most hard-stem neuter nouns is **-a**. For soft-stem neuter nouns this ending is **-я**. The following tables show how to form the plural of Russian nouns.

MASCULINE AND FEMININE NOUNS			
	Singular	*Plural*	
Hard stem	чемода́н - Ø газе́т- **a**	чемода́н- **ы** газе́т - **ы**	**-ы**
Soft stem	музе́ - **й** слова́р - **ь** деклара́ци - **я** за́пис - **ь**	музе́ - **и** словар - **й́** деклара́ци - **и** за́пис - **и**	**-и**

NEUTER NOUNS			
	Singular	*Plural*	
Hard stem	óтчеств - **о**	óтчеств - **а**	**-а**
Soft stem	плáть - **е**	плáть - **я**	**-я**

Spelling rules: Russian spelling does not allow some combinations of letters. For example, after the letters **к, г, х, ш, щ, ж,** and **ч,** it is not possible to write the letter **-ы.** This is called the **7-letter spelling rule.** Whenever an **-ы** or **-и** sound follows one of the seven letters, it is spelled **-и.** For example, кассéтник - Ø ➡ кассéтник - **и;** кни́г - а ➡ кни́г - **и.**

Learn the 7-letter spelling rule now. You will have many chances to apply it as you continue your study of Russian.

The 7-letter spelling rule:

After the letters **к, г, х, ш, щ, ж, ч,** do not write **-ы,** write **-и** instead.

Notes

1. Whenever you change endings on Russian nouns and adjectives, the following three rules are essential.

    a. Delete the old ending before adding a new one.
    b. Add the ending that will allow the stem to retain its hard or soft nature (unless this would cause you to break a spelling rule).
    c. Never break a spelling rule.

2. Sometimes there is an accent shift in the plural: словáрь ➡ словари́, письмó ➡ пи́сьма. Such words will be marked in the glossaries and word lists.

3. Some masculine nouns with **-е** or **-о** in the semi-final position lose this vowel whenever an ending is added.

подáр	о	к

подáр	↓	ки
	о	

In the word lists and glossaries in this textbook, such words will be listed like this: подáр(о)к.

4. Some masculine nouns take stressed **а** as the plural ending. In this unit you will use three such words: **дом, сви́тер, пáспорт.** In the word lists and glossaries in this textbook, the plural of such words will be indicated.

singular	*plural*
дом	домá
сви́тер	свитерá
пáспорт	паспортá

5. Words of foreign origin ending in **-о, -и,** or **-у** never change their form. They are called indeclinable. The nominative plural form of such a word is the same as the nominative singular form. For example: **ра́дио, пальто́, такси́, кенгуру́.**

Упражнение

2. Give the nominative plural form of the following nouns.

а. магнитофо́н	д. фотоаппара́т	и. чемода́н
б. маши́на	е. шко́ла	й. ма́ма
в. слова́рь	ж. студе́нтка	к. пода́рок
г. о́тчество	з. пла́тье	л. пальто́

➤ Complete Oral Drill 1 and Written Exercise 1 in the Workbook.

2.3   THE PERSONAL PRONOUNS: *ОН, ОНА, ОНО, ОНИ*

You now know that Russian nouns are divided into three classes: masculine, feminine, and neuter. The pronouns used to replace these nouns are also masculine, feminine, or neuter. The choice of pronoun depends on the grammatical gender of the noun.

— Где **Бори́с Миха́йлович?**	— Вот **он.**	There *he is.*
— Где **па́па?**	— Вот **он.**	There *he is.*
— Где **Мари́на Ива́новна?**	— Вот **она́.**	There *she is.*
— Где **Аня и Гри́ша?**	— Вот **они́.**	There *they are.*

[handwritten top margin:] вот : looking for something, and then find it. (there) там : over there   это : this is, these are.

The English word *it* has several possible Russian equivalents, depending on the context.

— Где твой **чемода́н?**	— Вот **он.**	There *it is.*
— Где твоя́ **кни́га?**	— Вот **она́.**	There *it is.*
— Где твоё **ра́дио?**	— Вот **оно́.**	There *it is.*
— Где твои́ **часы́?**	— Вот **они́.**	There *it is.*

In the plural, the personal pronoun is **они́**—it does not matter what gender the noun is.

| — Где твои́ **кни́ги?** | — Вот **они́.** | There *they are.* |
| — Где твои́ **чемода́ны?** | — Вот **они́.** | There *they are.* |

Упражне́ние

3. How would you answer these questions, following the models given above?

а. Где ва́ша ви́за?
б. А па́спорт?

в. А докуме́нты?
г. А чемода́н?

[handwritten:] твой m твой / твоя́ f твоя́ / твоё n / твои pl

➤ Complete Oral Drills 2–3 and Written Exercise 2 in the Workbook.

2.4   THE POSSESSIVE PRONOUNS: *МОЙ, ТВОЙ, НАШ, ВАШ* AND THE QUESTION WORD *ЧЕЙ*

[handwritten:] мой m / моя́ f / моё n / мои pl

| — **Чья** э́то **ви́за?** |
| — Это **моя́ ви́за.** |

| — **Чьё** э́то **ра́дио?** |
| — Это **моё ра́дио.** |

| — **Чьи** э́то **кни́ги?** |
| — Это **мои́ кни́ги.** |

[handwritten:] Whose: чей Чей m он / чья Чья f она / чьё Чьё n оно / чьи Чьи pl они

The Russian words **мой, твой, наш, ваш,** and **чей** agree with the nouns they modify. The chart below lists all the nominative case forms of these words.

Nominative Case of *ЧЕЙ, МОЙ, ТВОЙ, НАШ, ВАШ*

Modifying masculine nouns	*Modifying neuter nouns*	*Modifying feminine nouns*	*Modifying plural nouns*
чей *whose*	чьё	чья	чьи
мой *my* *(sing. inform)*	моё	моя́	мой
твой чемода́н	твоё ра́дио	твоя́ ви́за	твой кни́ги
наш *our*	на́ше	на́ша	на́ши
ваш *yours (formal, plural)*	ва́ше	ва́ша	ва́ши

Matches word it modifies.

ВАША СОБАКА, ВАШИ СОБАКИ

The possessive pronouns **его́**—*his* (with the **г** pronounced like a **в**), **её**—*her*, and **их**—*their* never change their form:

his — его — его   *her — её ее*   *their — их — ux*

Это **его́** чемода́н.
Это **его́** кни́га.
Это **его́** ра́дио.
Это **его́** кни́ги.

Это **её** чемода́н.
Это **её** ви́за.
Это **её** ра́дио.
Это **её** кни́ги.

Это **их** чемода́н.
Это **их** ви́за.
Это **их** ра́дио.
Это **их** кни́ги.

Упражнение

Какой : what kind of

кавой es слон : who has an elephant?

4. Fill in the blanks, using the correct form of the appropriate possessive pronoun.

— Чьи это докуме́нты? _____ (yours, formal)?

— Да, _мой_ (mine).

— Так. А это _ваш_ (your) чемода́н?

— Нет. Не _мой_ (mine). Это, наве́рное, _его_ (his) чемода́н.

Вот э́тот большо́й чемода́н _мой_ (mine). И ещё су́мка

моя (mine).

— _Чьи_ (whose) это кни́ги?

— Это _____ (our) кни́ги. Нет, подожди́те мину́точку. Эта кни́га не

наша (ours). Это не _твоя_ (your, informal) кни́га?

— Нет не _моя_ (mine).

— Интере́сно, _чья_ (whose) это кни́га?

➤ Complete Oral Drills 4-9 and Written Exercises 3-5 in the Workbook.

2.5   ADJECTIVES (NOMINATIVE CASE)

Russian adjectives always *agree in gender, number, and case with the nouns they modify*. Like nouns, adjective stems are either hard or soft. Remember that all endings you add should allow the stem to preserve its hardness or softness. In the nominative singular the ending for masculine adjectives is **-ый** or **ий** (**-ой** if the ending is accented). The ending for feminine adjectives is **-ая** or **-яя**. The ending for neuter adjectives is **-ое** or **-ее**. The nominative plural ending of adjectives is **-ые** or **-ие**.

кошка : cat (F)

какая (what kind of?)

маленкая
красивая
молодая
интересная
хорошая

Masculine	но́в - ый больш - о́й	-ий -ий -ый ый -о́й ой
Feminine	но́в - ая	-ая ая
Neuter	но́в - ое	-ое ое
Plural	но́в - ые	-ые ые -ие

[м] какой
большой
красивый
старый
неинтересный
хороший
плохой

серый : grey j

ая/яя = something   (сог in workbook)

The 7- letter spelling rule

After the letters **к, г, х, ш, щ, ж, ч,** do not write **-ы**, write **-и** instead.

The 5- letter spelling rule

After the letters **ш, щ, ж, ч, ц,** do not write unstressed **-о**, write **-е** instead.

Упражнения

5. Make a list of the clothing you own. Use adjectives with as many items as you can.

6. Create grammatically correct sentences by combining words from the three columns below. Be sure to make the adjectives agree with the nouns.

	но́вый	джи́нсы
	хоро́ший	магнитофо́н
	ста́рый	ра́дио
Это	краси́вый	пла́тье
У вас есть	плохо́й	кроссо́вки
У меня́ есть	некраси́вый	руба́шка
		телеви́зор
		кассе́ты

➤ Complete Oral Drills 10–12 and Written Exercises 6–10 in the Workbook.

2.6 *WHAT: ЧТО* vs. *КАКОЙ*

Both **что** and **какой (кака́я, како́е, каки́е)** mean *what*, but they are not interchangeable. Look at the examples:

Что в чемода́не?   *What* is in the suitcase?
Кака́я кни́га в чемода́не?   *What (which) book* is in the suitcase?

When *what* is followed by a noun, it is adjectival and therefore rendered by **какой.** When *what* stands alone it is translated as **что.**

Упражнение

7. Fill in the blanks with the correct Russian equivalent of *what*.

a. What is that? ___что___ э́то?

b. What documents are those? ___какие___ э́то докуме́нты?

c. What do you have there? ___что___ тут у вас?

d. What book is that? ___кака́я___ э́то кни́га?

e. What kind of television is this? ___какы́й___ э́то телеви́зор?

➤ Complete Written Exercise 11 in the Workbook.

2.7 THIS IS/THESE ARE vs. THIS/THESE:
ЭТО vs. *ЭТОТ (ЭТА, ЭТО, ЭТИ)*

Both the unchanging form **э́то** and the modifier **э́тот (э́та, э́то, э́ти)** can be rendered in English as *this / these*. However, they are not interchangeable. Study these examples and then work through the exercise that follows. At this stage of learning Russian, you should develop an awareness of the distinction. You will become more comfortable with it and will be able to control its use only after you have read and heard a great deal more authentic Russian.

This is … / These are …

Это мой чемода́н.
Это моя́ ви́за.
Это моё ра́дио.
Это мой докуме́нты.

This … / These …

Этот чемода́н мой. *Этот*
Эта ви́за моя́. *Эта*
Это ра́дио моё. *Это*
Эти докуме́нты мой. *Эти*

Is this … ?/ Are these … ?

Это ваш чемода́н?
Это но́вая ви́за?
Это его́ ра́дио?
Это твой докуме́нты?

Is this (x) … ?/ Are these (x's) … ?

Этот чемода́н ваш?
Эта ви́за но́вая?
Это ра́дио его́?
Эти докуме́нты твой?

Упражнение

7. Fill in the blanks with **э́то** or a form of **э́тот**.

a. *This is* my book.   *Это*   моя́ кни́га.

b. *This book* is mine.   *Эта*   кни́га моя́.

c. *These are* my suitcases.   *Это*   мои́ чемода́ны.

d. *This suitcase* is yours.   *Этот*   чемода́н ваш.

e. *This small suitcase* is also yours. *Этот*   ма́ленький чемода́н то́же ваш.

f. *These books* are interesting. *Эти*   кни́ги интере́сные.

g. *These interesting books* are yours. *Эти*   интере́сные кни́ги ва́ши.

h. *These are* interesting books. *Это*   интере́сные кни́ги.

i. *Are these* interesting books? *Это*   интере́сные кни́ги?

j. Are *these books* interesting?   *Эти*   кни́ги интере́сные?

2.8   INDICATING HAVING SOMETHING:
У МЕНЯ́ ЕСТЬ, У ТЕБЯ́ ЕСТЬ, У ВАС ЕСТЬ

for,   inf.

You have learned how to say you have something (**У меня́ есть пода́рок**) and how to ask others if they have things (**У вас есть докуме́нты? У тебя́ есть ви́за?**). Here, as in many places in your learning of Russian, it is important to observe and imitate the structure of the Russian sentences rather than trying to translate directly from English or other languages you know. In the Russian sentences the thing one has is the grammatical subject of the sentence. That is why it is in the nominative case. And that is why you were asked to use this structure to learn and practice the nominative singular and plural of nouns and adjectives. This also explains why you were not asked to produce sentences indicating things you do not have. Such sentences would require the use of a form you do not yet know. Although you do not have the tools yet to say that you don't have something (*I don't have a book*), if asked whether you have certain things, you can answer no by using the phrase **Нет, у меня́ не́ту** (*I don't have one of those*).

Упражнение

9. Ask what clothing your partner owns. Use *У тебя́ есть …?/У вас есть …?* in your questions. Then answer the same questions using your own information.

➤ Complete Orals Drills 13–16 and Written Exercises 12–13 in the Workbook.

ОБЗОРНЫЕ УПРАЖНЕНИЯ

A. **День рождéния.** What ten things would you like to get for your birthday? Use adjectives with at least five items on your list.

B. **Поéздка в Москвý.** Sasha and Lena have invited you to visit them in Moscow for two weeks in December.

1. Make a list of ten things to pack.
2. Act out your arrival in Moscow, passing through customs and greeting your friends. Classmates and your teacher will play the other roles.
3. Introduce yourself to one of Lena's parents. Find out about him or her, and tell about yourself.

C. **На тамóжне.** Below you will find lines of a conversation between Nancy and a Russian customs official. Read through the lines and put them in order. Then listen to the recording and see if you were correct.

_____	**Рабóтник:**	Так. Понятно. Литератýру везёте?
_____	**Нэнси:**	Да, вот этот чёрный. А это персонáльный компьютер.
_____	**Рабóтник:**	Хорошó. Закрóйте чемодáн. Проходите.
_____	**Нэнси:**	Тóлько рýсские учéбники и словари.
_____	**Рабóтник:**	Покажите, пожáлуйста, деклар áцию.
_____	**Нэнси:**	Да, двáдцать кассéт.
_____	**Рабóтник:**	Это вáши чемодáны?
_____	**Нэнси:**	Пожáлуйста.
_____	**Рабóтник:**	Персонáльный, да? А кассéты везёте?

D. **Пóсле тамóжни.** Listen to the conversation with the following questions in mind.

1. What does Valera say about Jim's suitcase?
2. What does Jim have in the lighter suitcase?
3. What does Jim have in the heavier suitcase?
4. What gift has Jim brought for Valera?
5. What is Valera's surprise?

НОВЫЕ СЛОВА И ВЫРАЖЕНИЯ

NOUNS

ви́за	visa
газе́та	newspaper
деклара́ция	customs declaration
докуме́нт	document, identification
дом (*pl.* дома́)	home, apartment building
журна́л	magazine
за́пись (*fem.*)	recording
кни́га	book
музе́й	museum
па́спорт (*pl.* паспорта́)	passport
письмо́ (*pl.* пи́сьма)	letter
пода́р(о)к	gift
слова́рь (*pl.* словари́)	dictionary
сюрпри́з	surprise
тамо́жня	customs
уче́бник	textbook
чемода́н	suitcase

те́хника	**gadgets**
видеокассе́та	video cassette
видеомагнитофо́н	video cassette recorder
кассе́та	cassette
кассе́тный магнитофо́н (кассе́тник)	cassette player
компью́тер	computer
магнитофо́н	tape recorder
маши́на	car
при́нтер	printer
ра́дио (радиоприёмник)	radio
телеви́зор	television
фотоаппара́т	camera

оде́жда	**clothing**
блу́зка	blouse
брю́ки (*pl.*)	pants
ва́режки (*pl.*)	mittens
га́лстук	tie
джи́нсы (*pl.*)	jeans
колго́тки (*pl.*)	pantyhose
костю́м	suit
кроссо́вки (*pl.*)	athletic shoes sneakers
купа́льник	woman's bathing suit
ку́ртка	short jacket
ма́йка	T-shirt
носки́ (*pl.*)	socks

очки́ (*pl.*)	eyeglasses
пальто́ (*indecl.*)	overcoat
перча́тки (*pl.*)	gloves
пиджа́к	suit jacket
пла́вки (*pl.*)	swimming trunks
пла́тье	dress
руба́шка	shirt
сапоги́ (*pl.*)	boots
сви́тер (*pl.* свитера́)	sweater
ту́фли	shoes
футбо́лка	jersey
ю́бка	skirt
часы́ (*pl.*)	watch

PRONOUNS

он	he, it
она́	she, it
оно́	it
они́	they
э́то	this is, that is, those are, these are

POSSESSIVE PRONOUNS

чей (чья, чьё, чьи)	whose?
мой (моя́, моё, мои́)	my
твой (твоя́, твоё, твои́)	your (*informal*)
наш (на́ша, на́ше, на́ши)	our
ваш (ва́ша, ва́ше, ва́ши)	your (*formal or plural*)
её	her
его́	his
их	their

ADJECTIVES

како́й (кака́я, како́е, каки́е)	what, which
большо́й–ма́ленький	large–small
но́вый–ста́рый	new–old
хоро́ший–плохо́й	good–bad
(не)интере́сный	(un)interesting
(не)краси́вый	pretty–ugly
америка́нский	American
ру́сский	Russian
э́тот (э́та, э́то, э́ти)	this
чёрный	black

ADVERBS

там	there
то́лько	only
тут	here

QUESTION WORDS

како́й (кака́я, како́е, каки́е)	what
кто	who
чей (чья, чьё, чьи)	whose
что	what

CONJUNCTION

и	and

OTHER WORDS AND PHRASES

Вот …	Here is …
Всё.	That's all.
Есть …?	Is there …? Are there …?
Интере́сно …	I wonder …, It's interesting …
Закро́йте!	Close.
Как ты?	How are you? (*informal*)
Литерату́ру везёте?	Do you have literature with you?

Молод(е́)ц!	Well done!
нет	no
ну …	well …
ой	oh
Откро́йте.	Open.
Пожа́луйста. *пожалуйста*	You're welcome.
Поня́тно.	Understood.
Проходи́те.	Go on through.
С прие́здом! *с приездом*	Welcome! (*To someone from out of town*)
Спаси́бо.	Thank you.
У меня́ есть …	I have …
У меня́ не́ту.	I don't have any of those.
У вас есть … ?	Do you have … ? (*formal*)
У тебя́ есть …?	Do you have … ? (*informal*)
Хорошо́.	Fine. Good.

NUMBERS 11–20 (*for understanding*)

PERSONALIZED VOCABULARY

_____ *меня*

_____ *тебя*

_____

_____

Test

1) ~~Он она~~   Он, она, оне, они   replace nouns √ / pronouns.

2) ex: ваш ста́рый костю́м → plural form
5)

3) его, её, их ; мой, твой, ваш, наш   pos. pron.
6)

4) У меня есть, У ~~тебя~~ тебя есть, У вас есть, and answering....

8) a. vocab...
6)   Rishi → Lagi; ему → mestym

7) like WB #14 p 39

УРОК 3

КАКИЕ ЯЗЫКИ ВЫ ЗНАЕТЕ?

▼ КОММУНИКАТИВНЫЕ ЗАДАНИЯ

Talking about languages
Discussing ethnic and national
   backgrounds
Reading ads about language programs

▼ В ПОМОЩЬ УЧАЩИМСЯ

Verb conjugation
Position of adverbial modifiers
Prepositional case of singular
   modifiers and nouns
Languages: ру́сский язы́к vs.
   по-ру́сски
Conjunctions: и, а, но

Workbook: Numbers 21–30
            Intonation of yes-no
               questions (IC–3)

▼ МЕЖДУ ПРОЧИМ

Nationalities
Responding to compliments

Точка отсчёта

О чём идёт речь?

A. The following people are described in terms of their national origin and native language.

Это Джон и Джéссика.
Джон—**америкáнец.**
Джéссика—**америкáнка.**
Они говорят **по-англи́йски.**

Это Алёша и Кáтя.
Алёша—**рýсский.**
Кáтя—**рýсская.**
Они говоря́т **по-рýсски.**

Это Хуáн и Марисóль.
Хуáн—**испáнец.**
Марисóль—**испáнка.**
Они говоря́т **по-испáнски.**

B. What languages do you know or study? What is your ethnic background? What kind of last name do you have? What language(s) do you speak at home? Read through the questions and answers below. Pick out the responses that best apply to you. Consult your teacher for words that are not in the list.

1. Какие языки вы изучáете или знáете?

   Я изучáю …
   Я знáю …

   англи́йский язы́к
   арáбский язы́к
   испáнский язы́к
   китáйский язы́к (*Chinese*)

   немéцкий язы́к (*German*)
   рýсский язы́к
   францýзский язы́к
   япóнский язы́к (*Japanese*)

2. Кто по национáльности вáши роди́тели?

   Мой пáпа …
   Моя́ мáма …
   Они́ …

   америкáнец, америкáнка, америкáнцы
   англичáнин, англичáнка, англичáне
   арáб, арáбка, арáбы
   испáнец, испáнка, испáнцы
   итальянец, итальянка, итальянцы
   канáдец, канáдка, канáдцы
   китáец, китая́нка, китáйцы
   мексикáнец, мексикáнка, мексикáнцы
   нéмец, нéмка, нéмцы
   рýсский, рýсская, рýсские
   францýз, францýженка, францýзы
   япóнец, япóнка, япóнцы

понятия
не имею

3. На каком языке́ вы говори́те до́ма?

Дома мы говори́м ...

по-англи́йски	по-неме́цки
по-ара́бски	по-ру́сски
по-испа́нски	по-францу́зски
по-кита́йски	по-япо́нски

4. Ва́ша фами́лия ру́сская?

Да, ру́сская.
Нет, ...

англи́йская	неме́цкая
ара́бская	францу́зская
испа́нская	япо́нская
кита́йская	

C. **Разгово́ры.** Read the questions. Then listen to the dialogs. Don't worry if you can't understand everything. You have completed the assignment when you can answer the questions.

Разгово́р 1: Вы зна́ете англи́йский язы́к?
(Разгова́ривают Пе́тя и секрета́рь филологи́ческого факульте́та Моско́вского университе́та)

1. What language is being discussed?
2. Does Petya know this language?
3. What does he want to find out?
4. How does the secretary help him?

Wanted folklore
at lab ...
Russian folklore at 12:30

Разгово́р 2: Вы говори́те по-францу́зски?
(Рагова́ривают Вади́м и Анто́н Васи́льевич)

1. What language is being discussed?
2. Does the professor know this language?
3. What is Vadim trying to find out?
4. Does the professor help him?

Разгово́р 3: Ты изуча́ешь испа́нский язы́к?
(Разгова́ривают Ко́ля и Ве́ра)

1. What two languages does Kolya study?
2. Which language does Kolya know better?
3. Can Kolya understand fast speech in his second foreign language?
4. What language does Vera study?

ДИАЛОГИ

❶ Вы зна́ете испа́нский язы́к?

— Жа́нна, вы зна́ете испа́нский язы́к?
— Чита́ю хорошо́, говорю́ пло́хо.
— Я тут чита́ю испа́нский журна́л и не понима́ю одно́ сло́во …
— Како́е?
— Вот э́то. Как по-ру́сски «aduana»?
— По-ру́сски э́то бу́дет «тамо́жня».
— Большо́е спаси́бо!
— Пожа́луйста.

❷ Вы о́чень хорошо́ говори́те по-ру́сски.

— Джейн, вы о́чень хорошо́ говори́те по-ру́сски.
— Нет, что вы! Я хорошо́ понима́ю, но говорю́ и пишу́ ещё пло́хо.
— Нет-нет, вы говори́те о́чень хорошо́. Роди́тели ру́сские?
— Па́па ру́сский, а ма́ма—америка́нка. Но до́ма мы говори́м то́лько по-англи́йски.
— А отку́да вы зна́ете ру́сский язы́к?
— Я его́ изуча́ю в университе́те. И живу́ в ру́сском до́ме.
— В ру́сском до́ме? Что э́то тако́е?
— Это общежи́тие, где говоря́т то́лько по-ру́сски.
— Поня́тно.

> Note the use of the **они́** form of the verb without the pronoun **они́**. *That's a dormitory where* [they] *speak only Russian / where only Russian is spoken.*

❸ Дава́йте познако́мимся.

— Дава́йте познако́мимся. Полищу́к Алекса́ндр Дми́триевич.
— Са́ра Нью́элл. Очень прия́тно. Полищу́к—э́то украи́нская фами́лия, да?
— Да, оте́ц—украи́нец. А мать ру́сская. В па́спорте стои́т, что я то́же ру́сский.
— А до́ма вы говори́те по-украи́нски?
— Не всегда́. Иногда́ по-украи́нски, а иногда́ по-ру́сски.
— Интере́сно.

4 **Разреши́те предста́виться.**

— Разреши́те предста́виться. Боб Джонс.
— Смирно́ва Ли́дия Миха́йловна. Очень прия́тно.
— Очень прия́тно.
— Вы англича́нин, да?
— Нет, америка́нец.
— Ой, прости́те. Вы так хорошо́ говори́те по-ру́сски.
— Нет-нет, что вы! Я говорю́ ещё пло́хо.
— Но вы всё понима́ете по-ру́сски, да?
— Нет, не всё. Я понима́ю, когда́ говоря́т ме́дленно.
— А я не бы́стро говорю́?
— Нет, норма́льно.

> Note again the use of the **они́** form of the verb without the pronoun **они́**. *I understand when it is spoken slowly.*

5 **Очень прия́тно познако́миться.**

— Дава́йте познако́мимся. Пе́гги Сно́у.
— Аганя́н Гайда́р Була́тович.
— Говори́те ме́дленнее, пожа́луйста. Я пло́хо понима́ю по-ру́сски.
— Аганя́н Гайда́р Була́тович.
— Зна́чит, ва́ше и́мя Аганя́н?
— Нет, Аганя́н—фами́лия. Зову́т меня́ Гайда́р Була́тович.
— Поня́тно. Гайда́р не ру́сское и́мя?
— Не ру́сское. По национа́льности я армяни́н. Живу́ в Ерева́не. Извини́те, Пе́гги, о́чень прия́тно познако́миться, но у меня́ сейча́с ле́кция.
— До свида́ния.
— До свида́ния.

Ме́жду про́чим

Комплиме́нты. No matter how well Russians speak English, they will probably respond to a compliment about their ability to speak a foreign language with denials, such as **Нет-нет, что вы!** (*Oh, no! Not at all!*)

Па́спорт и национа́льность. Russia is a multinational state. At age sixteen each citizen receives a passport that serves as a national ID. The passport contains the person's address, marital and military status, and **национа́льность** or ethnic group, which is based on the ethnic origin of either parent.

A. Как по-ру́сски …? Ask your partner how to say the following words in Russian. Follow the example.

Образе́ц: — Я забы́л, как по-ру́сски «dress».
  — По-ру́сски э́то бу́дет «пла́тье».

> The expression **я забы́л(а)** (*I forgot*) is marked for gender. A man says **я забы́л**, and a woman says **я забы́ла**.

a. shirt	f. suit	k. blouse
b. coat	g. tie	l. skirt
c. shoes	h. jacket	m. glasses
d. jeans	i. T-shirt	n. pants
e. sneakers	j. watch	o. overcoat

B. Кто они́ по национа́льности? Identify the people in the pictures. Then indicate their nationalities. Follow the model.

Образе́ц:

Это—Джордж Ха́ррисон.
Он англича́нин.

1.

2.

3.

4.

5.

6.

ЯЗЫК В ДЕЙСТВИИ

ДАВАЙТЕ ПОГОВОРИМ

A. **Подгото́вка к разгово́ру.** Review the dialogs. How would you do the following?

- ask if someone knows Spanish, English, French, etc.
- describe your level in speaking, reading, and understanding in a language you know
- find out the meaning of a word you don't know in Spanish (French, Russian, etc.)
- praise someone's language ability
- respond to a compliment about your Russian
- ask where someone learned Russian (English, Spanish, etc.)
- find out if someone's name is Russian (French, Spanish, etc.)
- indicate that you don't understand fast speech
- find out if you are speaking too fast

B. **Иностра́нные языки́.** Working in pairs, find out as much as you can about each other's knowledge of foreign languages. Then survey the other pairs in your class to find out what languages they know, and compile a list of all the languages known.

C. **Немно́го о карти́нах.** Describe one of the pictures below to a partner in as much detail as you can, using the material from this unit. Your partner will ask you for additional information. Reverse roles for the other picture.

1.

2.

D. **Игровы́е ситуа́ции.** Imagine that you are in Moscow and act out the following situations.

1. You are applying for a translating job and are asked to describe your language background. Your prospective employer may be interested in one skill more than another (for example, reading over speaking).

2. Start a conversation with a Russian on any topic. If you find it goes too fast for you, slow it down.

3. You have just started a conversation with a Russian in Russian, but your language is still too limited to talk about much. Find out if you share another language.

4. Working with a partner, prepare and act out a situation of your own that deals with the topics of this unit.

E. **Устный перево́д.** You are an interpreter for a foreigner visiting Moscow. At a party, the foreigner, who speaks no Russian, is interested in meeting a Russian who speaks no English. Help them out.

English speaker's part

1. Hi. Let me introduce myself. My name is …. What's your name?
2. Pleased to meet you. [Name and patronymic of the Russian] do you know English?
3. No, I don't know Russian. I understand a little French and Italian.
4. Yes, I go to school at a small university in California. How about you?
5. Do you live in St. Petersburg?
6. Goodbye.

ДАВАЙТЕ ПОЧИТАЕМ

A. **Ку́рсы иностра́нных языко́в.**

1. Look at this newpaper ad with the following questions in mind.

   - What is the name of the company?
   - What languages are being offered?
   - Who are the instructors?

2. Go back to the ad and underline all the cognates (words that sound like English words).

3. If the root **-скор-** means fast, what is the meaning of the adjective **ускóренный?**

Фи́рма «ЛИ́НГВА»
объявляет открытие курсов иностранных языков

◆ **английского**

◆ **французского**
◆ **немецкого**

Приглашаем взрослых и учащихся старших классов. Обучаем быстро, интересно, основательно.

Лучшие учебные пособия, лингофонные и видеокурсы, а, главное, высококвалифицированные, опытные преподаватели из Англии, США, Германии, Франции и Канады. Для коммерсантов мы предлагаем ускоренные бизнес-курсы: девять недель по шесть часов в день.

Телефон: 158-06-90 (с 16 до 19 часов ежедневно, кроме субботы и воскресенья). Адрес: ул. Врубеля, 8, ст. метро «Сокол».

B. **Иностра́нные языки́.** Working in pairs or small groups, go through the newspaper ad and extract from it as much information as you can. Compare the information you got with other groups. What clues did you use to get the information?

ВЫ ЕДЕТЕ В АМЕРИКУ? А ЯЗЫК?

Фирма «НТМ» поможет вам быстро освоить **английский язык** с использованием современных методик и пособий США и Канады. Мы предлагаем

· курсы ускоренного обучения
· бизнес-курсы
· курсы для иммигрантов

Оплата по наличному и безналичному расчёту.

Тел. 236-98-78, 236-66-96

ДАВАЙТЕ ПОСЛУШАЕМ 📼

Рекла́ма по ра́дио.

1. Listen to the radio ad and decide what is being advertised. Then name three key points you expect to find in it.

2. Listen to the ad again with the following questions in mind:

   a. At which segment of the listening audience is the ad aimed (children, teenagers, adults, etc.)?
   b. What services are offered?
   c. What is the advertiser's strongest drawing card?
   d. Name one other feature of the services provided.
   e. Where can you get more information?

В ПОМОЩЬ УЧАЩИМСЯ

3.1 VERB CONJUGATION

Verbs, like nouns and adjectives, are made up of **stems** and **endings.**

For most Russian verbs, the infinitive is easily recognized by its ending: **-ть.** The infinitive form is the one listed in Russian dictionaries. The infinitive is also used in several specific contexts, such as **Я хочу́ чита́ть** (*I want to read*); **Я люблю́ чита́ть** (*I like to read*). For the time being, you will not use infinitives, but rather the conjugated forms of Russian verbs.

In the present tense, the endings on Russian verbs change to agree with the subject: я **чита́ю,** ты **чита́ешь,** он **чита́ет,** она́ **чита́ет,** мы **чита́ем,** вы **чита́ете,** они́ **чита́ют.** This is called **verb conjugation**.

In Russian there are two basic conjugation patterns: first and second conjugation. When you learn a Russian verb, you must learn its conjugation in addition to its infinitive (dictionary) form. The conjugation of verbs cannot be predicted from the infinitive until you know more about Russian.

3.2 FIRST-CONJUGATION VERBS:
-Ю (-У),-ЕШЬ, -ЕТ, -ЕМ, -ЕТЕ, -ЮТ(-УТ)

The following chart shows the endings for first-conjugation verbs.

	знать	чита́ть	понима́ть	изуча́ть	
я	зна́ - ю	чита́ - ю	понима́ - ю	изуча́ - ю	**-ю**
ты	зна́ - ешь	чита́ - ешь	понима́ - ешь	изуча́ - ешь	**-ешь**
он/она́	зна́ - ет	чита́ - ет	понима́ -ет	изуча́ -ет	**-ет**
мы	зна́ - ем	чита́ - ем	понима́ - ем	изуча́ - ем	**-ем**
вы	зна́ - ете	чита́ - ете	понима́ - ете	изуча́ - ете	**-ете**
они́	зна́ - ют	чита́ - ют	понима́ - ют	изуча́ - ют	**-ют**
	to know	*to read*	*to understand*	*to study*	

по - русски = in Russian
русский язык

и: both, and
a: but (mild) (I know Russian, but he know English: no contradiction).
но: but
I study Russian, but I read it badly

For some verbs, such as **писа́ть**—*to write* (**я пишу́, ты пи́шешь**) and **жить**—*to live* (**я живу́, ты живёшь**), the stem of the present tense is not the same as the stem of the infinitive. For this reason you must learn both the infinitive and the conjugation of the given verb.

The verbs **писа́ть** and **жить** illustrate another feature of the first conjugation. When the last letter written in the present tense stem is a consonant instead of a vowel, the ending for the **я** form is spelled **-у** instead of **-ю**. The ending for the **они́** form is spelled **-ут** instead of **-ют**.

писа́ть	
я	пиш - **у́**
ты	пиш - **ешь**
он/она́	пиш - **ет**
мы	пиш - **ем**
вы	пиш - **ете**
они́	пиш - **ут**
	to write

я говорю́ : I speak
я зна́ю русский язык : I know Russian

When the present tense ending is stressed, the vowel in the **ты, он/она́, мы,** and **вы** forms is spelled **ё** rather than **e**.

жить	
я	жив - **у́**
ты	жив - **ёшь**
он/она́	жив - **ёт**
мы	жив - **ём**
вы	жив - **ёте**
они́	жив - **у́т**
	to live

зна́ю
понима́ю } direct object ___ + русский язык
изуча́ю

In this form, means understand, can speak fluently

Упражне́ние

1. а. Ива́н бы́стро __читает__ (чита́ть) по-ру́сски, а я __читаю__ (чита́ть) ме́дленно.

   б. — На каки́х языка́х вы __понимаете__ (понима́ть)?
   — Мы __понимаем__ (понима́ть) по-англи́йски и немно́го по-ру́сски.

   в. — Кто _____ (жить) здесь?
   — Здесь _____ (жить) на́ши студе́нты.

   г. — Вы хорошо́ _____ (писа́ть) по-ру́сски?
   — Да, я _____ (писа́ть) непло́хо.

   д. — Каки́е языки́ вы _____ (знать)?
   — Я _____ (чита́ть) по-испа́нски и по-неме́цки, но пло́хо _____ (понима́ть).

   е. Кристи́на _____ (жить) во Фра́нции, но она́ пло́хо _____ (знать) францу́зский язы́к. Она́ дово́льно хорошо́ _____ (понима́ть), но пло́хо _____ (чита́ть).

   ж. — Ты _____ (жить) в Ме́ксике? Зна́чит, ты _____ (знать) испа́нский язы́к?
   — Зна́ешь, я по-испа́нски хорошо́ говорю́ и _____ (понима́ть), но пло́хо _____ (писа́ть) и _____ (чита́ть).

➤ Complete Oral Drills 1–6 and Written Exercises 1–5 in the Workbook.

3.3 SECOND-CONJUGATION VERBS:
-Ю, -ИШЬ, -ИТ, -ИМ, -ИТЕ, -ЯТ

The following chart shows the endings for second-conjugation verbs. You already know one verb in this family: **говори́ть**.

говори́ть		
я	говор - ю́	**-ю**
ты	говор - и́шь	**-ишь**
он/она́	говор - и́т	**-ит**
мы	говор - и́м	**-им**
вы	говор - и́те	**-ите**
они́	говор - я́т	**-ят**
	to speak, to talk	

How to tell if a verb belongs to the first or second conjugation

The vowel in the **ты, он/она́, мы,** and **вы** forms remains constant. For first-conjugation verbs this vowel is always **е** (ё if stressed); for second- conjugation verbs it is **и.** Therefore, if you know the **ты** form of the verb, you will be able to predict the **он/она́, мы,** and **вы** forms. When a new verb is introduced in future units, the word list at the end of the unit will give the infinitive followed by the **я, ты,** and **они́** forms. For example: **жить (живу́, живёшь, живу́т); говори́ть (говорю́, говори́шь, говоря́т).**

Упражнения

2. Fill in the blanks with the correct form of the verb **говори́ть**.

Мы _____ по-англи́йски, а Ди́ма и Ве́ра _____ по-ру́сски.

3. Make ten truthful statements using the words from the columns below. Conjugate the verb **говори́ть** as needed.

я		по-ру́сски
роди́тели		по-англи́йски
мы	(не) говори́ть	по-испа́нски
ты		по-украи́нски
вы		по-францу́зски
		по-ара́бски
		по-неме́цки

➤ Complete Oral Drills 7–8 and Written Exercise 6 in the Workbook.

3.4 THE POSITION OF ADVERBIAL MODIFIERS IN RUSSIAN SENTENCES

Compare the position of the adverbial modifiers in the following Russian and English sentences.

Ты **хорошо́** говори́шь по-ру́сски.	You speak Russian *well.*
Он **о́чень** лю́бит ру́сский язы́к.	He likes Russian *very much.*

Adverbial modifiers such as **хорошо́, пло́хо,** and **немно́го** usually precede verbs. However, if one is responding to the question **как** (*how*), the adverb comes last. This conforms to the tendency in Russian for new or stressed information to come at the end of the sentence. For example:

— **Как** вы говори́те по-ру́сски?	*How* do you speak Russian?
— Я говорю́ **хорошо́.**	I speak it *well.*

➤ Review Oral Drill 8 in the Workbook.

3.5 TALKING ABOUT LANGUAGES—*ЯЗЫКИ*

Learning a language means not only learning words. You must also learn how the words are related to one another in a sentence, because putting words together randomly does not produce meaningful sentences. Many Russian verbs are always used in a particular grammatical construction. That is, they always occur in a particular grammatical *environment*. When learning such verbs, you must learn their grammatical environment as well.

The Russian verbs for speaking, reading, writing, knowing, understanding, and studying a language have different grammatical environments. The verbs **говори́ть** (*to speak*), **чита́ть** (*to read*), and **писа́ть** (*to write*) require one kind of grammatical structure. **Знать** (*to know*) and **изуча́ть** (*to study*), on the other hand, require a different grammatical structure.

- The examples on the next page show that questions with the verbs **говори́ть, чита́ть,** and **писа́ть** require the question phrase in the prepositional case: **На како́м языке́ ...?** (*What language ...?*) and **На каки́х языка́х ...?** (*What languages ...?*). Statements with these verbs require a special form of the language: **по-ру́сски, по-испа́нски, по-италья́нски,** etc.

На каки́х языка́х …?

— На каки́х языка́х вы **говори́те?**
— Я говорю́ **по-ру́сски** и **по-англи́йски.**

— На каки́х языка́х вы **чита́ете?**
— Я чита́ю **по-испа́нски** и **по-францу́зски.**

— На како́м языке́ вы хорошо́ **пи́шете?**
— Я хорошо́ пишу́ **по-англи́йски.**

• Questions asked with the verbs **знать** and **изуча́ть** require the question phrase in the accusative case: **Како́й язы́к …?** (*What language …?*) and **Каки́е языки́ …?** (*What languages …?*). Statements with these verbs require forms like: **англи́йский язы́к, испа́нский язы́к, италья́нский язы́к,** etc.

Каки́е языки́ …?

— Каки́е языки́ вы **зна́ете?**
— Я зна́ю **англи́йский и испа́нский языки́.**

— Како́й язы́к вы **изуча́ете** в университе́те?
— Я изуча́ю **францу́зский язы́к.**

• The verb **понима́ть** can be used with either structure.

— Каки́е языки́ **понима́ет** твоя́ ма́ма?
— Она́ понима́ет **испа́нский и неме́цкий языки́.**

— На како́м языке́ **понима́ет** ваш па́па?
— Он понима́ет **по-испа́нски.**

The next chart summarizes when to use which form.

	по-...ски *по* -й *and по* язы́к	...ский язы́к *Must have* -й *and* язы́к
Говори́ть **Чита́ть** **Писа́ть**	Я говорю́ по-ру́сски. Я чита́ю по-ру́сски. Я пишу́ по-ру́сски.	
Зна́ть **Изуча́ть**		Я зна́ю ру́сский язы́к. Я изуча́ю ру́сский язы́к.
Понима́ть	Я понима́ю по-ру́сски. *OR*	Я понима́ю ру́сский язы́к.

Упражнения

4. Answer the following questions in Russian.

   а. Какие языки вы знаете?
   б. Какие языки вы понимаете?
   в. На каких языках вы хорошо говорите? Читаете?
   г. Какие языки знают ваши родители?
   д. На каком языке вы говорите дома?
   е. Какие языки вы изучаете?

5. How would you express the following in Russian?

   a. What languages do you know?
   b. We understand English and German.
   c. We read Spanish.
   d. And we are studying Russian.

➤ Complete Oral Drills 9–15 and Written Exercises 7–9 in the Workbook.

3.6   TALKING ABOUT NATIONALITIES

When identifying a non-Russian by nationality, Russian uses a noun. In English you may say *She is an American* (noun) or *She is American* (adjective). In Russian there is only one way to express this idea: **Она американка** (noun). In Russian the adjective is used only if the nationality term modifies another noun. For example: **Это американская студентка** (*This is an American student*).

There is no noun of nationality for a Russian person; adjectives are used.

Он русский.   **Она русская.**   **Они русские.**

Nouns and adjectives referring to nationalities are not capitalized in Rusian, unless they start a new sentence.

Упражнение

6. Answer the following questions in Russian.

   а. Кто по национальности ваша мама?
   б. Кто по национальности ваш папа?
   в. На каком языке вы говорите дома?

➤ Complete Written Exercise 9 in the Workbook.

3.7 THE PREPOSITIONAL CASE

You have been using the prepositional case after the preposition **в** to indicate location. For example: **Я живу́ в Аме́рике.**

The prepositional singular ending for masculine and neuter modifiers is **-ом** (**-ем** where necessary to avoid breaking the 5-letter spelling rule or to keep a soft stem soft.) The prepositional singular ending for feminine modifiers is **-ой** (**-ей** where necessary to avoid breaking the 5-letter spelling rule or to keep a soft stem soft.) For most declinable singular nouns the prepositional singular ending is **-е**. In two cases this ending is **-и**: (1) to avoid writing **-ие** as the last two letters in the prepositional singular, and (2) for feminine nouns ending in **-ь**. The plural forms are given here for those who want to know them now. They will be dealt in more detail in a later unit.

[handwritten: in the suitcase: в чемода́не   in the new suitcase: в но́вом чемода́не]

	ADJECTIVES		NOUNS	
singular masculine and neuter	но́в - ом после́дн - ем	**-ом** **-ем**	чемода́н - е письм - е́	**-е**
singular feminine	но́в - ой после́дн - ей	**-ой** **-ей**	кварти́р - е	**-е**
plural	но́в - ых после́дн - их	**-ых** **-их**	язык-а́х общежи́ти - ях	**-ах** **-ях**

[handwritten left margin: When the last syllable is stressed, the ending is ой: большо́й]

[handwritten: в кварти́ре: in the apartment;   в но́вой кварти́р : in the new apartmen.   в больш́ой шко́ле : in the large school]

Notes

1. a. Always delete the old ending before adding a new one.
   b. Add the ending that will allow the stem to retain its hard or soft nature (unless this would cause you to break a spelling rule).
   c. Never break a spelling rule. The 5-letter spelling rule is important here. After **ш, щ, ж, ч, ц**, do not write **о** if unstressed, write **е** instead: **В хоро́шем университе́те.**

2. For prepositional singular nouns, never write **-ие** as the last two letters; write **-ии** instead: **общежи́тие** ⟶ **в общежи́тии, Росси́я** ⟶ **в Росси́и.**

3. The prepositional singular ending for feminine nouns ending in **-ь** is **-и**: **Сиби́рь** ⟶ **в Сиби́ри.**

4. Some masculine nouns with **е** or **о** in the semi-final position lose this vowel whenever an ending is added: **пода́рок** ⟶ **в пода́рке.**

5. Words of foreign origin ending in **-о, -и**, or **-у** are indeclinable. They never change their form: **Ога́йо** ⟶ **в Ога́йо, Цинцинна́ти** ⟶ **в Цинцинна́ти**

6. The prepositional case endings for the possessive pronouns **чей, мой, твой, наш, ваш** and the demonstrative **э́тот** are given below. These are not irregular, but because they involve stress shifts, soft endings, and applications of spelling rules, you may wish simply to memorize them.

Язык=language (handwritten)
русски язык=Russian language (handwritten)

masculine and neuter singular	мо - ём тво - ём наш - ем	ваш - ем чь - ём эт - ом
feminine singular	мо - ей тво - ей наш - ей	ваш - ей чь - ей эт - ой
plural	мо - их тво - их наш - их	ваш - их чь - их эт - их

The possessive pronouns **его́, её,** and **их** never change their form:
Кни́га в **его́ (её, их)** ко́мнате.

Упражнение

7. Make sentences that tell where the following people live.

    a. студе́нты—большо́е общежи́тие, на́ше общежи́тие, э́то общежи́тие
    б. Ди́ма—ма́ленькая кварти́ра, хоро́шая кварти́ра, их кварти́ра
    в. Лари́са—ста́рый го́род, наш го́род, э́тот го́род, интере́сный го́род
    г. они́—Но́вая Англия
    д. Хосе́—Испа́ния
    е. Курт—Эсто́ния
    ж. Мари́—Фра́нция
    з. Мари́я—Ме́ксика
    и. Джордж—Цинцинна́ти
    й. Дже́ннифер—Сан-Франци́ско
    к. Ке́вин—Миссу́ри
    л. Михаи́л—хоро́ший дом, большо́й дом
    м. ба́бушка—ваш дом
    н. Ната́ша—их дом
    о. Анна—большо́й штат, наш штат, э́тот штат

➤ Complete Oral Drills 16–18 and Written Exercises 10–11 in the Workbook.

3.8 CONJUNCTIONS: *И , А , НО*

This table shows in what situations the conjunctions **и, а,** and **но** are used.

	И	А	НО
compound subject	Ка́тя **и** Яша ру́сские.		
compound predicate	Они́ чита́ют **и** пи́шут по-ру́сски.		
but rather		Это не Ки́ра, **а** Ка́тя. Ки́ра говори́т не по-неме́цки, **а** по-ру́сски.	
first word in continuing question		— До́ма они́ говоря́т по-ру́сски. — **А** отку́да они́ зна́ют ру́сский язы́к?	
to combine two clauses • to make the *same comment* about two different subjects	Ка́тя ру́сская, **и** Яша ру́сский.		
• to make *different comments* about two different topics		Ка́тя ру́сская, **а** Энн америка́нка.	
• to indicate that the information in the second clause is a logical result of the first	Яша ру́сский, **и** он хорошо́ зна́ет ру́сский язы́к.		
• to indicate that the information in the second clause is un-expected, or that it in some way limits the information in the first clause			Я изуча́ю ру́сский язы́к, **но** говорю́ ещё пло́хо.

Упражнения

8. Review the dialogs on pages 72-73. Find sentences with the conjunctions **и, а,** and **но.** Group them in appropriate columns.

9. How would you express the following paragraph in Russian? Pay special attention to the underlined conjunctions.

Masha <u>and</u> Styopa are Russians. They live in Moscow <u>and</u> go to the university. She studies French <u>and</u> he studies English. She knows French, <u>but</u> reads slowly. Styopa knows not Spanish, <u>but</u> English.

ОБЗОРНЫЕ УПРАЖНЕНИЯ

A. You are the administrator of a new foreign language program whose budget is large enough to offer instruction in five languages. Which languages would you include? Next to each language on your list, write a sentence indicating why you would include it.

B. You are a guide for a group of Russian tourists who are going to visit Europe. You need to find out in which countries they will need an interpreter. Write a brief list of questions to give them.

C. **На како́м языке́ вы говори́те до́ма?** Listen to the conversation and fill in the missing words.

Вади́м: Здра́вствуй! Что э́то у тебя́, уче́бник ру́сского языка́? Но ты уже́ свобо́дно _____ по-ру́сски. У тебя́ ведь роди́тели _____ .

Анна: Нет, то́лько ма́ма ру́сская. Па́па _____ . И до́ма мы говори́м _____ .

Вади́м: Да, но ведь _____ ты _____ практи́чески всё. Заче́м тебе́ уче́бник?

Анна: В то́м-то и де́ло. Я всё понима́ю, но _____ пло́хо. И поэ́тому я _____ ру́сский язы́к _____ . Тепе́рь до́ма _____ с ма́мой то́лько по-ру́сски.

Вади́м: А как же твой па́па? Он понима́ет, что вы говори́те?

Анна: Нет! Поэ́тому он говори́т, что то́же хо́чет изуча́ть _____ в университе́те.

D. **Интервью.** You have been asked to interview a Russian visitor.

1. List a few questions you could ask the visitor about his or her language or ethnic background.

2. Role play a meeting with a Russian visitor in which you ask your questions.

3. Write a short letter to a Russian pen pal telling what you learned about the visitor.

E. **Сочинéние—Мои родúтели.** Write a short composition about your parents' nationality and knowledge of languages. Give as much information as you can, keeping within the bounds of the Russian you know.

НОВЫЕ СЛОВА И ВЫРАЖЕНИЯ

NOUNS

америка́н(е)ц/америка́нка	American
англича́нин (*pl.* англича́не)/англича́нка	English
ара́б/ара́бка	Arab
армяни́н (*pl.* армя́не)/армя́нка	Armenian
Ерева́н	Yerevan (city in Armenia)
испа́н(е)ц/испа́нка	Spanish
италья́н(е)ц/италья́нка	Italian
кана́д(е)ц/кана́дка	Canadian
кита́(е)ц (*pl.* кита́йцы)/китая́нка	Chinese
кварти́ра	apartment
ле́кция	lecture
ма́ма	mom
мать (*fem.*) (*pl.* ма́тери)	mother
мексика́н(е)ц/мексика́нка	Mexican
не́м(е)ц/не́мка	German
общежи́тие	dormitory
от(е́)ц	father
па́па	dad
роди́тели	parents
ру́сский/ру́сская	Russian
семья́ (*pl.* се́мьи)	family
сло́во (*pl.* слова́)	word
украи́н(е)ц/украи́нка	Ukrainian
францу́з/францу́женка	French
язы́к (*pl.* языки́)	language
япо́н(е)ц/япо́нка	Japanese

PRONOUNS

всё	everything
мы	we

ADJECTIVES

англи́йский	English
ара́бский	Arabic
испа́нский	Spanish
италья́нский	Italian
кита́йский	Chinese
неме́цкий	German
после́дний	last
ру́сский	Russian
Санкт-Петербу́ргский	(of) St. Petersburg
украи́нский	Ukrainian
францу́зский	French
япо́нский	Japanese

VERBS

говори́ть (говорю́, говори́шь, говоря́т)	to speak, to say
жить (живу́, живёшь, живу́т)	to live
знать (зна́ю, зна́ешь, зна́ют)	to know
изуча́ть (изуча́ю, изуча́ешь, изуча́ют)(*что*)	to study (*requires direct object*)
писа́ть (пишу́, пи́шешь, пи́шут)	to write
понима́ть (понима́ю, понима́ешь, понима́ют)	to understand
чита́ть (чита́ю, чита́ешь, чита́ют)	to read

ADVERBS

бы́стро	quickly
всегда́	always
дово́льно	quite
ещё	still
иногда́	sometimes
ме́дленно	slowly
немно́го, немно́жко	a little
непло́хо	pretty well
норма́льно	in a normal way
о́чень	very
пло́хо	poorly
по-англи́йски	English
по-ара́бски	Arabic
по-испа́нски	Spanish
по-италья́нски	Italian
по-кита́йски	Chinese
по-неме́цки	German
по-ру́сски	Russian
по-украи́нски	Ukrainian
по-францу́зски	French
по-япо́нски	Japanese
свобо́дно	fluently
сейча́с	now
так	so
хорошо́	well

CONJUNCTIONS

где	where
когда́	when
но	but
что	that

NEGATIVE PARTICLE

не   not (*negates following word*)

OTHER WORDS AND PHRASES

Большо́е спаси́бо.	Thank you very much.
В па́спорте стои́т …	In my passport it says …
Говори́те ме́дленнее.	Speak more slowly.
До свида́ния.	Goodbye.
до́ма	at home
Извини́те.	Excuse me.
Как по-ру́сски …?	How do you say … in Russian?
Кто … по национа́льности?	What is …'s nationality?
На каки́х языка́х вы говори́те до́ма?	What languages do you speak at home?
На како́м языке́ вы говори́те до́ма?	What language do you speak at home?
одно́ сло́во	one word
Отку́да вы зна́ете ру́сский язы́к?	How do you know Russian?
пожа́луйста	please
по национа́льности	by nationality
Разреши́те предста́виться.	Allow me to introduce myself.
Что́ вы (ты)!	*response to a compliment*
Что э́то тако́е?	(Just) what is that?
Я забы́л(а).	I forgot.

NUMBERS

21–30 (*for understanding*)

PERSONALIZED VOCABULARY

_____

_____

_____

_____

УНИВЕРСИТЕТ

▼ **КОММУНИКАТИВНЫЕ ЗАДАНИЯ**

Talking about where and what
    people study
Presentation about yourself
Reading and writing academic
    schedules
Reading diplomas and transcripts

▼ **В ПОМОЩЬ УЧАЩИМСЯ**

Учи́ться vs. **изуча́ть (что)**
The 8-letter spelling rule
На како́м ку́рсе …?
на + prepositional case for location
Accusative case of modifiers
    and nouns
Conjunctions: **где, что, как,**
    потому́ что

▼ **МЕЖДУ ПРОЧИМ**

Higher education in Russia: univer-
    sities and institutes
Russian diplomas
Using the 24-hour clock for schedules

ТОЧКА ОТСЧЁТА

О ЧЁМ ИДЁТ РЕЧЬ?

A. Taking turns with a partner, ask and answer the following questions about where you go to college, what year of study you are in, what your major is, and what courses you are currently taking. Follow the models.

1. — Где вы сейча́с у́читесь?
   — Я учу́сь …

в Калифорни́йском (госуда́рственном) университе́те
в Виско́нсинском (госуда́рственном) университе́те
в Пенсильва́нском (госуда́рственном) университе́те

в Джорджта́унском университе́те
в Га́рвардском университе́те
в Дю́кском университе́те

в Университе́те (и́мени) Джо́рджа Ва́шингтона
в Университе́те (и́мени) Джо́нса Го́пкинса

> **Имени** means *named for* and is often omitted.

в Мичига́нском госуда́рственном университе́те
в Госуда́рственном университе́те шта́та Ога́йо
в Госуда́рственном университе́те шта́та Нью-Йо́рк

Your teacher will tell you the name of your college or university.

2. — На како́м ку́рсе вы у́читесь?
   — Я учу́сь …

	пе́рвом	
	второ́м	
на	тре́тьем	ку́рсе
	четвёртом	
	пя́том	
в	аспиранту́ре.	

национальность
anything ending with -ность is feminine.

3. — Кака́я у вас специа́льность?
   — Моя́ специа́льность …
   ↑ feminine

англи́йская
литерату́ра

архитекту́ра

биоло́гия

исто́рия

ру́сский язы́к

фи́зика

медици́на

му́зыка

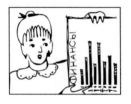

фина́нсы

хи́мия

эконо́мика

юриспруде́нция

Други́е специа́льности:

антрополо́гия
вычисли́тельная те́хника
матема́тика
междунаро́дные отноше́ния
педаго́гика
полити́ческие нау́ки

психоло́гия
ру́сское странове́дение
социоло́гия
филоло́гия
филосо́фия

4. — Что вы изуча́ете?
   — Я изуча́ю …

англи́йскую литерату́ру	психоло́гию
антрополо́гию	ру́сский язы́к
архитекту́ру	ру́сское странове́дение
биоло́гию	социоло́гию
вычисли́тельную те́хнику	фи́зику
исто́рию	фина́нсы
матема́тику	филоло́гию
междунаро́дные отноше́ния	филосо́фию
медици́ну	хи́мию
му́зыку	эконо́мику
педаго́гику	юриспруде́нцию
полити́ческие нау́ки	

B. Make three lists of subjects: those you have taken, those you are taking now, and those you need to take.

C. Make a list of the subjects you like the best and the least.

D. **Разгово́ры.** Listen to the conversations with the following questions in mind.

Разгово́р 1: В общежи́тии
(Разгова́ривают ру́сский и иностра́нец)

1. A Russian is speaking with a foreigner. What nationality is the foreigner?
2. What is he doing in Russia?
3. Where does he go to school in his home country?
4. In which year of university study is he?

Разгово́р 2: В библиоте́ке
(Разгова́ривают ру́сский и америка́нка)

1. What is the American student doing in Russia?
2. What is her field of study?
3. What does the Russian say about the American's Russian?
4. What is the man's name?
5. What is the woman's name?

Разгово́р 3: Я вас не по́нял!
(Разгова́ривают ру́сский и иностра́нец)

1. One of the participants is a foreigner. What makes that obvious?
2. Where is the foreigner from?
3. What is he doing in Russia?
4. What interests does the foreigner have besides Russian?
5. What are the names of the two speakers?

🔊 ДИАЛОГИ

1 **Где вы у́читесь?**

— Где вы у́читесь?
— В Моско́вском университе́те.
— Вот как?! А на како́м ку́рсе?
— На тре́тьем.
— Кака́я у вас специа́льность?
— Журнали́стика.
— Кака́я интере́сная специа́льность!
— Да, я то́же так ду́маю.

2 **Вы у́читесь и́ли рабо́таете?**

— Вы у́читесь и́ли рабо́таете?
— Я учу́сь.
— В университе́те?
— Нет, в Институ́те иностра́нных языко́в.
— А каки́е языки́ вы зна́ете?
— Я хорошо́ говорю́ по-англи́йски. Немно́жко чита́ю и понима́ю по-францу́зски.
— Молоде́ц! А я то́лько немно́жко говорю́ по-ру́сски.

> If you are no longer a student, you will want to be able to answer the question **Где вы учи́лись?** *(Where did you study/go to college?)* The answer to this question is marked for gender. A woman says **Я учи́лась в … университе́те.** A man says **Я учи́лся в … университе́те.**

3 **Я изуча́ю ру́сский язы́к.**

— Ли́нда, где ты у́чишься в Аме́рике?
— В Иллино́йском госуда́рственном университе́те.
— Кака́я у тебя́ специа́льность?
— Ещё не зна́ю. Мо́жет быть, ру́сский язы́к и литерату́ра.
— А что ты изуча́ешь здесь, в Росси́и?
— Я изуча́ю ру́сский язы́к.
— Но ты уже́ хорошо́ говори́шь по-ру́сски!
— Нет, что ты! Ру́сский язы́к о́чень тру́дный!

4 **Я изуча́ю англи́йский язы́к.**

— Вале́ра! Что ты чита́ешь?
— Америка́нский журна́л «Тайм». Очень интере́сный журна́л.
— Ты хорошо́ чита́ешь по-англи́йски. Молоде́ц!
— Не о́чень хорошо́. Я сейча́с изуча́ю англи́йский язы́к.
— Где?
— На филологи́ческом факульте́те, на ка́федре англи́йского языка́.
— Там хоро́шие преподава́тели?
— Коне́чно!

5 **Вы у́читесь в Аме́рике?**

— Вы в Аме́рике у́читесь?
— Я не по́нял. Как вы сказа́ли?
— Вы у́читесь в Аме́рике?
— В Аме́рике? Да, учу́сь. В Джорджта́унском университе́те.
— А что вы там изуча́ете?
— Европе́йскую исто́рию, ру́сский язы́к, полити́ческие нау́ки, эконо́мику. Я люблю́ ру́сский язы́к. Ой, у меня́ сейча́с ле́кция. До свида́ния!
— До свида́ния! Я ваш сосе́д. Живу́ здесь, в общежи́тии.

> **Я не по́нял (поняла́)** *I didn't catch that.* This phrase is marked for gender. A man says **Я не по́нял**; a woman says **Я не поняла́.**

A. **Уче́бный день.** Following the example of the daily planner below, make a schedule of your day. Adjust the times to reflect those of your own classes. Note that most university classes in Russia last an hour and a half.

9.00	*англи́йский язы́к – фоне́тика*
10.30	*англи́йский язы́к – пра́ктика*
12.00	*америка́нская литерату́ра*
13.30	*обе́д*
15.00	*дискуссио́нный клуб*
16.30	*аэро́бика*
19.30	*кинофи́льм*

> Russians use the 24-hour clock for all schedules. Note that periods, not colons, are used between minutes and seconds.

B. **Предме́ты.** With your partner, discuss your opinion about the following school subjects. Use adjectives from the column on the right. Make sure they agree with the subject in gender and number.

Образе́ц: — Я ду́маю, что ру́сский язы́к о́чень тру́дный.
— Я то́же так ду́маю.

и́ли

— Я ду́маю, что ру́сский язы́к не тру́дный.

биоло́гия
фи́зика
испа́нский язы́к   тру́дный
неме́цкий язы́к   не тру́дный
эконо́мика   интере́сный
филосо́фия   не интере́сный
фина́нсы

ВЫСШЕЕ ОБРАЗОВАНИЕ В РОССИИ

Пя́тый курс. Russian students normally spend five years in the university.

Университе́ты и институ́ты. What is called college in the U.S. might be an **университе́т** or an **институ́т** in Russia. There are fewer universities in Russia than in the United States. Only the largest cities have more than one. On the other hand, cities may have several institutes, each devoted to its own discipline: **медици́нский институ́т, энергети́ческий институ́т, институ́т ру́сского языка́,** and so forth. Admission, based on high school grades and entrance exams, is extremely competitive, especially in the case of the more prestigious universities such as **Моско́вский госуда́рственный университе́т.** Students declare their major upon application and, if admitted, take a standard set of courses with virtually no electives. Graduation is likely to lead to a job in one's major field, usually in the city where the school is located if the student grew up there.

Факульте́т. Russian universities are made up of units called **факульте́ты,** which are somewhere in size between what Americans call divisions and departments. A typical university would normally include **математи́ческий факульте́т, филологи́ческий факульте́т** (languages, literatures, linguistics), **истори́ческий факульте́т, юриди́ческий факульте́т,** etc.

Ка́федра. It is roughly equivalent to a department. For instance, the **филологи́ческий факульте́т** may include **ка́федра ру́сского языка́, ка́федра англи́йского языка́,** and other individual language **ка́федры.**

Язык в действии

ДАВАЙТЕ ПОГОВОРИМ

A. **Подготóвка к разговóру.** Review the dialogs. How would you do the following?

- tell someone where you go (or went) to school
- say what year of college you are in
- tell someone what your major is
- tell someone what languages you know and how well
- tell someone where you live
- tell someone what courses you are taking
- express agreement with an opinion
- respond to a compliment
- state that you missed something that was said

B. **На какóм кýрсе ты ýчишься?** Ask what year your classmates are in. Find out what courses they are taking. Report your findings to others in the class.

C. **Автобиогрáфия.** You are in a Russian classroom on the first day of class. The teacher has asked everybody to tell a bit about themselves. Be prepared to talk for at least one minute without notes. Remember to say what you can, not what you can't!

D. **Игровы́е ситуáции.** Imagine that you are in Russia and act out the following situations.

1. Start up a conversation with someone at a party and make as much small talk as you can. If your partner talks too fast, explain the state of your Russian to slow the conversation down. When you have run out of things to say, close the conversation properly.

2. You are talking to a person who knows several languages. Find out as much as you can about your new friend's language background.

3. Now imagine that you are in your own country. You are a reporter for your campus newspaper. Interview a Russian exchange student whose English is minimal.

4. Working with a partner, prepare and act out a situation of your own that deals with the topics of this unit. Remember to use what you know, not what you don't.

E. **Устный перевод.**

The verbs **говори́ть** *(to say)*, **ду́мать** *(to think)*, **спра́шивать** *(to ask),* and **отвеча́ть** *(to answer)* allow you to assume the point of view of a third person in the interpreting exercises: *She says that ..., He thinks ..., They are asking ...,* etc. Below you see some lines that might come up in interpreting. Practice changing them from direct speech into indirect speech.

American and Ukrainian	*Interpreter*
— What's your name and patronymic?	— Он спра́шивает, как ва́ше и́мя-о́тчество.
— **Меня́ зову́т Кири́лл Па́влович.**	— He says his name is Kirill Pavlovich.

— What's your last name?
— **Са́венко.**
— Is that a Ukrainian last name?
— **Украи́нская.**
— Where do you live?
— **Здесь, в Москве́. А вы, ка́жется, америка́нец?**
— Yes.
— **Вы хорошо́ говори́те по-ру́сски!**
— Not really. Russian is very hard.

Now use the verbs you have just practiced in the interpreting situation below.

A reporter for your college newspaper wants to conduct an interview with a visiting Russian student and has asked you to interpret.

English speaker's part

1. What is your name?
2. What is your last name?
3. Where do you go to school?
4. Which university?
5. That is very interesting. In what department?
6. So your major is history?
7. That's very good. Do you know English?
8. Are you studying English now?
9. Goodbye.

ДАВАЙТЕ ПОЧИТАЕМ

A. **Дипло́м Моско́вского университе́та.**

1. Working in pairs, write down two or three things you would expect to find in a university diploma.

2. Now read the diploma to see if you can find these pieces of information. What else did you find out? Share the information with other pairs.

ДИПЛОМ

В-I № 324028

настоящий диплом выдан .... *Беловой*

.... *Ирине Валентиновне* ....

в том, что он *а* в 19 *82* году поступил *а*

в *Московский государственный*

педагогический ин-т иностр. языков

и в 19 *88* году окончил *а* полный курс ....

названного

института

по специальности ....

иностранный

язык

Решением Государственной экзаменационной комиссии

от « *22* » .... *июля* .... 19 *88* г.

присвоена квалификация *преподавателя*

английского языка ....

Председатель Государственной
экзаменационной комиссии

Ректор

---

3. Go back to the diploma and find the exact name of the university.

4. Review the diploma and find the verbs **поступи́л(а)** and **око́нчил(а).** What are the forms of the Russian past tense?

    a. verbs with masculine subjects   _____

    b. verbs with feminine subjects   _____

5. Underline the Russian equivalents of the following words. What makes these words easy to recognize?

    a. diploma
    b. testing (*adjective*)
    c. qualification
    d. commission

Между прочим

Михаи́л Васи́льевич Ломоно́сов, a founder of Moscow University in 1755, was a scientist, tinkerer, poet, and linguist (somewhat like Benjamin Franklin). He also wrote one of the first Russian grammars.

B. **Приложе́ние к дипло́му.**

1. Jot down the kinds of courses you would expect to find in an official transcript for an Engish major in your country. Which courses are required for everyone receiving a university degree? Which are specific to an English major?

_____

_____

_____

_____

_____

_____

2. Now read through the transcript issued in the 1970's by a Soviet university.

   a. Which subjects listed in the transcript are similar to those taken by English majors in your country?
   b. Which subjects would not normally be taken by English majors in your country?
   c. Which subjects do you think were required in the Soviet system of education?
   d. What do these courses tell you about the goals of Soviet higher education in the 1970's?

Между прочим

THE RUSSIAN GRADE SYSTEM

The following grades are recorded in Russian transcripts:

> **отли́чно (5)**
> **хорошо́ (4)**
> **удовлетвори́тельно (3)**
> **неудовлетвори́тельно (2)**

Students can take courses on a pass/fail basis. A passing grade in this document is recorded as **зачет.**

When talking about grades, students most often refer to them by number:

> **Я получи́л(а)**   **пятёрку (5)**
> **четвёрку (4)**
> **тро́йку (3)**
> **дво́йку (2)**
> **едини́цу (1)**

Although a **едини́ца (1)** is technically the lowest grade a student can receive, in reality a **дво́йка (2)** is a failing grade and **едини́цы** are rarely given.

ПРИЛОЖЕНИЕ К ДИПЛОМУ № 645789
В Ы П И С К А
из зачетной ведомости (без диплома недействительно)

Рыжков Иван Денисович за время пребывания на филологическом факультете Ленинградского ордена Ленина государственного университета им. А. А. Жданова с 1976 по 1978 год сдал экзамены и зачеты по следующим дисциплинам по специальности английский язык и литература.

1. История КПСС ч. I	хорошо
2. История КПСС ч. II	удовлетв.
3. Политическая экономия ч. I	хорошо
4. Политическая экономия ч. II	удовлетв.
5. Диалектический материализм	удовлетв.
6. Исторический материализм	удовлетв.
7. История философии	хорошо
8. Введение в языкознание	хорошо
9. Современный русский язык	удовлетв.
10. Английский язык	хорошо
11. Немецкий язык	хорошо
12. История английского языка	удовлетв.
13. Введение в английскую филологию	хорошо
14. Теоретическая грамматика англ. языка	удовлетв.
15. Теоретическая фонетика	удовлетв.
16. Лексикология	хорошо
17. Латинский язык	хорошо
18. История Англии	удовлетв.
19. География Англии	хорошо
20. Педагогика	хорошо
21. Педагогическая практика	хорошо
22. Методика преподавания	зачет
23. История русск. литературы XIX века I	хорошо
24. История русск. литературы XIX века II	хорошо
25. История русск. литературы XX века и советской литературы	удовлетв.
26. История зарубежной литературы средних веков и эпохи Возрождения	хорошо
27. История зарубежной литературы XIX века	удовлетв.
28. Логика	зачет
29. Психология	зачет
30. Теория литературы	хорошо
31. Курсовая работа	удовлетв.
32. Спецкурс	зачет
33. Спецсеминар	зачет

3. Read the transcript again and see if you can determine the following.

   a. To whom was the transcript issued?
   b. What university issued it?
   c. What kind of grades did this student receive?

4. Go over the transcript again and find all the courses having to do with the study of foreign languages.

5. Find Russian equivalents for these words.

   a. history
   b. geography
   c. pedagogy
   d. logic
   e. philosophy
   f. psychology

6. List five courses you would be most and least interested in taking.

   Most interested   Least interested

   _____   _____

   _____   _____

   _____   _____

   _____   _____

   _____   _____

   дедушка : grandfather

   мальчик : boy

   осёл : donkey

   мельник : miller

Санкт-Петербу́ргский университе́т. You will hear segments of an opening talk from an assistant dean of St. Petersburg University to visiting American students.

1. Imagine that you are about to make a welcoming speech to a group of foreign students who have just arrived at your university. What four or five things would you tell them?

2. The assistant dean's remarks can be broken up into a number of topic areas. Before you listen to the talk, arrange the topics in the order you think they may occur.

   a. composition of the student body
   b. foreign students
   c. foreign students from North America
   d. good luck wishes
   e. opening welcome
   f. structure of the university
   g. student stipends and internships

   Now listen to the talk to see if you were correct.

3. Listen to the talk again with these questions in mind.

   a. How many departments does the university have?
   b. How many institutes are there?
   c. Name one university resource.
   d. How big is the library?
   e. How many students are there?
   f. Name five things that students can major in.
   g. Is the student population limited to the St. Petersburg area? What led you to your conclusion?
   h. What department hosts most of the students from the U.S. and Canada?
   i. Name two other departments that have hosted North American students.
   j. The assistant dean says that two Americans are pursuing interesting individual projects. Name the topic of at least one of the two projects.

4. Listen to the speech again and determine the meaning of these words from context:

   большинство́
   нау́чно-иссле́довательская ста́нция
   пра́ктика

В ПОМОЩЬ УЧАЩИМСЯ

4.1   УЧИТЬСЯ

— Вы **у́читесь** и́ли рабо́таете?   *Do* you *go to school* or work?
— Я **учу́сь.**   *I go to school.*

You are already somewhat familiar with the verb **учи́ться** from Unit 1. The **-ся** or **-сь** at the end of this verb makes it look different from other verbs you have learned. The verb endings before this particle, however, are regular second-conjugation endings, with application of the 8-letter spelling rule. You will learn more **-ся** verbs later.

Here is the complete conjugation of **учи́ться**:

[handwritten: Reflexive: indicates self.]

[handwritten: учить : to teach]
[handwritten: учиться : Teach self.]

учи́ться	
я	уч - **у́** - сь
ты	у́ч - **ишь** - ся
он/она́	у́ч - **ит** - ся
мы	у́ч - **им** - ся
вы	у́ч - **ите** - сь
они́	у́ч - **ат** - ся

> ### *The 8-letter spelling rule*
> After the letters **к, г, х, ш, щ, ж, ч, ц,** write **-у** instead of **-ю,** and **-а** instead of **-я.**

*[handwritten:
я учусь   мы учимся
ты учишься   вы учитесь
он/она учится   они учатся]*

Упражнение

1. Fill in the blanks with the appropriate form of the verb **учи́ться.**

— Ты ___учишься___ и́ли рабо́таешь?
— Я ___учусь___ в университе́те.
— Пра́вда? А мой брат то́же там ___учится___ !
— А я ду́мала, что твой брат рабо́тает.
— Мы с бра́том рабо́таем ве́чером, а днём мы ___учимся___ .

➤ Complete Oral Drills 1–2 in the Workbook.

4.2   THE PREPOSITIONAL CASE: *HA*

You already know that the prepositional case is used after the preposition **в** to indicate location. In this unit you will find several words that are used with the preposition **на** plus the prepositional case to indicate location. The preposition **на** is used instead of **в** in the following situations:

- with activities: **на ле́кции** in class

- with certain words: **на факульте́те** in the division (of a college)
  на ка́федре in the department (of a college)
  на ку́рсе in a year (first, second, etc.) of college

Упражнения

2. Form at least ten sentences in Russian combining words from the columns below. Pay special attention to which words will be used with **в** and which with **на**. Be sure to put the words following **в** or **на** into the prepositional case.

я			филологи́ческий факульте́т
мы			Моско́вский университе́т
профе́ссор	учи́ться	в	пе́рвый курс
э́тот студе́нт	рабо́тать	на	Росси́я
вы			Институ́т иностра́нных языко́в
			ка́федра англи́йского языка́

3. Fill in the blanks with either **в** or **на**.

Ната́ша у́чится _____ четвёртом ку́рсе _____ институ́те _____ Росси́и. Там она́ у́чится _____ филологи́ческом факульте́те, _____ ка́федре испа́нского языка́. Живёт она́ _____ Смоле́нске _____ большо́м общежи́тии.

➤ Complete Oral Drill 3 and Written Exercises 1–5 in the Workbook.

4.3   STUDYING: *УЧИТЬСЯ* vs. *ИЗУЧАТЬ*

— Где вы **у́читесь?**   Where do you *go to school*?
— Я **учу́сь в Га́рвардском университе́те.**   *I go* to Harvard.
— А что вы там **изуча́ете?**   What do you *study* there?
— Фи́зику.   Physics.
— Вы хорошо́ **у́читесь?**   Do you *do* well in school?
— Да, хорошо́.   Yes, I do.

Russian has several verbs that correspond to the English verb *study*. These Russian verbs are used in different situations. The verb **учи́ться** is used to express that someone is a student or goes to school somewhere. It can also be used to indicate what kind of a student someone is. The verb **изуча́ть,** on the other hand, is used to indicate what subject one is taking; the subject studied *must always* be mentioned when this verb is used.

The chart below summarizes in which situations these Russian verbs are used.

	УЧИТЬСЯ	ИЗУЧАТЬ (ЧТО)
No complement	Я учу́сь. *I'm a student.*	
Place	Я учу́сь **в Моско́вском университе́те.** *I go to Moscow University.*	
Adverb (how)	Я **хорошо́** учу́сь. *I do well in school.*	
Direct object (e.g. school subject)		Я изуча́ю **фи́зику.** *I take physics.*

Упражнения

4. How would you express the following in Russian?

— Where do you (**ты**) study?
— At Columbia University.
— What do you (**ты**) take?
— Spanish.
— Do you do well?
— Yes, I do well.

5. Answer the following questions.

   а. Вы у́читесь и́ли рабо́таете? Где? Что вы изуча́ете?
   б. Ва́ша сестра́ у́чится? Где? Что она́ изуча́ет?
   в. Ваш брат у́чится? Где? Что он изуча́ет?
   г. Ва́ши роди́тели учи́лись? Где?

➤ Review Oral Drills 1–3 and Complete Oral Drill 4 in the Workbook.

4.4   THE ACCUSATIVE CASE

(handwritten notes:) (Fem) бе́лка : squirrel   ✓ Inanimate   дом : home   слон : elephant   пальто : something neuter (?)

In Russian the accusative case is used for **direct objects.** A direct object is a noun or a pronoun that receives the action of the verb. The direct objects in the following Russian sentences are in boldface.

Я изуча́ю **ру́сский язы́к.**	I study *Russian (language).*
Я люблю́ **ру́сскую литерату́ру.**	I love *Russian literature.*
Я изуча́ю **ру́сское странове́дение.**	I take *Russian area studies.*
Ты чита́ешь **интере́сные кни́ги.**	You read *interesting books.*

(handwritten:) Я ви́жу бе́лку   Я ви́жу дом   Я ви́жу слона́   Я ви́жу пальто;

Упражне́ние

6. Indicate which of the following words are direct objects. (Note that a sentence may have no direct object.)

   On Friday we heard an interesting lecture on Russian art. The speaker has studied art for several decades. She concentrated on nineteenth-century paintings.

(handwritten:) Я ви́жу чудо́вище   Я ви́жу коня́ ← (from конь : male horse).   Я ви́жу большо́го коня́.

The accusative case of modifiers and nouns

The accusative singular endings for feminine phrases are **-ую** for adjectives (**-юю** if the adjective has a soft stem) and **-у** for nouns (**-ю** if the noun stem is soft; **-ь** for feminine **-ь** words).

For all other phrases (masculine singular, neuter singular, all plurals) the accusative endings are the same as the nominative endings *if the phrase refers to something inanimate* (not alive). The animate/inanimate distinction plays an important role only in the accusative case. The masculine singular animate endings are given in the table for those who want to know them. They will be dealt with in more detail in Unit 7. The accusative plural endings for animate phrases will be introduced later.

(handwritten:) Я ви́жу большу́ю бе́лку   Я ви́жу большо́й дом   Я ви́жу большо́го слона́   Я люблю́ Аню

	ADJECTIVES		NOUNS	
Masculine singular inanimate	но́в - ый после́дн - ий	**-ый** **-ий**	журна́л - Ø слова́р - ь	**-Ø** **-ь**
animate	но́в - ого после́дн - его	**-ого** **-его**	студе́нт - а преподава́тел - я	**-а** **-я**
Neuter singular nouns	но́в - ое после́дн - ее	**-ое** **-ее**	письм - о́ пла́ть - е	**-о** **-е**
Feminine singular nouns	но́в - ую после́дн - юю	**-ую** **-юю**	ма́м - у, газе́т - у Мари́ - ю, ле́кци - ю	**-у** **-ю**
Inanimate plural nouns	но́в - ые после́дн - ие	**-ые** **-ие**	журна́л - ы словар - и́ газе́т - ы ле́кци - и пи́сьм - а пла́ть - я	**-ы** **-и** **-а** **-я**

Notes

1. Some masculine nouns have end stress whenever an ending is added: оте́ц ➡ отца́.

2. Some masculine nouns with **e** or **o** in the semi-final position lose this vowel whenever an ending is added: америка́нец ➡ америка́нца, оте́ц ➡ отца́.

3. The accusative singular of feminine nouns ending in **-ь** is the same as the nominative case: мать ➡ мать, дочь ➡ дочь.

4. Remember that nouns ending in **-а** or **-я** that refer to men and boys decline like feminine nouns, but they are masculine and they take masculine modifiers: Мы зна́ем ма́ленького Ди́му.

5. Remember that masculine singular adjectives with stress on the ending have the ending **-о́й: большо́й, плохо́й**.

6. Some accusative forms of the possessive modifiers **мой, твой, наш,** and **ваш,** and a small number of other modifers have noun-like rather than adjective-like endings. For this reason they are often called special modifiers. The accusative case of the special modifiers you know is given in the next chart.

The accusative case of special modifiers

Masculine singular inanimate	мо - й тво - й наш	ваш чей	э́тот оди́н тре́т - ий
animate	мо - его́ тво - его́ на́ш - его	ва́ш - его чь - его	э́т - ого одн - ого́ тре́ть - его
Neuter singular	мо - ё тво - ё на́ш - е	ва́ш - е чь - ё	э́т - о одн - о́ тре́ть - е
Feminine singular	мо - ю́ тво - ю́ на́ш - у	ва́ш - у чь - ю	э́т - у одн - у́ тре́ть - ю
Plural inanimate	мо - и́ тво - и́ на́ш - и	ва́ш - и чь - и	э́т - и одн - и́ тре́ть - и

7. Recall that the possessive pronouns **его́**–*his,* **её**–*hers,* and **их**–*theirs* never change their form: Вы зна́ете **его́** ма́му? Я чита́ю **её** журна́л. Она́ чита́ет **их** письмо́.

Упражнение

7. Fill in the blanks with adjectives and nouns in the accusative case.

— Ко́стя, ты чита́ешь _____ (ру́сские газе́ты)?

— Да, я чита́ю _____ _____ («Моско́вские но́вости») и _____ («Вече́рняя Москва́»).

Я люблю́ _____ (ру́сские журна́лы) то́же. Я, наприме́р, регуля́рно чита́ю _____ («Но́вый мир») и _____ («Огонёк»).

— А _____ (каки́е газе́ты) ты чита́ешь?

— Я чита́ю _____ («Литерату́рная газе́та»), потому́ что я люблю́ _____ (ру́сская литерату́ра).

➤ Complete Oral Drills 8–10 and Written Exercises 6–8 in the Workbook. Do Written Exercise 6 before you do the Oral Drills.

4.5   CONJUNCTIONS

(1st cong)

Жéня спрáшивает, **где** ýчится Ивáн.	Zhenya asks *where* Ivan goes to school.
Я дýмаю, **что** Ивáн ýчится здесь.	I think (*that*) Ivan goes to school here.
Я отвечáю, **что** Ивáн ýчится здесь.	I answer *that* Ivan goes to school here.
Но я не знáю, **как** он ýчится.	But I don't know *how* he studies. (*how* good a student he is).
Он ýчится на филологи́ческом факультéте, **потомý что** он лю́бит литератýру.	He studies in the department of languages and literatures *because* he loves literature.

As you can see from the examples, you can use clauses such as **я говорю́, мы дýмаем, онá знáет** to start sentences such as *I say that …, We believe that …, She knows that …,* etc.

Note that Russian uses **что** where English uses *that*. But whereas in this context the word *that* is optional in English, the Russian **что** is obligatory.

Also note that in Russian a comma is used before the conjunctions **где, что, как,** and **потомý что**. In fact, in Russian a comma is always used between clauses.

Упражнение

8. How would you express the following in Russian?

Mila says Kolya studies English. Kolya speaks English well because he and his parents speak English at home.

По- Английский

➤ Complete Oral Drills 11–12 in the Workbook.

спрашиваю

отначаю
отначаешь
отначает
отначаеся
отначаете
отначают

ОБЗОРНЫЕ УПРАЖНЕНИЯ

A. **Пи́сьма на кассе́тах.** Instead of a letter, you got a cassette recording from a Russian student seeking an American pen pal.

1. Before you listen, jot down a couple of things you expect to find in such a letter. Then listen to the recording and write down as many facts as you can. Compare your notes in class.

2. Answer the letter. Remember to use what you know, not what you don't know.

B. **Письмо́.** Sara Frankel has prepared a letter for a Russian pen-pal organization, and has asked you to translate it into Russian. Before you start translating, remember that a good translator tries to find the best functional equivalent, rather than translate word for word.

October 5

Hello! Let me introduce myself. My name is Sara. I go to Georgetown University, where I am a freshman. I live in a dorm. My major is American literature, but I also take history, international relations, French, and Russian. I study Russian because I think it is very beautiful, but I know it poorly.

The library at our university is large. We read American and French newspapers and magazines in the library. I like the university very much.

Where do you go to school, and where do you live? Do you know English? Do you like music? I like American and Russian rock.

Yours,

Sara Frankel

Words you will need:

October 5	**5. 10**
also	**ещё**
library	**библиоте́ка**
you like	**вы лю́бите**
rock	**рок**

Note: Capitalize all forms of **Вы** and **Ваш** in the letter.

C. **Статья́ в газе́те.** You have been asked to write a feature article on a visiting Russian exchange student for your campus newspaper.

1. To prepare for your interview with an exchange student (**стажёр**), make a list of questions in Russian.

2. Your teacher will play the role of the visiting student. Find out the answers to your questions. Keep notes during the interview, so you can reconstruct it afterwards.

3. Write your short article. The article will be <u>in English</u>, and will show the extent to which you understood the visiting student's answers.

4. Now write a short letter <u>in Russian</u> to a Russian friend telling about the exchange student you interviewed.

D. **Интервью́.** Listen to a recording of an interview with a foreign student studying in Russia. For some reason the interviewer's questions were erased. Write down the questions that must have been asked.

Вопро́с 1: _____

Вопро́с 2: _____

Вопро́с 3: _____

Вопро́с 4: _____

Вопро́с 5: _____

Вопро́с 6: _____

Вопро́с 7: _____

Вопро́с 8: _____

НОВЫЕ СЛОВА И ВЫРАЖЕНИЯ

NOUNS

антрополо́гия	anthropology
архитекту́ра	architecture
аспиранту́ра	graduate school
биоло́гия	biology
вычисли́тельная те́хника	computer science
журнали́стика	journalism
Институ́т иностра́нных языко́в	Institute of Foreign Languages
исто́рия	history
ка́федра (на)	department
ка́федра ру́сского языка́	Russian department
ка́федра англи́йского языка́	English department
курс (на)	course, year in university or institute
литерату́ра	literature
матема́тика	mathematics
междунаро́дные отноше́ния	international affairs
медици́на	medicine
му́зыка	music
нау́ка	science
полити́ческие нау́ки	political science
образова́ние	education
вы́сшее образова́ние	higher education
педаго́гика	education (*a subject in college*)
преподава́тель	teacher in college
преподава́тель ру́сского языка́	Russian language teacher
психоло́гия	psychology
Росси́я	Russia
сосе́д (*pl.* сосе́ди)/сосе́дка	neighbor
социоло́гия	sociology
специа́льность (*fem.*)	major
стажёр	a student in a special course not leading to degree; used for foreign students doing work in Russia
странове́дение	area studies
ру́сское странове́дение	Russian area studies
факульте́т (на)	department
фи́зика	physics
фина́нсы	finance
филоло́гия	philology (*study of language and literature*)
филосо́фия	philosophy
хи́мия	chemistry
эконо́мика	economics
юриспруде́нция	law

ADJECTIVES

второ́й	second
госуда́рственный	state
европе́йский	European
иностра́нный	foreign
моско́вский	Moscow
пе́рвый	first
полити́ческий	political
пя́тый	fifth
тре́тий (тре́тье, тре́тья, тре́тьи)	third
тру́дный	difficult
филологи́ческий	philological (*relating to the study of language and literature*)
четвёртый	fourth

VERBS

ду́мать (ду́маю, ду́маешь, ду́мают)	to think
изуча́ть (*что*) (изуча́ю, изуча́ешь, изуча́ют)	to study, take a subject (*must have a direct object*)
отвеча́ть (отвеча́ю, отвеча́ешь, отвеча́ют)	to answer
рабо́тать (рабо́таю, рабо́таешь, рабо́тают)	to work
спра́шивать (спра́шиваю, спра́шиваешь, спра́шивают)	to ask
учи́ться (учу́сь, у́чишься у́чатся)	to study, be a student (*cannot have direct object*)

ADVERBS

ещё	still
уже́	already

PREPOSITIONS

в (+ *prepositional case*)	in, at
на (+ *prepositional case*)	in, on, at

CONJUNCTIONS

где	where
и́ли	or
как	how
потому́ что	because
что	that, what

OTHER WORDS AND PHRASES

Вот как?!	Really?!
Как вы сказа́ли? (*formal*)	What did you say?
коне́чно	of course
люблю́ (я)	I like, I love
мо́жет быть	maybe
на како́м ку́рсе	in what year (*in university or institute*)
Я не по́нял (поняла́).	I didn't catch (understand) that.
Я получи́л(а).	I received.
Я учи́лся (учи́лась).	I was a student.

NUMBERS

31–50 (*for understanding*)

PERSONALIZED VOCABULARY

_____

_____

_____

_____

Test

① Answer questions in complete sentences

What's your name, do you work, what year are you? What's your major; do you live in house or dorm, where do your parents live?

② Put correct endings on words

③ Conjugate 3 verbs.

④ Write plural forms   интере́стни журна́л

⑤ Write grammatically correct sentences.
   Я жить в Норсман
   Я живу́ в Норсмане

⑥ Trans. Eng → Russian

on cheat sheet: plural of nouns + adj. (+) letters sister, 8 new word.)
prep case
acc case

УРОК 5

РАСПОРЯДОК ДНЯ

▼ **КОММУНИКАТИВНЫЕ ЗАДАНИЯ**

Talking about daily activities
    and schedules
Asking and telling time on the hour
Making and responding to simple
    invitations
Talking on the phone
Reading and writing notes and letters

▼ **В ПОМОЩЬ УЧАЩИМСЯ**

в + accusative case for clock time
    and days of the week
у́тром, днём, ве́чером, and но́чью
Занима́ться vs. учи́ться vs. изуча́ть
Going: идти́ vs. е́хать;
        идти́ vs. ходи́ть
Questions with где and куда́
в/на + accusative case for direction
Expressing neccesity: до́лжен,
    должна́, должны́
Introduction to past tense for reading

Workbook: Consonant devoicing
    and assimilation

▼ **МЕЖДУ ПРОЧИМ**

The Russian calendar
Russian students' daily schedule

ТОЧКА ОТСЧЁТА

О ЧЁМ ИДЁТ РЕЧЬ?

A. **Что я де́лаю?** Which activities are typical for you? Pick and arrange them in chronological order from the list below.

ложу́сь спать

иду́ на ле́кцию

слу́шаю ра́дио

за́втракаю

занима́юсь

чита́ю газе́ту

иду́ в библиоте́ку

у́жинаю

встаю́

смотрю́ телеви́зор

обе́даю

одева́юсь

принима́ю душ

иду́ домо́й

убира́ю ко́мнату

отдыха́ю

B. Now construct sentences indicating at what time of day you perform the activities shown in exercise A.

Утром я встаю́.

Днём я обе́даю.

Ве́чером я занима́юсь.

жарко : very hot
тепло : warm.
холодно : cold
горячо : boiling

холодно мороз : freezing

Но́чью я ложу́сь спать.

ночью

Между прочим

у́тром	around 3 a.m. till noon
днём	12 noon till about 5:00 p.m.
ве́чером	about 5 p.m. till around midnight
но́чью	around 12 midnight till about 3:00 a.m.

Note that **у́тром, днём, ве́чером,** and **но́чью** often come at the beginning of a Russian sentence.

Разгово́ры. Before listening to the conversations, look at the page from a Russian calendar. Note that the days are listed vertically and that the first day of the week is Monday. Also note that the days of the week are not capitalized in Russian.

понеде́льник		6	13	20	27
вто́рник		7	14	21	28
среда́	1	8	15	22	29
четве́рг	2	9	16	23	30
пя́тница	3	10	17	24	31
суббо́та	4	11	18	25	
воскресе́нье	5	12	19	26	

Разгово́р 1: В общежи́тии
(Разгова́ривают Сти́вен и Бори́с)

1. How is Steven's Russian?
2. Does Boris know any English?
3. What is Steven doing in Moscow?
4. What does Steven do Monday through Thursday?

Разгово́р 2: Биле́ты на рок-конце́рт
(Разгова́ривают Джим и Ва́ля)

1. What days are mentioned? Circle them on the calendar.
2. What is Valya doing on Wednesday?
3. What is she doing on Thursday?
4. Which day do they finally agree on?

Разгово́р 3: Пойдём в буфе́т!
(Разгова́ривают Ле́на и Мэ́ри)

1. In what order will the following activities take place?

   буфе́т
   ру́сская исто́рия
   разгово́рная пра́ктика

2. Where and when will Mary and Lena meet?

утро : morning ⟼ *утром*

ДИАЛОГИ

день : day ⟼ *днём*

вечер : evening ⟼ *вечером*

ночь : night ⟼ *ночью*

1   Ты сего́дня идёшь в библиоте́ку?

— Са́ша, ты сего́дня идёшь в библиоте́ку?
— Сейча́с поду́маю. Како́й сего́дня день?
— Сего́дня? Понеде́льник.
— Да, иду́. Днём. В два часа́.
— В два? Отли́чно! Дава́й пойдём вме́сте.
— Дава́й!

2   Куда́ ты идёшь?

— Здра́вствуй, Же́ня! Куда́ ты идёшь?
— На ле́кцию.
— Так ра́но?! Ско́лько сейча́с вре́мени?
— Сейча́с уже́ де́сять часо́в.
— Не мо́жет быть! А что у тебя́ сейча́с?
— Пе́рвая па́ра—ру́сская эконо́мика. Ты извини́, но я должна́ идти́. Я уже́ опа́здываю.
— Ну, иди́. Пото́м поговори́м.

> **Па́ра,** literally *pair*, refers to the 90-minute lectures at Russian universities (2 x 45 minutes), which run without a break.

3   Что ты де́лаешь в суббо́ту ве́чером?

— Алло́! Воло́дя, э́то ты?
— Я. Здра́вствуй, Роб.
— Слу́шай, Воло́дя. Что ты де́лаешь в суббо́ту ве́чером?
— Ничего́.
— Не хо́чешь пойти́ в кино́?
— С удово́льствием. Во ско́лько?
— В шесть часо́в.
— Договори́лись.

4   Когда́ у вас ру́сская исто́рия?

— Алло́, Ве́ра! Говори́т Са́ша.
— Здра́вствуй, Са́ша.
— Слу́шай, Ве́ра! Я забы́л, когда́ у нас ру́сская исто́рия.
— В сре́ду.
— Зна́чит, за́втра?! А во ско́лько?
— Втора́я па́ра. В аудито́рии но́мер три на второ́м этаже́.
— Зна́чит, втора́я па́ра, аудито́рия три, второ́й эта́ж. Спаси́бо. Всё.

5 **Что ты сейчас делаешь?**

— Алло! Джилл! Слушай, что ты сейчас делаешь?
— Я убираю комнату, а Энн смотрит телевизор. А что?
— Хотите все вместе поехать на дачу?
— Когда?
— В двенадцать часов.
— В двенадцать не могу. Я должна заниматься.
— А Энн?
— А Энн свободна весь день.
— Ты знаешь, давай поедем не днём, а вечером.
— Хорошо. Договорились.

> The short-form adjective **свободен** *(free)* is marked for gender and number:
> **он свободен**
> **она свободна**
> **они свободны**

A. **Какой сегодня день?** For each of the days given below, create a short conversation with a partner based on the model.

Образец: пятница

— Ты сегодня идёшь в библиотеку?
— Какой сегодня день?
— Сегодня? **Пятница.**
— Да, иду.

а. понедельник г. суббота
б. среда д. вторник
в. воскресенье е. четверг

B. **В какой день ...?** Working in pairs, find out what your partner does on which days. Then reverse roles. Use the questions and answers below to guide your discussion.

> Note that in Russian **в** + accusative case of the day of the week is used to express the idea *on a certain day*.

	Вопросы	*Ответы*
	ты (не) смотришь телевизор?	В понедельник.
	ты (не) занимаешься в библиотеке?	Во вторник.
В какой день	ты (не) убираешь комнату?	В среду.
В какие дни	ты (не) работаешь?	В четверг.
Когда	ты (не) слушаешь радио?	В пятницу.
	ты (не) читаешь газету?	В субботу.
	ты (не) слушаешь лекции?	В воскресенье.
	ты (не) отдыхаешь?	

Learn times...

С. Ско́лько сейча́с вре́мени?

Сейча́с **час.**

Ско́лько сейча́с вре́мени?

Сейча́с **два часа́.**

Сейча́с **три часа́.**

Сейча́с **четы́ре часа́.**

Note that Russian uses three different forms of the word **час** (*o'clock*) after numbers.

Сейча́с **пять часо́в.**

Сейча́с **шесть часо́в.**

Сейча́с **семь часо́в.**

Сейча́с **во́семь часо́в.**

Сейча́с **де́вять часо́в.**

Сейча́с **де́сять часо́в.**

Сейча́с **оди́ннадцать часо́в.**

Сейча́с **двена́дцать часо́в.**

With a partner, act out a short dialog for each of the pictures below. Follow the model.

Образе́ц:

— Извини́те, пожа́луйста, ско́лько сейча́с вре́мени?
— Сейча́с **три часа́.**
— Спаси́бо.

а.   б.   в.  г.

D. **Когда́? Во ско́лько?** In pairs, find out what time your partner does the following things on a typical day. Then reverse roles.

Образе́ц: — Во ско́лько ты за́втракаешь?
            — Я обы́чно за́втракаю в 7 часо́в.

> To tell what time something happens, use **в** + **the hour**.

Во ско́лько ты ... ?
    встаёшь
    принима́ешь душ
    одева́ешься
    чита́ешь газе́ту
    идёшь на заня́тия
    идёшь в библиоте́ку
    обе́даешь
    идёшь на уро́к ру́сского языка́
    идёшь домо́й
    у́жинаешь
    ложи́шься спать

E. **Моя́ неде́ля.** Make a calendar of your activities for next week. As always, use what you know, not what you don't.

F. **Са́мый люби́мый день.** What are your most and least favorite days of the week?

а. Како́й у вас са́мый люби́мый день? Почему́?
б. Како́й у вас са́мый нелюби́мый день? Почему́?

ЯЗЫК В ДЕЙСТВИИ

ДАВАЙТЕ ПОГОВОРИМ

A. **Куда́ я иду́?** For each of the pictures below, construct a sentence telling on what day(s) and at what time you go to these places.

Образец: В понеде́льник в во́семь часо́в я иду́ в университе́т.

в кинотеа́тр

в магази́н

в музе́й

в рестора́н

в библиоте́ку

в кафе́

на стадио́н

на дискоте́ку

в цирк

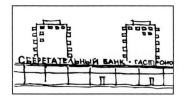

в банк

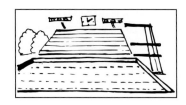

в бассе́йн

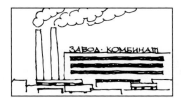

на рабо́ту

бассéйн. The following adverbs will help you describe how things. Like most adverbs in Russian, they normally precede

	often	**рéдко**	rarely
	usually	**никогдá не**	never
й **день**	every day	**всегдá**	always

/ou want to use these adverbs with regard to "going" somewhere in the present tense, use the form **я хожý: Я чáсто хожý** в кафé.

1. For each of the pictures in exercise A, construct a sentence indicating how often you go there.

   Образéц: Я **чáсто хожý** в университéт.
                Я **рéдко хожý** в цирк.

2. Working in pairs, find out what your partner does in a typical week and how often s/he does those things.

C. **Подготóвка к разговóру.** Review the dialogs. How would you do the following?

- ask what day it is
- tell what day today is
- ask what time it is
- tell what time it is now
- express surprise at something you hear
- start a telephone conversation with a friend
- ask what someone is doing (on Saturday, Sunday, now, etc.)
- invite a friend to go to the movies
- take someone up on an invitation to go to the movies (library, etc.)
- signal agreement to proposed arrangements
- identify yourself on the phone
- ask what day your Russian (math, English) class is
- tell what day your Russian (economics) class is
- ask what time your Russian (French, Spanish) class is
- tell what time your Russian (psychology) class is
- end a conversation with a friend
- say that you are (or someone else is) free (to do something)
- bring a conversation to an end by saying you have to go

D. Working with a partner, practice responding to the following. Then reverse roles.

       Какóй сегóдня день?
       Скóлько сейчáс врéмени?
       Когдá рýсский языќ?
       Кудá ты идёшь?
       Что ты сейчáс дéлаешь?
       Хóчешь пойти́ в магази́н?
       Давáй пойдём в кинó.
       Хóчешь пойти́ в библиотéку вмéсте?

E. **Игровы́е ситуáции.** Imagine that you are in Russia and act out the following situations.

1. Call up a friend and ask what he/she is doing. Invite him or her to go out.

2. Your friend calls you up and invites you to the library. Accept the invitation and decide when you will go.

3. A friend calls to invite you to a concert Thursday night. You are busy then. Decline the invitation and suggest an alternative.

4. Working with a partner prepare and act out a situation of your own that deals with the topics of this unit. Remember to use what you know, not what you don't know.

F. **Устный перевóд.** In Russia, you are asked to act as an interpreter between a tourist who does not speak any Russian and a Russian who does not speak any English.

English speaker's part

1. Hi. I'm an American student and my name is …
2. Where do you go to school?
3. What year are you in?
4. How interesting! My major is Russian history.
5. I am a sophomore. I am taking Russian, history, political science, mathematics, and economics.
6. I am a tourist.
7. That would be great! When?
8. That will be fine!

G. The following expressions will help you talk about your daily schedule and make your speech flow more naturally.

снача́ла ...	first
(а) пото́м ...	then
наконе́ц ...	finally

As you progress through the exercises in this unit, pay attention not only to content and grammatical accuracy, but to the flow of your speech as well. Try to vary the way you begin your sentences and pay special attention to where you might combine two smaller sentences into one longer one. Consider the following monologue:

Утром я встаю́. Я принима́ю душ. Я одева́юсь. Я за́втракаю. Я иду́ на заня́тия.

The monologue, which consists of a number of short sentences monotonously strung together, is boring. Let's convey the same information in a more coherent and interesting way:

Утром я встаю́ в семь часо́в. Снача́ла я принима́ю душ, а пото́м одева́юсь. В во́семь часо́в я за́втракаю и иду́ на заня́тия.

As you can see, we have turned a group of sentences into a short paragraph.

Based on the preceding example, turn the following groups of sentences into paragraphs. Then compare your paragraph to a partner's.

- В суббо́ту я отдыха́ю. Я встаю́. Я чита́ю газе́ту. Я принима́ю душ. Я одева́юсь. Я иду́ в кино́ и́ли в рестора́н.
- Ве́чером я у́жинаю. Я иду́ в библиоте́ку. Я занима́юсь. Я иду́ домо́й. Я ложу́сь спать.
- В воскресе́нье днём я обе́даю. Я отдыха́ю. Я занима́юсь. Я чита́ю газе́ту. Ве́чером я у́жинаю. Я занима́юсь. Я ложу́сь спать.

Now answer the following questions about yourself in as much detail as you can.

- Что вы обы́чно де́лаете в суббо́ту?
- Что вы обы́чно де́лаете в понеде́льник у́тром?
- Что вы обы́чно де́лаете в пя́тницу ве́чером?

ДАВАЙТЕ ПОЧИТАЕМ

A. **Расписа́ние.** You found a page from someone's daily calendar. Look through it quickly to get a general idea of who it might belong to. Jot down as many clues as you can find.

> 9.00 – английская литература
> 10.40 – фонетика
> 13.00 – обед
> 14.00 – грамматика
> 16.00 – театральный клуб
> 19.00 – кино

Look through the schedule again. List all the courses and academic activities mentioned in it.

B. **Запи́ски.** Imagine that the following notes were left for you. You do not know many of the words in the notes. On the basis of what you do understand, put a check mark next to the notes you believe need action on your part.

Хочешь пойти в кино в субботу вечером? У меня есть билет на Оклахому. Сеанс начинается в 19.30. Буду ждать тебя у станции метро Арбат.

Ирина

Я взял твой англо-русский словарь. Принесу его тебе в комнату сегодня вечером в 18.00

Володя

Ты идёшь в четверг в магазин? Давай пойдём вместе. Жду тебя у лифта на втором этаже в 16.00.

Вера

У меня хорошая идея. Давай пойдём в субботу на дискотеку. У меня новое платье. Поговорим вечером в кафетерии.

Нина

С. **Зна́ете ли вы ... ?** Match up the famous names with their achievements.

___ 1.	Анна Ахма́това	а.	Жил и рабо́тал в Африке.
___ 2.	Ри́чард Бирд	б.	Изуча́ла эффе́кты радиоакти́вности.
___ 3.	Фёдор Миха́йлович Достое́вский	в.	Организова́л па́ртию большевико́в.
___ 4.	Ире́н Жо́лио-Кюри́	г.	Организова́л экспеди́ции в Антаркти́ду.
___ 5.	Влади́мир Ильи́ч Ле́нин	д.	Написа́л рома́н «Бра́тья Карама́зовы».
___ 6.	Джон Ле́ннон и Пол Макка́ртни	е.	Писа́ла поэ́зию.
___ 7.	Пилигри́мы	ж.	Писа́ли пе́сни, кото́рые пе́ли Битлз.
___ 8.	Альберт Шве́йцер	з.	Пое́хали из Англии в Аме́рику.

Look at the verbs in the second column. What tense is being used?

What are the forms for...
    a. verbs with masculine subjects?
    b. verbs with feminine subjects?
    c. verbs with plural subjects?

ДАВАЙТЕ ПОСЛУШАЕМ 📼

Письмо́ на кассе́те. Nikolai sent a letter on cassette to his American friend, Jim. Listen to the recording with the following questions in mind.

1. What are Nikolai's hard days?
2. What are his easy days?
3. What does his schedule look like on a hard day?
4. What does he do on weekends?

5.1 NEW VERBS—*ЧТО ВЫ ДЕЛАЕТЕ?*

First-conjugation verbs

де́лать

де́ла - **ю**	Что вы **де́лаете?**	What *are you doing?*
де́ла - **ешь**	Что вы **де́лаете** у́тром?	What *do you do* in the morning?
де́ла - **ет**		
де́ла - **ем**		
де́ла - **ете**		
де́ла - **ют**		

to do

за́втракать

за́втрака - **ю**
за́втрака - **ешь**
за́втрака - **ет**
за́втрака - **ем**
за́втрака - **ете**
за́втрака - **ют**

to eat breakfast

обе́дать

обе́да - **ю**
обе́да - **ешь**
обе́да - **ет**
обе́да - **ем**
обе́да - **ете**
обе́да - **ют**

to eat lunch

у́жинать

у́жина - **ю**
у́жина - **ешь**
у́жина - **ет**
у́жина - **ем**
у́жина - **ете**
у́жина - **ют**

to eat dinner

The verbs above all conjugate just like the verb **чита́ть,** which you already know. Other new verbs with this conjugation are: **опа́здывать** (*to be late*), **отдыха́ть** (*to relax*), **принима́ть (душ)** (*to take a shower*), **слу́шать** (*to listen*), and **убира́ть (ко́мнату)** (*to clean a room*).

иду + в + accusative : walk to ____

они идут в
университет.

вставать

| встаю́ |
| вста - **ёшь** |
| вста - **ёт** |
| вста - **ём** |
| вста - **ёте** |
| вста - **ю́т** |

to get up

идти́

| ид - **у́** |
| ид - **ёшь** |
| ид - **ёт** |
| ид - **ём** |
| ид - **ёте** |
| ид - **у́т** |

to go (walk)

Notes

1. Remember that the vowel in the endings for the **ты, он/она́, мы,** and **вы** forms is **ё** when the ending is stressed.

2. When the endings are added after a consonant letter, the **я** and **они́** endings are **-у, -ут** instead of **-ю, -ют.**

Two first-conjugation verbs you learn in this unit have the particle **-ся.** The **-ся** particle is spelled **-ся** after consonants and **-сь** after vowels.

занима́ться

| занима́ - **ю** -сь |
| занима́ - **ешь** - ся |
| занима́ - **ет** - ся |
| занима́ - **ем** - ся |
| занима́ - **ете** - сь |
| занима́ - **ют** - ся |

to do homework

одева́ться

| одева́ - **ю** - сь |
| одева́ - **ешь** - ся |
| одева́ - **ет** - ся |
| одева́ - **ем** - ся |
| одева́ - **ете** - сь |
| одева́ - **ют** - ся |

to get dressed

Second-conjugation verbs

Two verbs you learn in this unit belong to the second conjugation.

ложи́ться

лож -	у́	-сь
лож -	и́шь	- ся
лож -	и́т	- ся
лож -	и́м	- ся
лож -	и́те	- сь
лож -	а́т	- ся

to go to bed

смотре́ть

смотр -	ю́
смотр -	ишь
смотр -	ит
смотр -	им
смотр -	ите
смо́тр -	ят

to watch

Notice that the stress in the **я** form of **смотре́ть** is on the ending, but in all other forms it is on the stem.

Упражнения

1. Fill in the blanks.

   а. Ки́ра встаёт в 7 часо́в, а я _____ в 8.
   б. Ки́ра принима́ет душ в 8 часо́в, а я _____ душ в 9.
   в. Ки́ра бы́стро* одева́ется, а я _____ ме́дленно*.
   г. Ки́ра за́втракает в 9 часо́в, а я _____ в 10 часо́в.
   д. Ки́ра не слу́шает ра́дио, а я его́ _____.
   е. Ки́ра смо́трит телеви́зор, а я не _____.
   ж. Ки́ра опа́здывает на ле́кцию, а я не _____.
   з. Днём Ки́ра отдыха́ет, а я не _____.
   и. Ки́ра не убира́ет ко́мнату, а я её _____.
   й. Ки́ра занима́ется, и я то́же _____.
   к. Ки́ра ложи́тся спать ра́но, а я _____ спать по́здно.

    *бы́стро–*quickly,* ме́дленно–*slowly*

2. How would you say the following in Russian?

— What do you do in the morning?
— I get up at 6 o'clock and get dressed.
— You don't eat breakfast?
— No. I study. Then at 10 o'clock I go to class.
— When do you eat lunch?
— At 1 o'clock. Then I go home. I relax and watch TV.
— And when do you go to bed?
— At 1 o'clock.

➤ Complete Oral Drills 5–6 and Written Exercise 4 in the Workbook.

5.2   *ЗАНИМАТЬСЯ* vs. *ИЗУЧАТЬ* vs. *УЧИТЬСЯ*

In this unit you learn and practice the verb **занима́ться.** In English it can be translated as *to study* in the sense of doing one's homework. It cannot take a direct object.

> — Где вы **у́читесь**?
> — Я **учу́сь** в университе́те.
> — Где вы **занима́етесь**?
> — Я **занима́юсь** в ко́мнате.
> — Что вы **изуча́ете**?
> — Я **изуча́ю** ру́сский язы́к.

Remember that the verb **учи́ться** means *to go to school,* and that the verb **изуча́ть** is used to indicate a subject one is taking. Neither **изуча́ть** nor **учи́ться** is a daily activity verb.

Упражнение

3. Use the correct verbs for *study* in this dialog.

> — Сла́ва, ты не зна́ешь, где _учится_ Со́ня?
> — Она́ _учится_ в экономи́ческом институ́те. Она́ хорошо́ _занимается_.
> Она́ всегда́ _занимает_.
>   or
> — Она́ _изучает_ америка́нскую фина́нсовую систе́му?   _учится_
> — Да, она́ _изучает_ эконо́мику США.

➤ Review Oral Drill 6 in the Workbook.

5.3   GOING

Russian distinguishes between going by foot and by vehicle:

 Са́ша **идёт** в библиоте́ку.

 Ма́рья **е́дет** в Москву́.

However, verbs for going by vehicle are used only when the context makes it absolutely clear that a vehicle is used, that is:

- when talking about going to another city or country, (Мы **е́дем** в Ки́ев).
- when the vehicle is physically present (e.g., one person sees another on a bicycle and asks **Куда́ ты е́дешь?**).
- when the specific vehicle being used is mentioned in the sentence.

In all other instances, verbs for going by foot are used.

иногда : sometimes   *часто : often*   *редко : seldom*   *всегда : always*   *каждый*

Both **идти** and **éхать** are regular first-conjugation verbs.

By foot, within city	**By vehicle, to ano...**

хожу : I walk (everyday... or periodical or repeated action)

иду : I walk.

идти		éхать	
ид - ý		éд - у	
ид - ёшь		éд - ешь	
ид - ёт		éд - ет	
ид - ём		éд - ем	
ид - ёте		éд - ете	
ид - ýт		éд - ут	
to go (walk)		*to go (ride)*	

Я хожу в вторник   *Я еду в Алабаму. ; Я еду в Нью Ерк*

Russian also distinguishes between going in one direction or setting out (**я идý**) and making trips back and forth (**я хожý**). With adverbs telling how often trips are made (**чáсто, рéдко, обы́чно, кáждый день,** etc.) the form **я хожý** is usually used.

⟹

каждый понидельник : every monday.

Я сейчáс **идý** в библиотéку.
В пять часóв я **идý** в библиотéку.

⟹   ⟹
⟸   ⟸

Я кáждый день **хожý** в библиотéку.

Я	хожу
Ты	ходишь
он	ходит
мы	ходим
вы	ходите
они	ходят

Упражнения

4. Fill in the blanks with the correct form of **идти** or **éхать**.

— Ви́тя, Мáша говори́т, что в суббóту ты ___едешь___ в США.
— Да, я ___еду___ .
— Как интерéсно! Мóжет быть ты …
— Лáра, извини́! Я ___иду___ на урóк и óчень опáздываю!

5. Fill in the blanks with **идý** or **хожý**.

а. Я сейчáс ___иду___ в парк.
б. Я кáждый день ___хожу___ в парк.
в. Я чáсто ___хожу___ в кинó, а рéдко ___хожу___ в музéй.
г. В 8 часóв я _____ на лéкцию. В час я ___иду___ домóй.

➤ Complete Oral Drills 7–8 and Written Exercise 5–6 in the Workbook.

In Russian, **где** is used to inquire about location and **куда́** is used to inquire about destination. Compare the following questions in English and in Russian:

— *Where* do you live?   — *Where* are you going?
— **Где** ты живёшь?   — **Куда́** ты идёшь?

location   *destination*

Verbs such as **жить, рабо́тать,** and **учи́ться** refer to location and require the use of **где** (*where*). Verbs like **идти́, е́хать,** and **опа́здывать** refer to destination and require the use of **куда́** (*where to*).

Упражнение

6. What would you say to find out … ?

- where your friend's parents live.
- where your neighbor works.
- where your teacher is going.
- what event your roommate is late for.
- where your friend is driving.
- where someone goes to school. (Be careful! Don't take the "go" of "goes to school" literally.)

➤ Complete Oral Drill 9 in the Workbook.

5.5   ANSWERING THE QUESTION *КУДА?*

You already know that **где** questions require answers with **в** or **на** plus the prepositional case:

— **Где** ты занима́ешься?
— Я занима́юсь **в библиоте́ке.**

Куда́ questions require answers with **в** or **на** plus the accusative case:

— **Куда́** ты идёшь?
— Я иду́ **в библиоте́ку.**

2 types of verbs: prep and acc, depends on case used to answer.

ГДЕ? (в/на + _prep_)	КУДА? (в/на + _acc_)	B or HA ?
в библиотéке в шкóле в аудитóрии в магазѝне в институ́те в музéе	в библиотéку в шкóлу в аудитóрию в магазѝн в институ́т в музéй	Place names usually take the preposition **в**.
на лéкции на концéрте на рабóте на урóке	на лéкцию на концéрт на рабóту на урóк	Activities take the preposition **на**.
на пéрвом этажé на кáфедре на стадиóне на факульте́те на дáче	на пéрвый этáж на кáфедру на стадиóн на факульте́т на дáчу	Some words that one would expect to take **в** in fact take **на**. They must be memorized.
дóма _дома_	домóй _домой_	Learn these special expressions for _home_

Acc Case gives direct object and direction
(куда + acc)

Упражнения

7. Supply the needed preposition. Indicate whether the noun following the preposition is in the prepositional case (P) or the accusative case (A).

   а. Утром я хожу́ ___в___ библиотéку (_A_). Я занимáюсь ___в___ библиотéке (_P_) три часá.
   б. Я опáздываю ___на___ лéкцию (_A_).
   в. В 2 часá я иду́ ___в___ институ́т (_A_). Я рабóтаю ___в___ институ́те (_P_) 4 часá. В 6 часóв я иду́ ___на___ кáфедру (_A_) ру́сского языкá.
   г. Вéчером я обы́чно хожу́ ___на___ концéрт (_A_) и́ли _____ кинó ( ).

8. Provide plausible answers to the questions you asked for exercise 6.

9. Answer the questions **Кудá вы идёте?** and **Где вы?** using the following prompts:

   dormitory, class, university, house, home (!)

➤ Complete Oral Drills 10–14 and Written Exercises 7–10 in the Workbook.

5.6 EXPRESSING NECESSITY:
ДОЛЖЕН, ДОЛЖНА, ДОЛЖНЫ + INFINITIVE

Ка́тя идёт
в библиоте́ку,
потому́ что она́
должна́ занима́ться.

Марк говори́т «До
свида́ния», потому́ что
он **до́лжен** идти́.

За́втра экза́мен.
Студе́нты **должны́**
занима́ться.

До́лжен, a short-form adjective, agrees with its subject and is always followed by an infinitive. It has only three forms. The form used after the **я** and **ты** forms depends on the gender of the person referred to. The form used after the **вы** form is always **должны́,** even when the **вы** refers to only one person.

Singular	Plural	
он **до́лжен**	мы	
она́ **должна́**	вы	**должны́**
	они́	

Упражне́ния

10. Use the correct form of the verb (either conjugated or the infinitive).

— Что вы (де́лаете—де́лать) сего́дня?
— Сего́дня мы должны́ (занима́емся—занима́ться) в библиоте́ке.
— А пото́м?
— А пото́м мы (идём—идти́) на уро́к.
— А ве́чером?
— А ве́чером мы должны́ (чита́ем—чита́ть) журна́л.

11. Who has to do what today? Name …

a. two things that you have to do today.
b. two more things someone else (male) has to do today.
c. still another two things someone else (female) has to do today.
d. one more thing that you and a friend have to do today.

12. How would you ask the following people what they have to do today?

a. your best friend (Watch out for gender!)
b. your Russian professor
c. two friends together

➤ Complete Oral Drill 15 and Written Exercise 11 in the Workbook.

ОБЗОРНЫЕ УПРАЖНЕНИЯ

A. **Разгово́р.**

Что ты де́лаешь в суббо́ту?
(*Разгова́ривают Ве́ра и Кэ́рол.*)

1. What days of the week are mentioned in the conversation?
2. What are Vera's plans for the first day mentioned? Arrange them in sequential order.
3. Where are the friends going on the second day mentioned?

B. **Уче́бный день.**

1. Make out a schedule for a typical day in your life during the academic year. Be as detailed as you can. Remember to use what you know, not what you don't know.

2. Then exchange your schedule with a classmate. Write a paragraph about your classmate's daily activities.

C. **Запи́ска.**

1. Write a short note inviting a classmate to go somewhere with you. Make sure to mention day and time. See page 133 for models.

2. Answer a classmate's note.

D. **Перепи́ска.** You received the following letter from your Russian pen pal Kostya. Earlier you had asked him to describe his academic schedule.

1. Before reading the letter, jot down two or three things you expect to find in it.

2. Now scan the letter. Do not expect to understand every word. Just look to see if it contains the things you expected. Did you learn any other information? What?

15.05.95

Здравствуй!

Спасибо за твое письмо. Я рад, что у тебя все хорошо в университете. Ты хочешь знать, как идут мои занятия. Сейчас я тебе все расскажу.

Как ты уже знаешь, я сейчас учусь в Киевском государственном университете. Моя специальность — политология , но я также очень люблю английский язык и литературу. В этом семестре у меня интересные курсы. Понедельник, среда и пятница у меня очень трудные дни. Я встаю в семь часов, одеваюсь и иду завтракать в столовую. Потом у меня три лекции. Первая лекция в девять часов. Это американская история. У нас очень хороший преподаватель. Он читает интересный курс. Потом в одиннадцать часов у меня семинар—экономика. Семинар трудный, но материал интересный. В час я иду обедать. В два часа у меня английский язык. Это мой любимый курс. На занятиях мы говорим только по-английски. Это хорошая практика. Потом я иду в лингафонный кабинет слушать английские кассеты. В пять часов я ужинаю, а потом занимаюсь в общежитии. Там я читаю, слушаю музыку или просто отдыхаю. Ложусь спать поздно: в двенадцать часов.

В субботу я встаю рано—в восемь часов. Утром я убираю комнату, днем иду в магазин, а вечером в кино, на дискотеку, на стадион или на концерт. В воскресенье утром я встаю поздно— в одиннадцать часов. Днем я иду в библиотеку. Там я занимаюсь. Иногда я хожу в гости.

Вот и вся моя неделя. Я очень хочу знать, как ты живешь. Жду письма.

Твой Костя

Homework: p. 142 , 10,11

3. Read the letter again. This time, make up a schedule of Kostya's typical day. How does his schedule compare to yours?

4. Look through the letter one more time to find answers to these questions:

   • Which courses does Kostya find to be difficult? interesting? his favorite?

   • How does Kostya spend his days off?

5. Answer Kostya's letter. Write a draft first.

E. **Автоотве́тчик.** You came home and found the following message for your Russian roommate on your answering machine (**автоотве́тчик**).

1. Take down as much information as you can (in English or in Russian).

2. When your roommate gets back, relay the content of the message.

F. **Выступле́ние.** You are in Moscow.

1. You have been asked to give a talk to a group of Russian students about Americans' weekly schedules. Jot down notes for your presentation in Russian.

2. Several students give their presentations to the class.

G. **Интервью́.** Listen to the recording of an interview with an American student studying in Russia. For some reason, the interviewer's questions were erased. You hear only the answers. Reconstruct five questions based on the answers you hear.

должен (m), должна (f); должно (n), должны (p) : must, should, have to...

должен + inf. verb = have to ___

читать ; Я должен читать : I have to read.

Я должен заниматься

Я должен писать мама

Я должен идти на лекцию.

Я должен писать книгу.

НОВЫЕ СЛОВА И ВЫРАЖЕНИЯ

NOUNS

аудито́рия	classroom
банк	bank
бассе́йн	swimming pool
библиоте́ка	library
воскресе́нье	Sunday
вто́рник	Tuesday
да́ча (на)	dacha
д(е)нь (*pl.* дни)	day
заня́тие (на)	class
кафе́ (*indeclinable*)	cafe
кино́ (*indeclinable*)	the movies
кинотеа́тр	movie theatre
му́зыка	music
но́мер	number
па́ра	class period
понеде́льник	Monday
пя́тница	Friday
рабо́та (на)	work
среда́ (в сре́ду)	Wednesday (on Wednesday)
стадио́н (на)	stadium
суббо́та	Saturday
уро́к (на)	class, lesson (*practical*)
уро́к ру́сского языка́	Russian class
центр	downtown
цирк	circus
час (2-4 часа́, 5-12 часо́в)	o'clock
четве́рг	Thursday

ADJECTIVES

все	everybody, everyone (*used as a pronoun*)
до́лжен (должна́, должны́) + *infinitive*	must
ка́ждый	each, every
ка́ждый день	every day
са́мый + *adjective*	the most + adjective
са́мый люби́мый	most favorite
са́мый нелюби́мый	least favorite
свобо́ден (свобо́дна, свобо́дны)	free, not busy

VERBS

вставáть (встаю́, встаёшь, встаю́т)   to get up
дéлать (дéлаю, дéлаешь, дéлают)   to do
éхать (éду, éдешь, éдут)   to go, set out by vehicle
зáвтракать   to eat breakfast
    (зáвтракаю, зáвтракаешь, зáвтракают)
занимáться   to study, do homework
    (занимáюсь, занимáешься, занимáются)
идти́ (иду́, идёшь, иду́т)   to go, walk, set out
ложи́ться спать   to go to bed
    (ложу́сь, ложи́шься, ложáтся)
обéдать (обéдаю, обéдаешь, обéдают)   to eat lunch
одевáться   to get dressed
    (одевáюсь, одевáешься, одевáются)
опáздывать   to be late
    (опáздываю, опáздываешь, опáздывают)
отдыхáть   to relax
    (отдыхáю, отдыхáешь, отдыхáют)
принимáть (душ)   to take a shower
    (принимáю, принимáешь, принимáют)
слу́шать (слу́шаю, слу́шаешь, слу́шают)   to listen
смотрéть (телеви́зор)   to watch (television)
    (смотрю́, смóтришь, смóтрят)
убирáть (дом, кварти́ру, кóмнату)   to clean (house, apartment, room)
    (убирáю, убирáешь, убирáют)
у́жинать (у́жинаю, у́жинаешь, у́жинают)   to eat dinner

OTHER VERBS

я забы́л(а)   I forgot
иди́(те)   go (*command form*)
могу́   I can
поговори́м   we'll have a talk
подýмаю   I'll think, let me think
слу́шай(те)   listen (*command form*)
я хожу́   I go (make trips)

ADVERBS

вéчером   in the evening
вмéсте   together
всегдá   always
днём   in the afternoon
зáвтра   tomorrow
кáждый день   every day
наконéц   finally
никогдá не   never
нóчью   at night

обы́чно	usually
отли́чно	excellent
по́здно	late
пото́м	later
ра́но	early
ре́дко	rarely
сего́дня	today
снача́ла	to begin with; at first
у́тром	in the morning
ча́сто	frequently

PREPOSITIONS

в + *accusative case of days of week*	on
в + *hour*	at
в + *accusative case for direction*	to
на + *accusative case for direction*	to

QUESTION WORDS

где	where (at)
когда́	when
куда́	where (to)

OTHER WORDS AND PHRASES

алло́	hello (*on telephone*)
весь день	all day
Во ско́лько?	At what time?
Дава́й(те) пойдём…	Let's go… (*on foot; someplace within city*)
Дава́й(те) пое́дем…	Let's go… (*by vehicle; to another city*)
Договори́лись.	Okay. (We've agreed.)
домо́й	(to) home (*answers* **куда́**)
Жду письма́.	Write! (I'm awaiting your letter.)
Како́й сего́дня день?	What day is it?
Не мо́жет быть!	That's impossible!
Не хо́чешь (хоти́те) пойти́ (пое́хать)…?	Would you like to go …?
ничего́	nothing
С удово́льствием.	With pleasure.
Ско́лько сейча́с вре́мени?	What time is it?

NUMBERS

оди́н, два, три, четы́ре, пять, шесть,
семь, во́семь, де́вять, де́сять,
оди́ннадцать, двена́дцать

PERSONALIZED VOCABULARY

_____

_____

_____

_____

Test (no conjugations...)

① Vocab (122-123)

② 4 adverbs : утром, днём, вечером, ночью.

③ иду, еду:

④ clock times...

⑤ verbs...

в понедельник
① математика ___?___ понедельник

② заниматься : compose sentences w/ this verb. (conj. sort of)

③ know infinitives

④ иду vs. еду + хожу

⑤ • где vs куда verbs.

HW ⟦2-27⟧
79 : 7
78 : 4
+ review : think about
short talk about self.

жить — где ты живёшь
Я живу Норманся

УРОК 6

ДОМ, КВАРТИРА, ОБЩЕЖИТИЕ

▼ **КОММУНИКАТИВНЫЕ ЗАДАНИЯ**

Talking about homes, rooms,
   and furnishings
Making and responding
   to invitations
Reading want ads

▼ **В ПОМОЩЬ УЧАЩИМСЯ**

Colors
Verbs of location: **виси́т/вися́т,
   лежи́т/лежа́т, стои́т/стоя́т**
Хоте́ть
Genitive case of pronouns, question
   words, and singular modifiers
   and nouns
Uses of the genitive case
   у кого́ + есть
   nonexistence: **нет чего́**
   possession and attribution ("of")
   at someone's place: **у кого́**

Workbook: Numbers 51–200
   Intonation of excla-
   mations (IC–5)

▼ **МЕЖДУ ПРОЧИМ**

Ты и вы
Russian apartments and furniture
Russian dormitories
Dachas

151

ТОЧКА ОТСЧЁТА

О ЧЁМ ИДЁТ РЕЧЬ?

A. **Дом.** Which words do you need to describe the rooms you have in your house or apartment?

спа́льня

черда́к

коридо́р

ле́стница

ку́хня

ва́нная

столо́вая

подва́л

кабине́т

гости́ная

Между прочим

The words **гости́ная, столо́вая,** and **ва́нная** are feminine adjectives in form. They modify the word **ко́мната,** which is normally left out of the sentence. Although they are used as nouns, they take adjective endings.

B. **Мебель.** Which words do you need to describe the furniture in your home?

холоди́льник

плита́

пи́сьменный стол

стул

ла́мпа

дива́н

крова́ть (f)

кре́сло

ковёр

C. **Цвета́.** List the colors below in order of your most to least favorite.

бе́лый – white
чёрный – black
кра́сный – red
си́ний – dark blue
голубо́й – light blue
се́рый – gray
жёлтый – yellow
зелёный – green
кори́чневый – brown

рыжий : red hair on person or animal

The adjective **си́ний** (*dark blue*) is the second soft-stem adjective you have seen. Any endings you add should preserve the softness of the stem.

D. What are you wearing today? List at least six items and say what color they are.

> *Образец:* Мои ботинки—чёрные.

E. Here are some architectural features commonly found in houses and apartment buildings. Describe these features in each of the rooms of your house, using appropriate modifiers.

F. **Разговóры.**

Разговóр 1: Фотогрáфии дóма
(Разговáривают Мúша и Кейт)

1. What does Misha want Kate to show him?
2. What does Misha think about the size of Kate's house?
3. How many rooms does Kate first say are on the first floor of her house?
4. How many rooms are there by Misha's count?
5. How many bedrooms are there in Kate's house?
6. Where is the family car kept?

Разговóр 2: Кóмната в общежúтии
(Разговáривают Óля и Майкл)

1. Where does Michael live?
2. Does he live alone?
3. How many beds are there in his room?
4. How many desks?
5. Does Michael have his own TV?

> Michael calls his closet a **шкаф**. Most Russian apartments, however, don't have built-in closets. The word **шкаф** normally refers to a free-standing wardrobe.

Разговóр 3: Пéрвый раз в рýсской квартúре
(Разговáривают Рóберт и Вáля)

1. What does Robert want to do before the meal?
2. Valya mentions two rooms. Which is hers?
3. Who lives in the second room?
4. What does Valya say about hanging rugs on walls?

ДИАЛОГИ

1 Фотогра́фия до́ма

— Марк, у тебя́ есть фотогра́фия твоего́ до́ма?

— Да. Хо́чешь посмотре́ть?

— Коне́чно.

— Вот э́то наш дом. Здесь живу́ я, сестра́ и роди́тели.

— То́лько одна́ семья́ в тако́м большо́м до́ме?! А ско́лько у вас ко́мнат?

— Сейча́с посмо́трим. На пе́рвом этаже́—гости́ная, столо́вая, ку́хня и туале́т. А на второ́м—три спа́льни и две ва́нные.

— А гара́ж у вас есть?

— Нет, гаража́ нет. Маши́на стои́т на у́лице. Вот она́, си́няя.

— Дом у вас о́чень краси́вый.

Между прочим

Ты и вы. As you know, Russians use the **ты** form to address people with whom they are on familiar speech terms, and the **вы** form for those with whom they are on formal terms, or when talking to more than one person. In many dialogs in this lesson, the speakers may seem to alternate between formal and informal address, but in fact they are using the **вы** forms to address more than one person (a whole family, the members of a cultural group).

Ско́лько у вас ко́мнат? **Есть** is omitted in "have" constructions when the focus is not on the existence of the item, but rather on some additional information about it. Mark's friend already knows that Mark has rooms in his house. His question is how many.

2 Фотогра́фия общежи́тия

— Джа́нет, ты живёшь в общежи́тии?

— Да. Хо́чешь посмотре́ть фотогра́фию?

— Да, хочу́. Ты живёшь одна́?

— Нет. У меня́ есть сосе́дка по ко́мнате. Ви́дишь, на фотогра́фии две крова́ти, два стола́.

— Кака́я краси́вая ме́бель. А э́то что тако́е?

— Это холоди́льник, а ря́дом шкаф.

— А телеви́зор?

— В ко́мнате телеви́зора нет. Телеви́зор у нас есть то́лько на этаже́. Ва́нные и туале́ты то́же.

3. Можно посмотреть квартиру?

— Добрый вечер, Саша. Я не опоздала?
— Нет, нет, Джоанна. Проходи в большую комнату. Мамы и папы ещё нет, но обед готов.
— А можно посмотреть квартиру?
— Конечно. Вот в той маленькой комнате живу я. А здесь живут родители.
— Какие большие окна! О, я вижу, что у вас иконы висят.
— Да, мы верующие.

> **Я не опоздал(а)?** Like other past tense forms, this phrase is marked for gender. Women say **Я не опоздала?** Men say **Я не опоздал?**

4. Ковёр на стене

— Валера, какая красивая комната!
— Да, что ты?! Она такая маленькая.
— Но уютная. Я вижу, что у тебя на стене висит ковёр. Это русская традиция?
— Да, а что? У вас такой традиции нет?
— Нет. Дома у меня такой же ковёр, только он лежит на полу.

5. Хотите поехать на дачу?

— Хотите, в воскресенье поедем на дачу?
— На дачу? У вас есть дача?
— Да, в пригороде.
— Она большая?
— Два этажа, четыре комнаты. Хотите посмотреть фотографию?
— Это ваша дача? Жёлтая?
— Да.
— Какая уютная! Почему вы живёте здесь, в городе, когда есть такой дом?
— Понимаете, на даче нет ни газа, ни горячей воды.
— Тогда понятно.

ЖИЛИЩНЫЕ УСЛОВИЯ В РОССИИ

Ру́сская кварти́ра. Russia suffers a housing shortage. Every citizen in the former USSR was officially allotted 9 square meters (approximately 100 square feet) of living space. Families received an extra 4.5 square meters (approx. 48 square feet) for the head of the family. Thus, a family of three was allowed 31.5 square meters (approx. 340 square feet) of living space. Even today most Russians live either in communal apartments or small one- or two-bedroom apartments. Those living in communal apartments usually have one room of their own, which serves as a combination bedroom/living room. They share kitchen and bath facilities with others in the apartment. After the break-up of the Soviet Union, the Russian government began selling apartments to residents.

Жилы́е ко́мнаты. When describing the number of rooms in a house or apartment, Russians count only those rooms where one sleeps or entertains (**жилы́е ко́мнаты**). They do not include the kitchen, bathroom, or entrance hall.

Гости́ная и столо́вая. The words **гости́ная** (*living room*) and **столо́вая** (*dining room*) are usually used to describe Western homes. Most Russian apartments are too small to have a dining room, and Russians usually refer to the room where they entertain (be it a combination bedroom/living room or the equivalent of a small living room) as **больша́я ко́мната.** If the bedroom is separate from the **больша́я ко́мната,** it is a **спа́льня.**

Ва́нная и туале́т. In most Russian apartments the toilet is in one room (**туале́т**) and the sink and bathtub in another (**ва́нная**).

Да́чи. **Да́чи** are summer houses located in the countryside surrounding most big cities in Russia. Many Russian families own one. These houses are usually not equipped with gas, heat, or running water. Toilets are in outhouses in the backyard. During the summer months Russians, especially old people and children, spend a lot of time at their dachas. Besides allowing them to get away from the city, dachas provide a place where people can cultivate vegetables and fruits to bottle for the winter.

Общежи́тие. Russian students studying at an institute in their home town are not given dormitory space. They usually live with their parents.

A. **Где я живу?** Describe where you live to a partner. Use the words and phrases below. Add as many descriptive words as you can.

Я живу́ в … (до́ме, кварти́ре, общежи́тии)

Наш дом … (большо́й, ма́ленький)
Моя́ кварти́ра о́чень … (ма́ленькая, краси́вая)

В на́шем до́ме … (оди́н эта́ж, два этажа́, три этажа́)
В мое́й кварти́ре … (одна́ ко́мната, две ко́мнаты, три ко́мнаты)
В мое́й ко́мнате … (больша́я крова́ть …)

На пе́рвом этаже́ … (гости́ная …)
На второ́м этаже́ … (ма́ленькая спа́льня …)

B. **Что у меня́ в ко́мнате?**

on the floor or on the table

As you can see in the pictures, the verbs **стои́т/стоя́т, лежи́т/лежа́т** and **виси́т/вися́т** are used to describe the position of objects.

В ко́мнате **стои́т** большо́й стол.
In the room a big table stands.

О, я ви́жу, что у вас ико́ны **вися́т.**
Oh, I see you have icons hanging.

До́ма у меня́ ковёр **лежи́т** на полу́.
At home I have a carpet lying on the floor.

Practice telling a partner what furniture you have in each room of your house or apartment. Use the verbs **стои́т/стоя́т, виси́т/вися́т,** and **лежи́т/ лежа́т** as in the example.

Образе́ц: В гости́ной **стоя́т** дива́н, кре́сла и ма́ленький стол. На полу́ **лежи́т** бе́лый ковёр, а на стене́ **вися́т** фотогра́фии.

		ла́мпа
		дива́н
		холоди́льник
		фотогра́фии
В гости́ной	стои́т/стоя́т	ковёр
В столо́вой	виси́т/вися́т	кре́сло
В спа́льне	лежи́т/лежа́т	стол
На ку́хне		стул
		плита́
		пи́сьменный стол
		шкаф
		крова́ть

Язык в действии

ДАВАЙТЕ ПОГОВОРИМ

A. **Подгото́вка к рагово́ру.** Review the dialogs. How would you do the following?

- ask if someone has something (a photograph, car, television)
- state what rooms are on the first and second floor of your house
- find out if someone lives in a house, apartment, or dormitory
- find out if someone has a roommate
- state what things you have in your dorm room
- state what things you don't have in your dorm room
- state that you have two of something (tables, beds, books)
- state that someone (Mom, Dad, roommate) is not present
- ask if you are late
- ask permission to look at someone's apartment (book, icons)
- compliment someone on his/her room (house, car, icons)
- respond to a compliment about your room (car, rug)

B. **Что у кого́ есть?** If you wanted to find out whether someone in your class lives in a large apartment, you could ask **Ты живёшь в большо́й кварти́ре?** or **Твоя́ кварти́ра больша́я и́ли ма́ленькая?** How would you find out the following?

- if someone lives in a small apartment
- if someone has a car
- if someone has a radio

Find answers to the following questions by asking other students and your teacher. Everyone asks and answers questions at the same time. Do not ask one person more than two questions in a row.

Кто живёт в большо́й кварти́ре?	У кого́ есть о́чень большо́й пи́сьменный стол?
Кто живёт в ма́ленькой кварти́ре?	У кого́ есть бе́лый сви́тер?
Кто живёт в общежи́тии?	У кого́ есть кра́сная маши́на?
У кого́ есть большо́й дом?	У кого́ нет маши́ны?
У кого́ нет телеви́зора?	У кого́ есть компью́тер и при́нтер?
У кого́ в ко́мнате есть кре́сло?	У кого́ нет телефо́на в ко́мнате?
У кого́ есть но́вая крова́ть?	У кого́ есть краси́вый ковёр?
У кого́ есть хоро́шее ра́дио?	У кого́ есть холоди́льник в ко́мнате?

C. **Плани́ровка до́ма.** Make a detailed floor plan of

- your home, or your parents' or grandparents' home.
- your dream home.

D. **Како́й у тебя́ дом?** How large is your home? What rooms does it have? How are they furnished?

1. Describe your home to a partner in as much detail as possible. Based on what you say, your partner will draw a detailed floor plan. You will then correct any mistakes your partner makes in it. Throughout this activity you should speak only Russian. The expressions below will help you describe your home.

Нале́во стои́т …	On the left there is …
Напра́во стои́т …	On the right there is …
Ря́дом стои́т …	Nearby there is …
Да́льше …	Further …

2. Tell a different partner as much as you can about where you live. Then find out as much as you can about your new partner's home.

E. **Игровы́е ситуа́ции.**

1. You have just arrived at a Russian friend's house. Ask your friend to show you the apartment. Ask as many questions as you can.

2. You have been invited to spend the weekend at a friend's dacha. Accept the invitation and find out as much as you can about where the dacha is and what it looks like.

3. A Russian friend is interested in where you live. Describe your living situation in as much detail as you can.

4. You've just checked into a hotel in Russia and are not pleased with your room. Complain at the hotel desk. There is no television. The lamp doesn't work. The table is very small, and there is no chair. You want a different room.

5. You want to rent a furnished apartment in St. Petersburg. Ask the owner some questions to find out as much as you can about the apartment.

6. Working with a partner, prepare and act out a situation of your own that deals with the topics of this unit.

F. **Устный перево́д.** You have been asked to interpret for a new Russian exchange student who is seeking accommodations at your university. He needs to talk to the housing director. As you interpret, bear in mind that your task is to communicate ideas, not to translate word for word.

English speaker's part

1. What did you say your last name was?
2. First name?
3. Oh, yes, here it is. You're in a dorm. Do you know where Yates Hall is? You're on the fifth floor.
4. No, you have two roommates.
5. Bathrooms and showers are on the hall.
6. No, there's no refrigerator, but every room has a bed, a desk, and a lamp. There's a refrigerator on each floor.
7. There's a telephone and TV on each floor.
8. You're welcome.

ДАВАЙТЕ ПОЧИТАЕМ

Прода́ю.

1. Look for these items in the classified ads on page 162. What number(s) would you call to inquire about their prices?

   - dacha   _____
   - bed   _____
   - dining room set   _____
   - refrigerator   _____
   - sleeper sofa   _____
   - television   _____

2. Circle a few ads for items that you would be interested in buying. List them below.

ПРОДАЮ

7537-540. Дачу (на участке, 120 км от Москвы). Звонить с 19 до 21 час. по тел. 377-64-32.

7668-360. Телевизор «Рекорд-334». Тел. 286-34-67.

7535-560. Двухкассетник «Шарп-575». Тел. 398-03-51.

7599-660. Старинное пианино «Новик». Тел. 152-64-83.

7446-52. Новый телевизор «Рекорд». ПАЛ/СЕКАМ-автомат. Тел. 461-15-87.

7396-350. Двухъярусную кроватку. Тел. 127-71-28.

7786-507. Тренажер для занятий атлетической гимнастики. Тел. 452-17-66.

7257-720. Двухтумбовый письменный стол Тел. 469-17-63.

7588-360. Холодильник «Минск-15». Тел. 532-69-71.

7542-1260. Дом (на участке, в 80 км от Москвы, г. Серпухов, для постоянного проживания). Тел. 268-74-30, звонить с 10 до 18 час., кроме субботы и воскресенья.

7625-360. Импортный диван-кровать (в хорошем состоянии). Тел. 165-69-34.

7557-360. Двухъярусную кровать. Тел. 464-61-55.

7632-340. Новую кухню. Тел. 997-58-38.

7426-388. Два кресла-кровати (ЧССР). Тел. 332-64-79.

7692-540. Стол и стулья из гарнитура «Севан» (Румыния). Тел. 654-77-94.

7600-532. Дом в деревне (140 км от Москвы). Звонить с 19 до 21 час. по тел. 378-74-85.

7610-543. Импортные диски рок-музыки. Тел. 289-30-24.

7132-67. Двухкассетный магнитофон. Тел. 239-89-36.

7353-721. Настенный холодильник «Сарма». Тел. 237-53-27.

---

3. What do the following words mean, given these building blocks?

двух- = two   **ту́мба** = pedestal
пи́сьменный = writing   **я́рус** = tier

двухту́мбовый пи́сьменный стол _____

двухкассе́тный магнитофо́н _____

двухкассе́тник _____

двухъя́русная крова́ть _____

4. Given that **на** means *on* and **стена́** means *wall*, what is a **настéнный холоди́льник?**

5. What is the difference between a **крéсло-крова́ть** and a **дива́н-крова́ть?**

Ищу́ кварти́ру.

1. Listen to the entire conversation. Decide which of the following statements best describes it.

   a. Someone has come to look over an apartment for rent.
   b. Someone has paid a visit to some new neighbors to see how they are doing.
   c. A daughter is helping her mother move into a newly-rented apartment.
   d. An apartment resident is selling her furniture.

   Write down an expression or two from the conversation that supports your conclusion.

2. Listen to the conversation again. Number the pictures to indicate the sequence of events.

___   ___   ___

___   ___   ___

___   ___

3. Now figure out the meaning of the following new expressions from context.

1. **микроволно́вая печь**
   a. microcomputer
   b. microwave oven
   c. minibike
   d. minicassette recorder

2. **Мы де́лали ремо́нт.**
   a. We had repairs done.
   b. We made a deal.
   c. We threw in the towel.
   d. We took out the garbage.

3. **остано́вки тролле́йбуса**
   a. trolley cars
   b. trolley traffic
   c. trolley repairs
   d. trolley stops

4. **сигнализа́ция**
   a. traffic light
   b. television signal
   c. anti-theft alarm
   d. microwave radiation

4. You now have enough information to answer these questions about renting the apartment.

   a. How many rooms does the apartment have (according to the way Russians count)?
   b. The woman renting the apartment is leaving some furniture behind for the renters to use. Which furniture stays with the house?
   c. What pieces will not be available to the renters?
   d. List at least two good points about this apartment.
   e. List at least two disadvantages.

В ПОМОЩЬ УЧАЩИМСЯ

6.1 ХОТЕТЬ

Learn the conjugation of the verb **хотеть** (*to want*). It is one of only four irregular verbs in Russian and must be memorized.

хотеть

хоч - **у́**
хо́ч - **ешь**
хо́ч - **ет**
хот - **и́м**
хот - **и́те**
хот - **я́т**
to want

Упражнения

1. Complete the dialog with the appropriate forms of **хоте́ть**.

— Алло́, Ли́за? Слу́шай, вы с Кристи́ной* не _хотите_ пойти́ сего́дня на конце́рт?
— Я _хочу_ . А Кристи́на говори́т, что она́ _хочет_ смотре́ть телеви́зор.
— Зна́ешь, у меня́ четы́ре биле́та. Если Кристи́на не _хочет_ , дава́й приглаcи́м Пи́тера и Ама́нду.
— Дава́й. Они́ у меня́ в ко́мнате и говоря́т, что _хотят_ пойти́.
— Прекра́сно.

*вы с Кристи́ной = you and Christina

2. Make sentences by combining words from the columns. The question marks mean that you may use a phrase of your own.

я			смотре́ть телеви́зор
наш преподава́тель	всегда́		писа́ть пи́сьма
мы	никогда́ не		слу́шать ра́дио
вы	сейча́с	хоте́ть	убира́ть ко́мнату
студе́нты	сейча́с не		чита́ть по-ру́сски
ты			у́жинать в кафе́
?			?

➤ Complete Oral Drill 4 and Written Exercise 1 in the Workbook.

6.2 GENITIVE CASE —FORMS

The genitive case of pronouns

— **У э́того ма́льчика** есть кни́га?
— Да, **у него́** есть кни́га.

— **У э́той де́вочки** есть кни́га?
— Да, **у неё** есть кни́га.

You already know how to express "having" by saying **У меня́ есть...,**
У тебя́ есть..., and **У вас есть ....** The word following the preposition **у** is in
the genitive case. The table below gives the genitive case forms for all the
pronouns.

NOMINATIVE CASE	У + GENITIVE CASE
КТО	у кого́
Я	у меня́
ТЫ	у тебя́
ОН	у него́
ОНА́	у неё
МЫ	у нас
ВЫ	у вас
ОНИ́	у них

Упражнение

3. Make sentences out of these words as in the model.

   Образе́ц: У/я/есть/телеви́зор. ➡ *У меня́ есть телеви́зор.*

   а. У/вы/есть/те́хника.
   б. У/я/есть/ра́дио и магнитофо́н.
   в. Это Анто́н. У/он/есть/маши́на.
   г. У/мы/есть/компью́тер.
   д. Это мои́ роди́тели. У/они́/есть/компью́тер и при́нтер.
   е. Это Ка́тя. У/она́/есть/да́ча.
   ж. У/ты/есть/но́вое пла́тье.

➤ Complete Oral Drills 5–6 and Written Exercise 2 in the Workbook.

The genitive case of modifiers and nouns

The genitive endings for singular masculine and neuter phrases are **-ого** for adjectives (**-его** to avoid breaking the 5-letter spelling rule or if the adjective has a soft stem) and **-а** for nouns (**-я** if the noun stem is soft).

The genitive endings for singular feminine phrases are **-ой** for adjectives (**-ей** to avoid breaking the 5-letter spelling rule or if the adjective has a soft stem) and **-ы** for nouns (**-и** if the noun stem is soft).

	ADJECTIVES		NOUNS	
masculine and neuter singular	нóв - ого послéдн - его	**-ого** **-его**	студéнт - а письм - á преподавáтел - я общежѝти - я	**-а** **-я**
feminine singular	нóв - ой послéдн - ей	**-ой** **-ей**	мáм - ы кýхн - и	**-ы** **-и**

Notes

1. Some masculine nouns have end stress whenever an ending is added: **стол ➡ столá, гарáж ➡ гаражá.**

2. Some masculine nouns with **е** or **о** in the semi-final position lose this vowel whenever an ending is added: **отéц ➡ отцá.**

3. The words **мать** and **дочь** have a longer stem in every case except the nominative and accusative singular. Their genitive singular forms are **мáтери** and **дóчери.**

4. Remember that nouns ending in **-а** or **-я** that refer to men and boys decline like feminine nouns, but they are masculine and take masculine modifiers:
   У мáленького Дѝмы есть кнѝга.

5. The genitive endings for the special modifiers are not irregular, but because they involve accent shifts, soft endings, and application of the 5-letter spelling rule, you may wish simply to memorize them.

masculine and neuter singular	мо - **егó** тво - **егó** нáш - **его**	вáш - **его** сво - **егó** чь - **егó**	э́т - **ого** одн - **огó** трéть - **его**
feminine singular	мо - **éй** тво - **éй** нáш - **ей**	вáш - **ей** сво - **éй** чь - **ей**	э́т - **ой** одн - **óй** трéть - **ей**

6. Recall that the possessive pronouns **егó, её,** and **их** never change their form:
   У **егó** мáмы есть кнѝга?   У **её** брáта есть журнáл.   У **их** бáбушки есть письмó.

Упражнение

4. Put the following words into the genitive case.

а. наш оте́ц
б. моя́ мать
в. э́тот америка́нец
г. ста́рая сосе́дка
д. большо́е общежи́тие

е. его́ брат
ж. твоя́ сестра́
з. на́ша семья́
и. интере́сный журна́л
й. хоро́шая кни́га

➤ Complete Oral Drill 7 and Written Exercises 3–4 in the Workbook.

6.3 EXPRESSING OWNERSHIP, EXISTENCE, AND PRESENCE: *ЕСТЬ ЧТО*

Russian expresses ownership by using **у + genitive case + есть.**

The preposition **у**, which is always followed by a phrase in the genitive case, means *by* or *next to*. Russians don't say *Ivan has a book*. Instead they say *There is a book by Ivan* (**У Ива́на есть кни́га**). This literal translation might help you understand the grammar of this construction better. Note that in the sentence *There is a book by Ivan*, the word *book* (**кни́га**) is the subject of the sentence. That is why it is in the nominative case.

Russians often answer questions about ownership with the short answer **Да, есть.** Note that **есть** has several different English translations depending on context.

— **У них есть** компью́тер?   *Do they have* a computer?
— Да, **есть.**   Yes, they *do*.

— **У твое́й сестры́ есть** пальто́?   *Does your sister have* a coat?
— Да, **есть.**   Yes, she *does*.

In Russian, simple presence (*There is … / There are …*) is also expressed by using **есть.**

— Здесь **есть** кни́га?   *Is there* a book here?
— Да, **есть.**   Yes, *there is*.

Just as in English, the object or person present is the subject of the sentence, and therefore it is in the nominative case.

5. Make questions and statements about things people have by combining words from the columns below.

Образец: У твоего отца есть дача?

я	дача
мы	компьютер
ваш сосед	большой диван
твой отец	красивая лампа
твоя сестра	японский телевизор
эта американка	большой стол
её дочь	новая машина
здесь	

➤ Review Oral Drills 5–7 and Written Exercises 2–4 in the Workbook. Complete Oral Drill 8.

6.4   EXPRESSING NONEXISTENCE AND ABSENCE: *НЕТ ЧЕГО*

When the word **есть** is negated, the result is the contraction **нет**. To express nonexistence, the negation of **есть**, Russian uses **нет** *plus the genitive case*. (Здесь **нет книги.** Здесь **нет общежития.** Здесь **нет студента.**) Sentences with this contraction have no grammatical subject.

~~не есть~~   ➡   **нет** + *genitive case*

— Где Катя?	— Где Миша?	— Где родители?
— **Её** здесь **нет.**	— **Его** здесь **нет.**	— **Их** здесь **нет.**

Note that the genitive case of **он, она,** and **они** in the example sentences above differ slightly from the forms introduced before: **у него, у неё, у них.** These third person pronouns begin with the letter **н** only when they follow a preposition.

The contraction **нет** + *genitive case* is also used to say that someone does *not* have or own something.

HAVING	NOT HAVING
есть + *nominative noun*	**нет** + *genitive noun*
У меня́ есть брат.	У меня́ **нет бра́та.**
У нас есть кассе́та.	У нас **нет кассе́ты.**
У неё есть пла́тье.	У неё **нет пла́тья.**

Упражнения

6. Answer the following questions in the negative, following the model.

   Образе́ц: У вас есть но́вый телеви́зор? ➡ **Нет, у нас нет но́вого телеви́зора.**

   а. У вас есть да́ча?
   б. У вас есть маши́на?
   в. У вас есть сестра́?
   г. Здесь есть кре́сло?
   д. Здесь есть телефо́н?
   е. Здесь есть компью́тер?

7. Answer the questions, indicating that the following people are not present.

   Образе́ц: Где Анна Никола́евна? ➡ **Не зна́ю, её здесь нет.**

   а. Где Никола́й Константи́нович?
   б. Где Татья́на Петро́вна?
   в. Где Анна Серге́евна и Влади́мир Петро́вич?
   г. Где Алекса́ндра Ви́кторовна?
   д. Где Вади́м Серге́евич?
   е. Где ва́ши роди́тели?

8. Working with a partner, ask and answer questions about what you have or don't have in your dormitory room or at home.

➤ Complete Oral Drills 9–14 and Written Exercises 5–7 in the Workbook.

6.5 POSSESSION AND ATTRIBUTION ("OF")—GENITIVE CASE OF NOUN PHRASE

- To express possession Russian uses the genitive case where English uses a noun + **'s**.

Это кварти́ра **Вади́ма.**   This is *Vadim's* apartment.

- In English **'s** is usually used to answer the question *whose*. In Russian the genitive case is used to answer the question **чей** when the answer is a noun.

— **Чья** э́то кварти́ра?   *Whose* apartment is this?
— Это кварти́ра **Вади́ма.**   This is *Vadim's* apartment.
— Это кварти́ра **Ки́ры.**   This is *Kira's* apartment.
— Это кварти́ра **на́шего сосе́да.**   This is *our neighbor's* apartment.

- In English the question *whose* can be answered with a noun + **'s** *or* with a possessive modifier (my, his, our, etc.). Possessive modifiers can be used in Russian as well.

— **Чья** э́то кварти́ра?   *Whose* apartment is this?
— Это кварти́ра **Вади́ма.**   This is *Vadim's* apartment.
— Это **его́** кварти́ра.   This is *his* apartment.

- In Russian the genitive case is also used where English uses *of.*

Это фотогра́фия **Ка́ти.**   This is *Katya's* picture
                                         or   This is a photograph *of Katya.*

Note the word order in the Russian sentence. In English, the word *Katya* can either precede the word picture (*Katya's* picture) or follow it (a picture *of Katya*). In Russian, however, the word in the genitive case can come only at the end of the phrase. The only possible word order is: **Это фотогра́фия Ка́ти.**

Упражне́ние

9. Express the following short dialog in Russian.

— Do you have a picture of your house?
— Yes, I do. This is my family's house. This is my room, and this is my sister's room.
— Is that your car?
— That's my father's car. My mother's car is on the street.

➤ Complete Oral Drill 15 and Written Exercises 8–9 in the Workbook.

6.6   SPECIFYING QUANTITY

оди́н, одна́, одно́

The Russian word **оди́н** is a modifier. It agrees with the noun it modifies.

оди́н брат, журна́л, студе́нт, стол

одно́ окно́, пла́тье, общежи́тие

одна́ сестра́, газе́та, студе́нтка, крова́ть

Compound numerals ending in **оди́н (одна́, одно́)** follow the same pattern. The noun following the numeral is in the nominative singular.

два́дцать **оди́н журна́л**
три́дцать **одна́ газе́та**
пятьдеся́т **одно́ окно́**

2, 3, 4 + genitive singular noun

A noun following **два, три,** or **четы́ре** will be in the genitive singular:

2   бра́та, журна́ла, студе́нта, стола́
3   окна́, пла́тья, общежи́тия
4   сестры́, газе́ты, студе́нтки, крова́ти

The numeral **2** is spelled and pronounced **два** before masculine and neuter nouns, but **две** before feminine nouns:

два { бра́та, журна́ла, студе́нта, стола́
      окна́, пла́тья, общежи́тия

две { сестры́, газе́ты,
      студе́нтки, крова́ти

Compound numerals ending in **два (две), три,** or **четы́ре** follow the same pattern:

В э́том до́ме **два́дцать три этажа́.**

Other expressions of quantity

The genitive plural, which you will learn later, is used after all other numbers (5-20, tens, hundreds, thousands, etc., and compound numbers ending in 5, 6, 7, 8, or 9). For the time being, avoid specifying quantity unless the number ends in **оди́н, два, три,** or **четы́ре** and avoid using adjectives with numbers other than one.

Упражнение

10. Make sentences out of the following strings of words.

   а. У/мы/два/компью́тер.
   б. У/я/два/сестра́.
   в. В/на́ша/кварти́ра/четы́ре/ко́мната.
   г. У/ты/то́лько/оди́н/брат?
   д. В/наш/го́род/три/библиоте́ка.

➤ Complete Oral Drills 16–17 and Written Exercise 10 in the Workbook.

6.7 AT SOMEONE'S PLACE: *У КОГО*

To indicate *at someone's place* in Russian, use **y** + *genitive case*. Context dictates what the "place" is (house, office, city, or country).

Мы живём **у бра́та.**	We live *at my brother's (house).*
Студе́нт сейча́с **у преподава́теля.**	The student is now *at the teacher's (office).*
У нас интере́сно.	It's interesting *in our town.*

Упражнение

11. How would you express the following ideas in Russian? Pay special attention to the phrases in bold.

   a. There's no library **in our town.**
   b. Petya is **at Sasha's** today.
   c. I'm living **at my sister's place** right now.
   d. It's interesting **in our country.**

➤ Complete Oral Drill 18 and Written Exercise 11 in the Workbook.

REVIEW OF THE USES OF THE GENITIVE CASE

Read the following sentences. Underline the pronouns, adjectives, and nouns in the genitive case. Indicate (*a, b, c,* or *d*) why the genitive case was used.

a. Appears after **y** to indicate "have."
b. Follows the numbers **два/две, три,** or **четы́ре.**
c. Used in connection with **нет** to indicate absence.
d. Indicates possession or the notion "of."

Образе́ц: ___c___ Здесь нет <u>большо́й ко́мнаты.</u>

___a___ 1. У <u>моего́ бра́та</u> есть маши́на.
___d___   Это маши́на <u>моего́ бра́та.</u>

___b___ 2. В университе́те четы́ре <u>общежи́тия.</u>
___d___   Это ко́мната <u>Мари́и.</u>
___c___   Здесь нет <u>цветно́го телеви́зора.</u>
___a___   Но у <u>неё</u> есть кре́сло, стол и шкаф.
___b___   Здесь ещё два <u>сту́ла.</u>

___a___ 3. У <u>ма́тери</u> зелёный ковёр.

___a___ 4. У <u>кого́</u> есть фотогра́фии?
___a___   У <u>меня́</u> есть.
___d___   Вот фотогра́фия <u>мое́й сестры́.</u>
___b___   А э́то её де́ти—две <u>до́чери.</u>

___b___ 5. В на́шем университе́те четы́ре <u>библиоте́ки.</u>
___a___   У <u>нас</u> хоро́ший спорти́вный зал.
___c___   Но здесь нет <u>бассе́йна.</u>

ОБЗОРНЫЕ УПРАЖНЕНИЯ

A. **Разгово́ры.** Listen to the conversations with the following questions in mind.

Разгово́р 1. *Приглаша́ем на да́чу*
(Разгова́ривают На́дя и Ли́за)

1. Where is Nadya's dacha?
2. How many rooms does it have?
3. Why doesn't Nadya's family live at the dacha all the time?

Разгово́р 2: *Ко́мната в общежи́тии*
(Разгова́ривают Ми́тя и Кэ́ти)

1. In what city does Kathy live?
2. What sort of housing does she have?
3. What can you say about her room furnishings?
4. Kathy's Russian friend asks where she got her rug. What does her friend assume? Is this assumption correct?

B. **Но́вая кварти́ра в Москве́.** Your company has just purchased an unfurnished two-room apartment in Moscow. You have been asked to furnish it.

1. List at least ten items you would like to buy. Use at least one adjective with each item.

2. Read the ads on page 162 to see if they include any of the items on your list. If so, jot down the telephone numbers next to the appropriate items on your list.

3. For one of the advertised items on your list, place a phone call to find out whether it is still available, and whether it is suitable (e.g., if you wanted a red rug, ask if the rug advertised is red or some other color).

4. Assume that you have been able to purchase everything you wanted for the apartment. Write one short paragraph (5-7 sentences) describing the apartment to your colleagues.

НОВЫЕ СЛОВА И ВЫРАЖЕНИЯ

NOUNS

брат (*pl.* бра́тья)	brother
ва́нная (*declines like adj.*)	bathroom (bath/shower; no toilet)
ве́рующий (*declines like adj.*)	believer
вода́ (*pl.* во́ды)	water
газ	natural gas
гара́ж (*ending always stressed*)	garage
гости́ная (*declines like adj.*)	living room
да́ча (на)	summer home, dacha
дверь (*fem.*)	door
де́вочка	(little) girl
дива́н	couch
ико́на	religious icon
кабине́т	office
ков(ё)р (*ending always stressed*)	rug
коридо́р	hallway, corridor
кре́сло	armchair
крова́ть (*fem.*)	bed
ку́хня (на)	kitchen
ла́мпа	lamp
ле́стница	stairway
ма́льчик	(little) boy
ме́бель (*fem., always sing.*)	furniture
обе́д	lunch
окно́ (*pl.* о́кна)	window
плита́ (*pl.* пли́ты)	stove
подва́л	basement
пол (на полу́; *ending always stressed*)	floor (as opposed to ceiling)
при́город	suburb
сосе́д(ка) по ко́мнате	roommate
спа́льня	bedroom
стена́ (*pl.* сте́ны)	wall
стол (*ending always stressed*)	table
пи́сьменный стол	desk
столо́вая (*declines like adj.*)	dining room, cafeteria
стул (*pl.* сту́лья)	(hard) chair
това́рищ по ко́мнате	roommate (male)
тради́ция	tradition
туале́т	bathroom
у́лица (на)	street
фотогра́фия (на)	photograph
холоди́льник	refrigerator
черда́к (на) (*ending always stressed*)	attic

шкаф (в шкафу́) (*ending always stressed*) cabinet; wardrobe; free-standing closet
эта́ж (на) (*ending always stressed*) floor, story

ADJECTIVES

цвета́	colors
бе́лый	white
голубо́й	light blue
жёлтый	yellow
зелёный	green
кори́чневый	brown
кра́сный	red
се́рый	gray
си́ний	dark blue
цветно́й	color
чёрно-бе́лый	black and white
чёрный	black

Other adjectives

горя́чий	hot (*of things, not weather*)
оди́н (одна́, одно́, одни́)	one
пи́сьменный	writing
свой (своя́, своё, свои́)	one's own
тако́й	such, so (used with nouns)
тако́й же	the same kind of
тот (то, та, те)	that, those (*as opposed to э́том*)
ую́тный	cozy, comfortable (*about room or house*)

QUESTION WORDS

почему́	why
ско́лько	how many

VERBS

хоте́ть	to want
(хочу́, хо́чешь, хо́чет, хоти́м, хоти́те, хотя́т)	
есть (+ *nominative*)	there is
нет (+ *genitive*)	there is not
виси́т, вися́т	hang(s)
лежи́т, лежа́т	lie(s)
стои́т, стоя́т	stand(s)

ADVERBS

да́льше	further, next
ря́дом	alongside
тогда́	in that case
нале́во	on the left
напра́во	on the right

PHRASES AND OTHER WORDS

жили́щные усло́вия	living conditions
Мо́жно посмотре́ть кварти́ру?	May I look at the apartment?
ни… ни…	neither … nor …
Обе́д гото́в.	Lunch is ready.
Пое́дем…	Let's go …
Посмо́трим.	Let's see.
Проходи́(те).	Come in.
Ско́лько у вас ко́мнат?	How many rooms do you have?
у + *genitive*	at (somebody's) house
у + *genitive* + есть + *nominative*	(someone) has (something)
у + *genitive* + нет + *genitive*	(someone) doesn't have (something)
Хо́чешь посмотре́ть?	Would you like to see [it, them]?
Я ви́жу …	I see …
Я не опозда́л(а)?	Am I late?

NUMBERS

51–200 (*for understanding*)

PERSONALIZED VOCABULARY

_____

_____

_____

_____

(handwritten margin notes):

бе́лый
бе́лая
бе́лое
бе́лые

си́ний
си́няя
си́нее
си́ние

Test
1) Fill in blanks w/ висят, лежит, стоит + plural forms висят, лежат
2) List 5 items in my closet + 5 pieces of furniture in the dorm room; put color adjectives w/ each. (15 pt)
3) хотеть (all the verbs) (5 sentences)
4) English → Russian "I have…"
5) 50 points: reading

НАША СЕМЬЯ

▼ КОММУНИКАТИВНЫЕ ЗАДАНИЯ

Naming family members
Talking about people: names, ages,
    professions, where they were born,
    and where they grew up
Exchanging letters about families

▼ В ПОМОЩЬ УЧАЩИМСЯ

Любить
Stable vs. shifting stress in verb
    conjugation
Родился, вырос
Expressing age—the dative case
    of pronouns
Specifying quantity
    год, года, лет in expressions of age
    Сколько детей, братьев, сестёр?
Зовут
Accusative case of pronouns and
    masculine animate singular
    modifiers and nouns
О(б)+ prepositional case
Prepositional case of plural modifiers,
    nouns, question words, and per-
    sonal pronouns

Workbook: Numbers 200–1000
IC-2 for emphasis

▼ МЕЖДУ ПРОЧИМ

Russian families
Teachers vs. professors

ТОЧКА ОТСЧЁТА

О ЧЁМ ИДЁТ РЕЧЬ?

A. **Это на́ша семья́.**

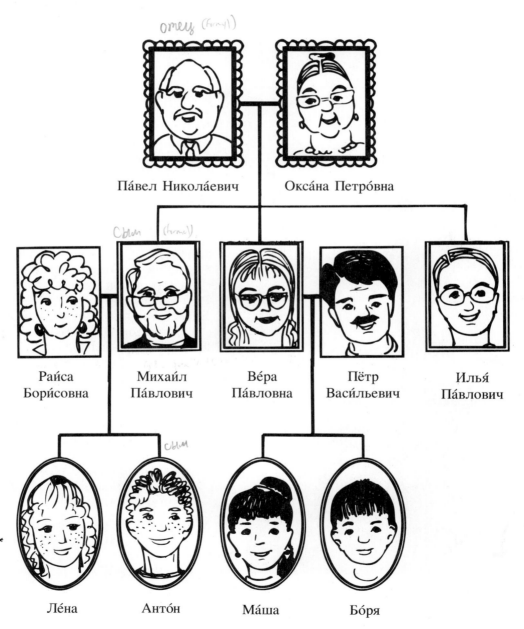

отец (*family*)

Па́вел Никола́евич   Окса́на Петро́вна

Сын (*family*)

Раи́са Бори́совна   Михаи́л Па́влович   Ве́ра Па́вловна   Пётр Васи́льевич   Илья́ Па́влович

Сын

Ле́на   Анто́н   Ма́ша   Бо́ря

Познако́мьтесь. Это мои́ роди́тели. Вот мать. Её зову́т Раи́са Бори́совна. А вот оте́ц. Его́ зову́т Михаи́л Па́влович. Анто́н мой брат. Я его́ сестра́.

Па́вел Никола́евич мой де́душка. Окса́на Петро́вна моя́ ба́бушка. Я их вну́чка, а Анто́н их внук.

Это мой дя́дя Илья́. У него́ нет жены́. А э́то моя́ тётя Ве́ра и её второ́й муж, Пётр Васи́льевич. Я их племя́нница, а мой брат Анто́н их племя́нник.

Это де́ти тёти Ве́ры. Вот её сын Бо́ря. Он мой двою́родный брат. А вот её дочь Ма́ша. Она́ моя́ двою́родная сестра́.

Чле́ны семьи́

оте́ц	мать
сын	дочь
дя́дя	тётя
де́душка	ба́бушка
внук	вну́чка
брат	сестра́
двою́родный брат	двою́родная сестра́
племя́нник	племя́нница
муж	жена́

роди́тели
де́ти

B. **У тебя есть...?** Find out if your partner has the family members shown on pages 180-181. Write down your partner's answers. Then reverse roles.

Образец: У тебя есть сестра?

C. **Профессии.** Find out what your partner's relatives do for a living. Use the pictures to help you with the names of some typical occupations. Ask your teacher for other professions if you need them. Write down your partner's answers.

Образец:
— Кто **по профессии** твой отец?
— **По профессии** мой отец **преподаватель.**

врач

учитель

учительница

секретарь

медсестра/медбрат

учёный

бизнесмен

музыкант

худо́жник　　**программи́ст**　　**зубно́й врач**　　**архите́ктор**

писа́тель　　**ме́неджер**　　**инжене́р**　　**фе́рмер**

библиоте́карь　　**журнали́ст**　　**продаве́ц/продавщи́ца**

salesma-

домохозя́йка　　**бухга́лтер**　　**юри́ст**

полицейский : police officer.

почтальон : postman.

УЧИТЕЛЬ—ПРЕПОДАВАТЕЛЬ—ПРОФЕССОР

Although these words all describe teachers, they are not interchangeable.

Учи́тель. Учителя́ work in a **шко́ла,** that is, a grade school or high school; a male teacher is an **учи́тель,** a female teacher is an **учи́тельница.**

Преподава́тель. Преподава́тели work at an **институ́т** or **университе́т.** Their job is most equivalent to the job of a lecturer or instructor in a U.S. college or university. Although the feminine form **преподава́тельница** exists, **преподава́тель** is usually used to identify either a man or a woman in this job.

Профе́ссор. Профессора́ also work at an **институ́т** or **университе́т.** They normally have a **до́кторская сте́пень,** which is considerably more difficult to obtain than a U.S. doctoral degree. The closest equivalent in the U.S. educational system is a full professor.

D. **Места́ рабо́ты.** Find out where your partner's relatives work. Review the prepositional case endings for adjectives and nouns in Unit 3 if necessary. Write down your partner's answers.

Образе́ц:

— Где рабо́тает твоя́ мать?
— Она́ рабо́тает **в больни́це.**

библиоте́ка

газе́та

комме́рческая фи́рма

теа́тр

лаборато́рия

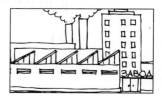

заво́д (на)

музе́й

фе́рма (на)

телеста́нция (на)

университе́т

шко́ла

учрежде́ние

поликли́ника

магази́н

юриди́ческая фи́рма

туристи́ческое бюро́

бюро́ недви́жимости

Между прочим

В УЧРЕЖДЕНИИ

We often say, "So-and-so works in an office." One can translate this phrase directly (**рабо́тать в учрежде́нии,** where **учрежде́ние** is any sort of white-collar setting), but by and large Russians describe jobs more specifically: **Ма́ма рабо́тает в бухгалте́рии небольшо́й фи́рмы** (*My mother works in the accounting department of a small company*).

Разгово́р 1: На́ша семья́
   (Разгова́ривают Мэ́ри и Ната́ша)

1. What does Natasha want to know about Mary's parents?
2. What does Mary's father do for a living?
3. What does Mary's mother do?
4. Does Mary have any siblings?
5. What does Natasha say about the size of Russian families?

Разгово́р 2: До́ма у Оле́га
   (Разгова́ривают Оле́г и Джон)

1. What is Oleg showing John?
2. What do Oleg's parents do for a living?
3. Who else lives with Oleg and his parents?

◄ Widowed grandmothers often live with their married children and take care of the grandchildren. This is the preferred childcare solution for many families.

Разгово́р 3: Немно́го о бра́те
   (Разгова́ривают На́дя и Дже́ннифер)

1. Who does Nadya want to introduce to Jennifer?
2. What does he do for a living?
3. What kind of person is he?
4. What do we learn about Jennifer's brother?

ДИАЛОГИ

1 Я родила́сь в Калифо́рнии.

— Дже́ннифер, где ты родила́сь?
— Я родила́сь в Калифо́рнии.
— И там вы́росла?
— Нет, я вы́росла в Нью-Йо́рке.
— А кто по профе́ссии твой оте́ц?
— Оте́ц? Он архите́ктор.
— А мать рабо́тает?
— Коне́чно. Она́ юри́ст.
— А как её зову́т?
— По́ла.
— А как зову́т отца́?
— Э́рик.

> роди́лся/родила́сь/родили́сь
> вы́рос/вы́росла/вы́росли
> Like all past tense verbs,
> these are marked for gender
> and number. See 7.3.

2 Немно́го о на́шей семье́

— Послу́шай, Марк! Я ничего́ не зна́ю о твое́й
  семье́. Расскажи́ мне, кто твои́ роди́тели.
— Ла́дно. Зна́чит так. Оте́ц у меня́ бизнесме́н.
  У него́ ма́ленькая фи́рма.
— Пра́вда? А мать?
— Ма́ма—врач. У неё ча́стная пра́ктика.
— Ты еди́нственный ребёнок?
— Нет, у меня́ есть ста́рший брат. Он у́чится
  в аспиранту́ре. Я его́ о́чень люблю́.

> When adult Russians speak
> of **моя́ семья́,** they normally
> speak of a spouse and chil-
> dren. When children or
> young adults speak about
> their parents and siblings,
> they are likely to refer to
> them as **на́ша семья́.**

3 Кто э́то на фотогра́фии?

— Мэ́ри! Кто э́то на фотогра́фии?
— Брат.
— А э́то?
— Это моя́ мла́дшая сестра́, Кэ́рол.
— А бра́та как зову́т?
— Дже́йсон. Он ещё у́чится в шко́ле. Он у́чится
  в оди́ннадцатом кла́ссе. Очень лю́бит спорт и
  му́зыку.
— Он, наве́рное, о́чень весёлый?
— Вы зна́ете, не о́чень. Он о́чень серьёзный,
  но симпати́чный.

4 В Аме́рике се́мьи больши́е?

— Фрэнк! Говоря́т, что в Аме́рике больши́е се́мьи. Это пра́вда?
— Да как сказа́ть? Есть больши́е, есть ма́ленькие. У нас, наприме́р, семья́ ма́ленькая: я, оте́ц и мать. Бра́тьев и сестёр у меня́ нет.
— А кто по профе́ссии твой оте́ц?
— Оте́ц? Он преподава́тель матема́тики в университе́те.
— А мать? Она́ то́же рабо́тает?
— Ма́ма по профе́ссии медсестра́. Рабо́тает в больни́це. Очень лю́бит свою́ рабо́ту.

> Russian families in large urban centers tend to be small. Couples rarely have more than one child.

5 Де́душка и ба́бушка

— Ване́сса! Кто э́то на фотогра́фии?
— Это моя́ ба́бушка. А вот э́то—мой де́душка.
— Они́ совсе́м не ста́рые! Ско́лько им лет?
— Ей шестьдеся́т пять. А ему́ се́мьдесят. Ба́бушка и де́душка на пе́нсии. Они́ живу́т во Флори́де. Они́ очень здоро́вые и энерги́чные. Лю́бят спорт.
— Интере́сно. А у нас ба́бушки и де́душки совсе́м не таки́е.

> Russians are often surprised by the youthfulness of American senior citizens.

A Draw your family tree, indicating not only your relative's names, but also their relationship to you. If you need words that are not in the textbook, consult your teacher.

B. In Russian, list ten of your relatives and friends. Indicate their profession and relationship to you.

Name	Relationship	Profession

C. Write three sentences about each of your family members.

Язык в действии

ДАВАЙТЕ ПОГОВОРИМ

A. **Немно́го о семье́.**

1. Find out how many brothers and sisters your partner has. Write down what you learn.

— Ско́лько у тебя́ бра́тьев и сестёр?   — У меня́ …

оди́н	брат
два, три, четы́ре	бра́та
пять	бра́тьев
одна́	сестра́
две, три, четы́ре	сестры́
пять	сестёр

2. Find out whether your partner's brothers and sisters go to school or work, and where. Write down what you learn.

3. Find out the names of your partner's parents and siblings. Write down the information.

— Как зову́т твоего́ отца́?
— Его́ зову́т Джон.

— Как зову́т твою́ мать?
— Её зову́т Мели́сса.

— Как зову́т твою́ сестру́?
— Её зову́т Кристи́на.

— Как зову́т твоего́ бра́та?
— Его́ зову́т Марк.

4. Describe one of your relatives to your partner, using the adjectives below. Then switch roles. Write down what you learn about your partner's relative.

энерги́чный—неэнерги́чный

серьёзный—несерьёзный

у́мный—*smart*

симпати́чный—несимпати́чный
(not) nice

весёлый—невесёлый
(not) cheerful

обыкнове́нный—необыкнове́нный
ordinary—unusual

здоро́вый—нездоро́вый
(un)healthy

5. Find out where the members of your partner's family were born. Then reverse roles. Write down what you learn.

6. Verify with your partner that the information you jotted down is correct. Your partner will respond appropriately.

То́чно!	**Нет, э́то не совсе́м так!**	**Нет, совсе́м не так!**
That's right!	*No, that's not completely right.*	*No, that's not it at all!*

Седьмой урок ГОЛОСА **191**

B. **Подготовка к разговору.** Review the dialogs. How would you do the following?

- ask where someone was born
- state where you were born
- ask where someone grew up
- state where you grew up
- ask what someone's father (mother, brother) does for a living
- state what you do for a living
- ask what someone's father's (mother's, sister's) name is
- ask if someone is an only child
- state you have an older brother or sister
- state you have a younger brother or sister
- say your mother (father, brother) really likes her (his) job
- describe the size and composition of your family

C. **Фотография семьи.** Bring a picture of your family to class. Pass it around. Your classmates will ask you questions about various members of your family. Answer in as much detail as you can.

D. **Игровые ситуации.**

1. Working with a partner, develop a list of questions for interviewing the following people about their families. Then act out one or more of the interviews with your teacher playing the role of the Russian.

   a. A Russian student who has just arrived on your campus.
   b. A new teacher from Russia who will be teaching Russian.
   c. A Russian rock musician who will be performing on your campus.

2. You were invited to an informal get-together of Russian students attending St. Petersburg University. They ask you about your family.

3. With a partner, prepare and act out a situation of your own that deals with the topics of this unit.

E. **Устный перевод.** You have been asked to interpret at a university reception for a group of visiting Russian students.

English speaker's part

1. Where do your parents live?
2. Where were they born?
3. What does your father do for a living?
4. Does your mother work?
5. What does she do for a living?
6. Do you have any brothers and sisters?
7. What are their names?
8. What a pretty Russian name!
9. That was very interesting.

ДАВАЙТЕ ПОЧИТАЕМ

A. **Рекла́ма.** Advertisements like these are common in local Russian newspapers.

1. For each ad, indicate
   - who placed it.
   - what kind of help is wanted.
   - any other details you understand.

1.

совместное
советско-американское предприятие «АМФАРМ»
приглашает на работу
фармацевтов
со знанием английского языка

Телефон для справок 151-38-44.

2.

ЭНЕРГИЧНЫЕ

- РЕДАКТОРЫ
- ДИЗАЙНЕРЫ
- ХУДОЖНИКИ
- ЖУРНАЛИСТЫ

Вас приглашает редакция нового журнала в области рекламы и информации о программных продуктах и компьютерной технике.
Телефон для справок: 903-04-57.

3.

РОССИЙСКАЯ ТОВАРНО-СЫРЬЕВАЯ БИРЖА ОБЪЯВЛЯЕТ КОНКУРС

для специалистов высокой квалификации:
бухгалтеров, менеджеров, консультантов,
юристов всех специализаций,
экономистов, финансистов,
специалистов по рекламе,
психологов,
переводчиков,
секретарей,
журналистов, редакторов, художников,
шоферов.

Просим составить резюме на одной странице, описание биографических данных, этапов карьеры и профессиональных навыков и вместе с 2 фотографиями выслать по адресу *Москва 125190 а/я 225.*

2. Find the abbreviation for **абоне́нтный я́щик**—*post office box.*

3. Look at the list of professions in the third ad. They are all in the genitive plural. What is the genitive plural ending for most masculine nouns? What is the genitive plural ending for nouns ending in **-ь**?

B. **Свиде́тельство о рожде́нии.** Look through the following text.

1. What kind of document is it?

2. Working with a partner, find as much information as you can in two minutes. Compare your notes with the rest of the class.

3. Find all the words that contain the element **род-/рожд-**, and determine their meaning from context.

СВИДЕТЕЛЬСТВО О РОЖДЕНИИ	РОДИТЕЛИ
Гражданин(ка) _Розенштейн_ _Александр Михайлович_	Отец _Розенштейн_ _Михаил Аврамович_
родился(лась) _16. 09. 1978 шестнадцатого сентября тысяча девятсот семьдесят восьмого года_	национальность _еврей_
	Мать _Розенштейн_ _Римма Григорьевна_
Место рождения _Украинская ССР г. Львов_	национальность _еврейка_
	Место регистрации _Дворец торжественных событий львовского горисполкома УССР_
Регистрация рождения произведена в соответствии с Законом 19_78_ года _ноября_ месяца _2_ числа	Дата выдачи _20 ноября_ 19 _80_
	Регистратор актов гражданского состояния _Л. Зубач_
	ДИЗ I-СI № 001029

C. **Здра́вствуйте далёкие друзья́!** The following letter is similar to many that were written in response to an American organization's request for Russian citizens to become pen pals with Americans. Although there is much in the letter that you will not yet understand, you will be able to get some basic information from it.

1. First look through the letter to find out which paragraphs contain the following information.

information	paragraph
the languages known by the writer	
where the writer lives	
the writer's family	
the writer's hobby (**увлече́ние**)	
her husband's hobby	

2. Now go through the letter again to answer the following questions.
   a. Who wrote the letter?
   b. What foreign languages does she know?
   c. Where does she live?
   d. The author discusses her nationality and that of family members. What nationalities does she mention?

3. Fill in the chart below with as much information as you can find about the author's family.

NAME   **RELATIONSHIP**   **PROFESSION**

_____

_____

_____

_____

_____

_____

Здравствуйте далёкие незнакомые друзья!

1. К сожалению, я не знаю английского языка, в школе учила французский. Пишу Вам из старинного города Ярославля. Наш город входит в Золотое кольцо России.

2. Немного о себе. Зовут меня Ольга, мне 46 лет, по профессии я инженер, работаю в проектном институте. Очень люблю свою работу. У меня два взрослых сына: один—профессиональный спортсмен, живёт в Киеве, женат, другой—достиг призывного возраста и служит в армии. Мы с мужем живём сейчас вдвоём. Мой муж Толя тоже инженер. Как опытный специалист, он работает в отделе экспертизы. С ним мы женаты 12 лет.

3. Наша семья интересна в национальном отношении: в моих жилах течёт польская и русская кровь. Мой первый муж и отец моих детей по национальности украинец. Жена старшего сына —наполовину эстонка.

4. У меня есть увлечение, я пишу стихи. Печататься я никогда не пыталась, писала для себя. Муж мой тоже имеет хобби: он поёт в хоре. Голос у него очень хороший и он поёт с удовольствием.

5. У нас есть небольшой участок земли на берегу реки Волги в лесу с небольшим домиком. Там мы выращиваем ягоды, ряд интересных растений и много цветов, особенно любим розы и клематисы. Вот такая наша жизнь.

6. Жду письма. Хотелось бы узнать о Вас, о Вашей семье.

С огромным приветом

Ольга Соколова

4. **Post-reading**
   a. Determine the meaning of the word **жена́т(ы)** from context (paragraph 2).
      Note: **Он жена́т, они́ жена́ты,** but **она́ за́мужем.**
   b. Find a synonym for the word **увлече́ние** (*hobby*).
   c. What is special about the way Russians write **вы, ваш** and all their forms in letters to one person?

Виктори́на. You are about to listen to the opening of a game show in which one family plays against another. As you tune in, the contestants are being introduced. Listen for the information requested below.

THE BELOVS: Head of the family—Name (and patronymic if given):
Age (if given):
Job:
Hobby (at least one):

Her brother—Name (and patronymic if given):
Age (if given):
Job:
Hobby (at least one):

Her sister—Name (and patronymic if given):
Age (if given):
Job:
Hobby (at least one):

Her aunt's husband—Name (and patronymic if given):
Age (if given):
Job:
Hobby (at least one):

THE NIKITINS: Head of the family—Name (and patronymic if given):
Age (if given):
Job:
Hobby (at least one):

His son—Name (and patronymic if given):
Age (if given):
Job:
Hobby (at least one):

His daughter-in-law—Name (and patronymic if given):
Age (if given):
Job:
Hobby (at least one):

His wife —Name (and patronymic if given):
Age (if given):
Job:
Hobby (at least one):

7.1 ЛЮБИТЬ

Люби́ть is a second-conjugation verb. Here is its full conjugation.

люби́ть

любл -	**ю́**
лю́б -	**ишь**
лю́б -	**ит**
лю́б -	**им**
лю́б -	**ите**
лю́б -	**ят**

to like or to love

Notes

1. The letter **-б-** becomes **-бл-** in the **я** form of the verb. This kind of change is called consonant mutation and is common in the **я** form of second-conjugation verbs.

2. The stress is on the ending in the infinitive and **я** form, but it is on the stem everywhere else.

Упражнение

1. Make grammatically correct statements and/or questions, using the words and phrases from the columns. Follow the model. Note that you need to conjugate the verb **люби́ть.** The verb that follows it is an infinitive.

   Образе́ц: Я люблю́ смотре́ть телеви́зор.

я		говори́ть по-ру́сски
ты		занима́ться в библиоте́ке
вы		учи́ться в университе́те
моя́ сосе́дка по ко́мнате		слу́шать му́зыку
мой това́рищ по ко́мнате	(не) люби́ть	писа́ть пи́сьма
мои́ друзья́		говори́ть о семье́
я и ма́ма		говори́ть о себе́
на́ша семья́		у́жинать в кафе́
студе́нты		убира́ть ко́мнату
		смотре́ть телеви́зор

➤ Complete Oral Drill 6 and Written Exercise 1 in the Workbook.

7.2   STABLE AND SHIFTING STRESS IN VERB CONJUGATIONS

Russian verb conjugations have three possible stress patterns:

1. Stress always on the ending, as in **говори́ть**.
2. Stress always on the stem, as in **чита́ть**.
3. Stress on the ending in the infinitive and **я** forms, and on the last syllable of the stem in all other forms, as in **люби́ть, писа́ть, смотре́ть,** and **учи́ться**.

Thus, if you know the stress on the infinitive and the **они́** form, you can predict the stress for the entire conjugation.

Stable stress
infinitive stress = stress
on all forms

Shifting stress
end stress on infinitive and **я** form;
stress on all other forms
one syllable closer to beginning of word

говор	и́ть	чита́	ть		пис	а́ть		уч	и́ться
говор	ю	чита́	ю		пиш	у́		уч	у́сь
говор	и́шь	чита́	ешь		пи́ш	ешь		у́ч	ишься
говор	и́т	чита́	ет		пи́ш	ет		у́ч	ится
говор	и́м	чита́	ем		пи́ш	ем		у́ч	имся
говор	и́те	чита́	ете		пи́ш	ете		у́ч	итесь
говор	я́т	чита́	ют		пи́ш	ут		у́ч	атся

Упражнение

2. How would you express the following in Russian? Pay special attention to the stress on all the verbs.

— Ты (like) ста́рые фи́льмы?
— Да, я их (like).

— Где ты (study)?
— Я (study) в университе́те. Мла́дший брат и сестра́ (study) в шко́ле, а ста́рший брат (study) в институ́те.

— Что вы (write)?
— Я (am writing) письмо́, а Ма́ша (is writing) сочине́ние.*

*сочине́ние—a composition

➤ Complete Oral Drill 7 and Written Exercise 2 in the Workbook.

7.3 WAS BORN, GREW UP

— Джéннифер, где ты **родилáсь?**	Jennifer, where *were you born*?
— Я **родилáсь** в Калифóрнии.	I *was born* in California.
— И там **вы́росла?**	And *did you grow up* there?
— Нет, я **вы́росла** в Нью-Йóрке.	No, I *grew up* in New York.

Марк **роди́лся** и **вы́рос** в Мичигáне.	Mark *was born* and *grew up* in Michigan.

Нáши роди́тели **роди́лись** и **вы́росли** во Флори́де.	Our parents *were born* and *grew up* in Florida.

Two past-tense verbs that are important for telling about your background are included in **Диалог 1** and repeated in the sentences above. On the basis of what you already know about the structure of Russian, you will not be surprised to see that these verbs have the past-tense marker -л for masculine singular, -ла for feminine singular, and -ли for plural forms. We will examine past tense verbs in full later. For the time being, learn these verbs according to the following charts.

was (were) born

singular	*plural*
он **роди́лся** онá **родилáсь**	мы вы **роди́лись** они́

grew up

singular	*plural*
он **вы́рос** онá **вы́росла**	мы вы **вы́росли** они́

Notes

1. The forms used after **я** and **ты** depend on the gender of the person referred to.

2. The forms used after **вы** are always **роди́лись** and **вы́росли,** even when referring to only one person.

Упражнения

3. How would you ask the following people where they were born and grew up?
   a. your best friend
   b. your Russian teacher

4. How would you say where you were born and grew up?

➤ Complete Oral Drill 8 and Written Exercise 3 in the Workbook.

— Кто э́то на фотогра́фии?
— Ба́бушка.
— Она́ совсе́м не ста́рая! **Ско́лько ей лет?**
— **Ей шестьдеся́т два го́да.**

— Ско́лько **им** лет?
— **Им** пять лет.

— Ско́лько **ему́** лет?
— **Ему́** шестьдеся́т лет.
— А **ей?**
— **Ей** четы́ре го́да.

Russian uses the dative case of the person to express age. Here are the forms for the personal pronouns in the dative case.

NOMINATIVE CASE	что	кто	я	ты	он	она́	мы	вы	они́
DATIVE CASE	чему́	кому́	мне	тебе́	ему́	ей	нам	вам	им

Упражне́ния

5. How would you ask the following people how old they are?
   a. a female friend
   b. a friend's father
   c. friends who are twins

6. How would you ask the following questions?
   a. How old is she?
   b. How old is he?
   c. How old are they?

➤ Complete Oral Drill 9 and Written Exercise 4 in the Workbook.

7.5   SPECIFYING QUANTITY

- In Unit 6 you learned that in Russian the nominative singular of nouns is used after 1, and the genitive singular after the numbers 2, 3, and 4. You also learned that the words for 1 (**один, одна, одно**) and 2 (**два, две**) are influenced by the gender of the following noun. After numbers 5 through 20, after the question word **сколько,** and after the quantity word **много,** Russian uses the genitive plural. You will learn all genitive plural forms in a later unit. In order that you can handle the age and family topics of this unit, however, the genitive forms for the words **год** *(year),* **брат** *(brother),* and **сестра** *(sister)* are presented below.

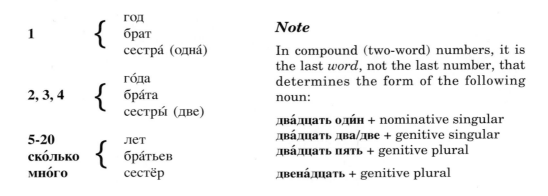

1 { год / брат / сестра (одна)

2, 3, 4 { года / брата / сестры (две)

5-20 / сколько / много { лет / братьев / сестёр

Note

In compound (two-word) numbers, it is the last *word,* not the last number, that determines the form of the following noun:

двадцать один + nominative singular
двадцать два/две + genitive singular
двадцать пять + genitive plural

двенадцать + genitive plural

Упражнения

7. Express the following people's ages in Russian.

он—13   она—31   они—3   вы—2   я—?

8. Complete the dialogs by using the correct forms of the words given in parentheses. Answer the question in the last dialog about yourself.

   а. — Дима, сколько у тебя (брат) и (сестра)?
       — У меня (2) (сестра) и (1) (брат).
       — Какая большая семья!

   б. — Саша, у тебя большая семья?
       — Только я и (1) (сестра).

   в. — Сколько у вас (сестра) и (брат)?
       — У меня …

➤ Complete Oral Drills 10–12 in the Workbook.

- **Дети.** When talking about the number of children in a family, Russians normally use special forms of numbers and the genitive plural of the word **дети** (*children*)—**детей.**

Сколько детей?

один ребёнок

двое детей

трое детей

четверо детей

пять детей

нет детей

Упражнение

9. Fill in the blanks.

— Сколько у новой соседки _____ (children)? Папа говорит, что у них _____ (five kids)!

— Нет, у них только _____ (three kids). Паша и его _____ (two sisters).

— И в соседней квартире тоже есть _____ (children)?

— Нет, там _____ (there aren't any children).

➤ Complete Oral Drills 13–14 and Written Exercises 5–6 in the Workbook.

7.6 THE ACCUSATIVE CASE OF PRONOUNS

Remember that the accusative case is used for all direct objects in Russian sentences. When the direct object is expressed by a pronoun, it is usually placed before the verb. This is in keeping with the tendency in Russian to give old information before new information.

Это мой ста́рший брат. Я **его́** о́чень люблю́.
Это на́ши роди́тели. Мы **их** о́чень лю́бим.
Вы понима́ете **меня́**, когда́ я говорю́ по-ру́сски?

Here are the forms of the question words and personal pronouns in the accusative case.

NOMINATIVE CASE	что	кто	я	ты	он	она́	мы	вы	они́
ACCUSATIVE CASE	что	кого́	меня́	тебя́	его́	её	нас	вас	их

Упражнения

10. What would you substitute for the words in parentheses?

— (Whom) ты зна́ешь в на́шем университе́те?
— Ве́ру Па́вловну. Ты (her) зна́ешь? Она́ чита́ет о́чень интере́сный курс.
— Я зна́ю. Я (it) слу́шаю.
— Зна́чит, ты, наве́рное, зна́ешь Са́шу Бело́ва. Он то́же слу́шает э́тот курс.
— Да, коне́чно я (him) зна́ю.

11. How would you express the following in Russian?

a. "Where is my magazine?"
"Masha is reading it."

b. "Do you know my sister?"
"No, I don't know her."
"Interesting... She knows you!"
"She knows me?"

➤ Complete Oral Drill 15 in the Workbook.

7.7 TELLING SOMEONE'S NAME: *ЗОВУТ*

Note the structure for asking and telling someone's name in Russian:

— Как **вас** зову́т?
— **Меня́** зову́т Кири́лл.
— А как зову́т **ва́шего бра́та** и **ва́шу сестру́**?
— **Их** зову́т Ди́ма и Со́ня.

The phrase **Как зову́т?** actually means *How do they call you?* The phrase **Меня́ зову́т Кири́лл** means *They call me Kirill.* This literal translation should help you to see that the words in boldface in the preceding dialog are direct objects, and therefore are in the accusative case.

Note the Russian word order. In questions with **Как зову́т,** nouns normally come at the end of the question (**Как зову́т *ва́шу сестру́*?**), whereas pronouns normally immediately follow the question word (**Как *вас* зову́т?**).

➤ Read 7.8. Then complete Oral Drill 16 in the Workbook.

7.8 THE ACCUSATIVE CASE

You already know that the accusative case is used:

• for direct objects

Меня́ зову́т Ива́н.
Я чита́ю **ру́сскую газе́ту**.

• after the prepositions **в** or **на** to answer the question **куда́**

Мы идём **в библиоте́ку**.
Студе́нты иду́т **на ле́кцию**.

The tables on the next page review the accusative endings you already know and introduce the accusative endings for singular masculine animate phrases.

• The accusative singular endings for feminine phrases are **-ую** for adjectives (**-юю** if the adjective has a soft stem) and **-у** for nouns (**-ю** if the noun stem is soft; **-ь** for feminine **-ь** words).

• For all other phrases (masculine singular, neuter singular, all plurals), the accusative endings are the same as the nominative endings if the phrase refers to something inanimate (not an animal or person), and the accusative endings are the same as the genitive endings if the phrase refers to something animate (alive). For the time being, you will not be asked to learn the animate plural accusative, which is like the genitive plural.

The accusative case of modifiers and nouns

	ADJECTIVES		NOUNS		
singular masc. animate	нóв - ого послéдн - его	**-ого** **-его**	студéнт - а преподавáтел - я	**-а** **-я**	⇐ like genitive
inanimate	нóв - ый голуб - óй послéдн - ий	**-ый** **-óй** **-ий**	журнáл - Ø портфéл - ь	**-Ø** **-ь**	
singular neuter	нóв - ое послéдн - ее	**-ое** **-ее**	окн - ó плáть - е	**-о** **-е**	⇐ like nomina
singular feminine	нóв - ую послéдн - юю	**-ую** **-юю**	мáм - у, лáмп - у Марú - ю, кýхн - ю	**-у** **-ю**	
plural inanimate	нóв - ые послéдн - ие	**-ые** **-ие**	журнáл - ы, лáмп - ы портфéл - и, кýхн - и óкн - а, плáть - я	**-ы, -и** **-а, -я**	⇐ like nomina

Notes

1. Some masculine nouns have end stress whenever an ending is added:
   отéц ➡ отцá.

2. Some masculine nouns with **e** or **o** in the semi-final position lose this vowel whenever an ending is added: **америкáнец ➡ америкáнца, отéц ➡ отцá.**

3. The accusative singular of feminine **-ь** nouns looks the same as the nominative case: **мать ➡ мать, дочь ➡ дочь.**

4. Remember that nouns ending in **-а** or **-я** that refer to men or boys decline like feminine nouns, but they are masculine and they take masculine modifiers: Мы знáем **вáшего пáпу.**

5. The accusative case of the special modifiers is given on the next page. For the time being, you will not be asked to learn the animate plural accusative, which is like the genitive plural.

singular masc. animate	мо - его тво - его наш - его	ваш - его сво - его чь - его	эт - ого одн - ого треть - его	⇐ like genitive
inanimate	мой твой наш	ваш свой чей	этот один трет - ий	
singular neuter	мо - ё тво - ё наш - е	ваш - е сво - ё чь - ё	эт - о одн - о́ треть - е	⇐ like nominative
singular feminine	мо - ю́ тво - ю́ наш - у	ваш - у сво - ю́ чь - ю	эт - у одн - у́ треть - ю	
plural inanimate	мо - и́ тво - и́ наш - и	ваш - и сво - и́ чь - и	эт - и одн - и́ треть - и	⇐ like nominative

6. Recall that the possessive forms **его, её,** and **их** never change. Examples: Вы зна́ете **его** ма́му? Я чита́ю **её** журна́л. Она́ чита́ет **их** письмо́.

Упражнения

12. How would you ask one of your classmates what the following people's names are?

Образе́ц: ваш но́вый сосе́д ➡ ***Как зову́т ва́шего но́вого сосе́да?***

э́тот молодо́й инжене́р
э́та молода́я продавщи́ца
ваш зубно́й врач
твоя́ но́вая учи́тельница
ваш люби́мый писа́тель
ты
э́та у́мная но́вая студе́нтка
симпати́чный музыка́нт
наш энерги́чный ме́неджер

твой брат
вы
твоя́ мать
твоя́ ба́бушка
твой де́душка
твой племя́нник
твоя́ племя́нница
они́
твоя́ сестра́

13. Construct meaningful and grammatically correct sentences from the following elements. Do not change word order, but do make verbs agree with their grammatical subjects, and use accusative endings on direct objects.

я	любить	мой брат и моя сестра́
на́ши роди́тели	чита́ть	ру́сская литерату́ра
мой преподава́тель	писа́ть	э́тот ру́сский писа́тель
моя́ сосе́дка по ко́мнате	знать	америка́нские газе́ты
мой това́рищ по ко́мнате	слу́шать	интере́сная кни́га
		но́вый рома́н (novel)
		интере́сные пи́сьма
		ру́сская му́зыка
		энерги́чный друг

➤ Complete Oral Drills 16–17 and Written Exercises 7–8 in the Workbook.

7.9   THE PREPOSITIONAL CASE: *O (ОБ)*

You already know that the prepositional case is used after the prepositions **в** and **на** to answer the question **где.**

The prepositional case is also used after the preposition **о** (**об** before a vowel sound) to express the notion *about.*

— **О ком** говори́т Дже́ннифер?　　　　*Who* is Jennifer talking *about?*
— Она́ говори́т **об отце́ и ма́тери.**　　She is talking *about her father and mother.*

— **О чём** вы говори́те?　　　　　　　*What* are you talking *about?*
— Мы говори́м **о на́шей но́вой да́че.**　We are talking *about our new dacha.*

As you can see in the examples above, the question words for the prepositional case are **о ком?** (*about whom?*) and **о чём?** (*about what?*).

You already know the endings for singular modifiers and nouns in the prepositional case. However, because you have not had occasion to use the words **мать** and **дочь** in the prepositional case, you have not yet learned that in the prepositional case (as in every case but the nominative and accusative singular) they have longer stems: **мать** (*prep. sg.* **о ма́тери**), **дочь** (*prep. sg.* **о до́чери**).

The prepositional case of plural modifiers, nouns, question words, and personal pronouns

You are also familiar with the prepositional case for plural adjectives and nouns from the question **На каки́х языка́х вы говори́те?** The prepositional plural ending for modifiers is **-ых** (**-их** where necessary to avoid breaking the 7-letter spelling rule or to keep a soft stem soft). The prepositional plural ending for nouns is **-ах** (**-ях** for soft-stem nouns).

ADJECTIVES		NOUNS	
нóв - ых	**-ых**	студéнт - ах	**-ах**
послéдн - их	**-их**	общежи́ти - ях	**-ях**

SPECIAL MODIFIERS		
мо - и́х	ва́ш - их	э́т - их
тво - и́х	сво - и́х	одн - и́х
на́ш - их	чь - их	тре́ть - их

Here are the forms of the question words and the personal pronouns in the prepositional case:

NOMINATIVE CASE	что	кто	я	ты	он	она́	мы	вы	они́
PREPOSITIONAL CASE	о чём	о ком	обо мнé	о тебé	о нём	о ней	о нас	о вас	о них

* Note that the preposition **о** becomes **обо** in the phrase **обо мне́.**

Упражнение

14. How would you express the following in Russian?

a. — Вы говори́те (about her older brothers)?
   — Да, мы говори́м (about them).
б. — Она́ ду́мает (about our energetic grandmother)?
   — Да, она́ ду́мает (about her).
в. — Что вы зна́ете (about our new teachers)?
   — Я ничего́ (about them) не зна́ю.
г. — Что пи́шут (about the Russian dorms)?
   — Ничего́ не пи́шут (about them).
д. — Вы говори́те (about me) и́ли (about my father)?
   — Мы говори́м (about him).

➤ Complete Oral Drill 18 and Written Exercises 9–11 in the Workbook.

ОБЗОРНЫЕ УПРАЖНЕНИЯ

A. **Выступле́ние.** Prepare a two-minute oral presentation on your family. Give it without looking at your notes.

 B. **Перепи́ска на кассе́тах.** You received a letter on cassette from a Russian pen pal with the photo shown below. Listen to the letter. Then prepare a response. Include as much information about your family as you can, while staying within the bounds of the Russian you know.

C. **Семья́ и кварти́ра.** Divide the class into small groups of 3-6 people. Each group is to be a family.

1. Using Russian only, decide what your names are and how you are related. On large sheets of paper, draw a diagram of the house or apartment where you live. Label the rooms and furniture.

2. Invite another "family" to your house. Introduce yourselves, and show them around your home.

НОВЫЕ СЛОВА И ВЫРАЖЕНИЯ

NOUNS

ро́дственники	relatives
ба́бушка	grandmother
брат (*pl.* бра́тья)	brother
двою́родный брат	male cousin
внук	grandson
вну́чка	granddaughter
де́душка	grandfather
де́ти (5 дете́й)	children
дочь (*gen. and prep. sg.* до́чери; *nom. pl.* до́чери)	daughter
дя́дя	uncle
жена́ (*pl.* жёны)	wife
мать (*gen. and prep. sg* .ма́тери; *nom. pl.* ма́тери)	mother
муж (*pl.* мужья́)	husband
от(е́)ц (*all endings stressed*)	father
племя́нник	nephew
племя́нница	niece
ребён(о)к (*pl.* де́ти)	child(ren)
сестра́ (*pl.* сёстры)	sister
двою́родная сестра́	female cousin
сын (*pl.* сыновья́)	son
тётя	aunt

профе́ссии	professions
архите́ктор	architect
библиоте́карь	librarian
бизнесме́н	businessperson
бухга́лтер	accountant
врач (*all endings stressed*)	physician
зубно́й врач	dentist
домохозя́йка	housewife
журнали́ст	journalist
инжене́р	engineer
коммерса́нт	businessperson
медбра́т (*pl.* медбра́тья)	nurse (male)
медсестра́ (*pl.* медсёстры)	nurse (female)
ме́неджер	manager
музыка́нт	musician
писа́тель	writer
программи́ст	computer programmer
продав(е́)ц (*all endings stressed*)	salesperson (man)
продавщи́ца	salsperson (woman)
секрета́рь (*all endings stressed*)	secretary

учёный (declines like an adjective)	scholar; scientist
учи́тель (pl. учителя́)	school teacher (man)
учи́тельница	school teacher (woman)
худо́жник	artist
юри́ст	lawyer

места́ рабо́ты — places of work

больни́ца	hospital
бюро́ (indecl.)	bureau, office
бюро́ недви́жимости	real estate agency
туристи́ческое бюро́	travel agency
заво́д (на)	factory
лаборато́рия	laboratory
магази́н	store
музе́й	museum
поликли́ника	health clinic
теа́тр	theater
телеста́нция (на)	television station
учрежде́ние	office
фе́рма (на)	farm
фи́рма	company, firm
комме́рческая фи́рма	trade office, business office
юриди́ческая фи́рма	law office

други́е слова́ — other words

год (2-4 го́да, 5-20 лет)	year(s) [old]
класс	grade (in school: 1st, 2nd, 3rd, etc.)
курс (на)	year (in college)
лет (see год)	years
пе́нсия	pension
на пе́нсии	retired
пра́вда	truth
пра́ктика	practice
ча́стная пра́ктика	private practice
профе́ссия	profession
спорт (always singular)	sports

ADJECTIVES

весёлый (не-)	cheerful (melancholy)
еди́нственный	only
здоро́вый (не-)	healthy (un-)
комме́рческий	commercial, trade
мла́дший	younger
молодо́й	young
обыкнове́нный (не-)	ordinary (unusual)
серьёзный (не-)	serious (not)

симпати́чный (не-)	nice (not)
ста́рший	older
ста́рый	old
туристи́ческий	tourist, travel
у́мный	intelligent
ча́стный	private (business, university, etc.)
энерги́чный (не-)	energetic (not)
юриди́ческий	legal, law

VERBS

люби́ть (люблю́, лю́бишь, лю́бят)	to love

only past tense forms of these verbs

вы́расти	to grow up
вы́рос, вы́росла, вы́росли	
роди́ться	to be born
роди́лся, родила́сь, родили́сь	

ADVERBS

ла́дно	okay
наве́рное	probably
совсе́м	completely
совсе́м не	not at all …
то́чно	precisely

PREPOSITION

о, об (чём)	about (*The form* **об** *is used before words beginning with the vowels* **а, э, и, о,** *or* **у.**)

PHRASES AND OTHER WORDS

Говоря́т, что…	They say that …; It is said that …
Да, как сказа́ть?	How should I put it?
Зна́чит так.	Let's see …
Как зову́т (*кого́*)	What is …'s name?
Кто по профе́ссии (*кто*)	What is …'s profession?
люби́ть свою́ рабо́ту	to like one's work
наприме́р	for example
Послу́шай(те)!	Listen!
Расскажи́(те) (мне) …	Tell (me) … (*request for narrative, not just a piece of factual information*)
Ско́лько (*кому́*) лет?	How old is …?
(*Кому́*) … год (го́да, лет).	… is … years old.
Я ничего́ не зна́ю.	I don't know anything.

NUMBERS 200–1000 (*for understanding*)

COLLECTIVE NUMBERS

двóе, трóе, чéтверо 2, 3, 4 (*apply to children in a family*)

PERSONALIZED VOCABULARY

_____

_____

_____

_____

Test

(1) prep case : о(б) + dative [(about)]

(2) dative case of pronouns (learn them)

(3) given the answer, state the question

65 points : Hcmm#work о себé : (13 sentences (at least)

В МАГАЗИНЕ

▼ КОММУНИКАТИВНЫЕ ЗАДАНИЯ

Asking for advice about purchases
Making simple purchases
Birthday greetings

▼ В ПОМОЩЬ УЧАЩИМСЯ

Past tense
Был
Past tense of **есть** and **нет**
Ходи́л vs. **пошёл**
Dative case of modifiers and nouns
Uses of the dative case
    Expressing age
    Indirect objects
    The preposition **по**
    Expressing necessity and
      possibility: **ну́жно, на́до, мо́жно**
Review of question words and pronouns

Workbook: Soft consonants [д], [т],
      [л], [н]
      IC–3 and pauses

▼ МЕЖДУ ПРОЧИМ

Russian stores
Shopping etiquette
Metric clothing sizes
Evgeny Zamyatin

шкатулка : made in Палехска. ложка : spoon

Точка отсчёта

поднос : tray (decorative, wooden) (literally: under your nose)

О ЧЁМ ИДЁТ РЕЧЬ?

А. **Что продаю́т в э́том универма́ге?**

ОТДЕЛ	ЭТАЖ	ОТДЕЛ	ЭТАЖ
галантере́я	1-ый	носки́-чулки́	3-ий
головно́й убо́р	2-ой	о́бувь	1-ый
грампласти́нки	1-ый	пальто́	1-ый
же́нская оде́жда	3-ий	спорттова́ры	2-ой
мужска́я оде́жда	3-ий	сувени́ры	2-ой
това́ры для дете́й	2-ой		

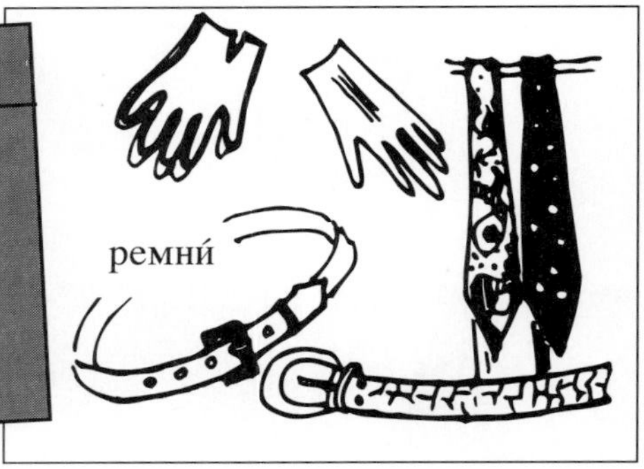

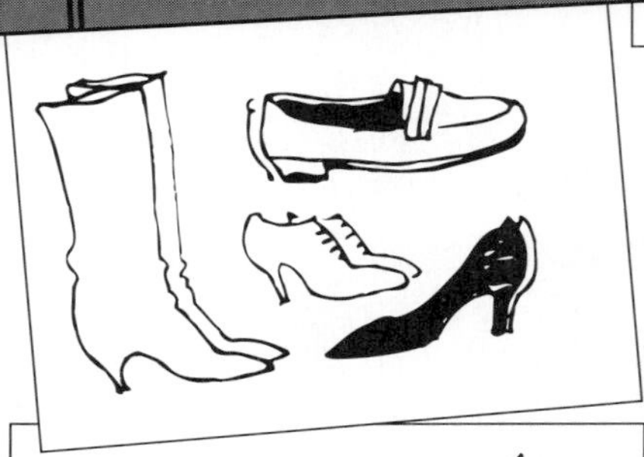

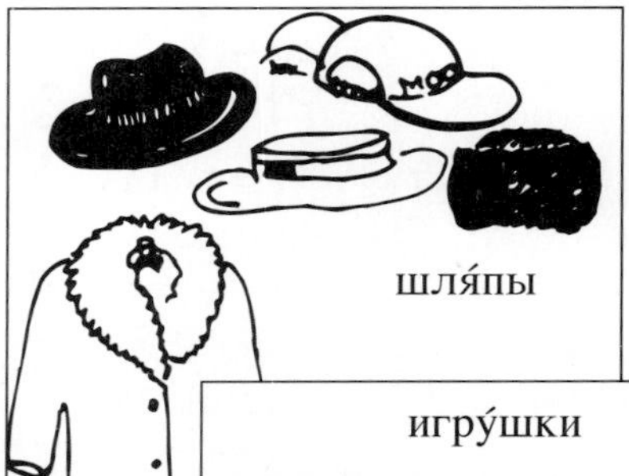

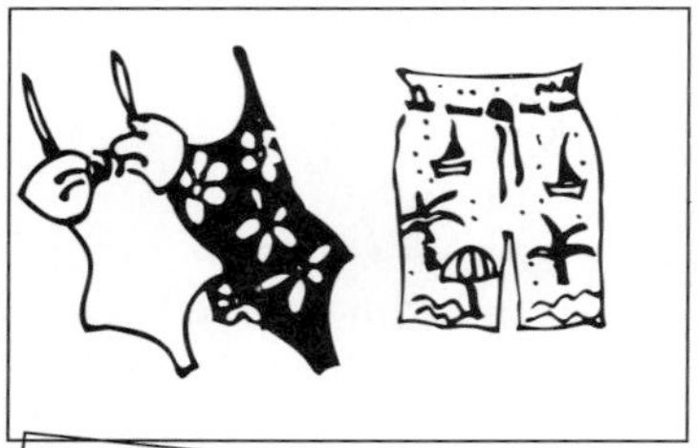

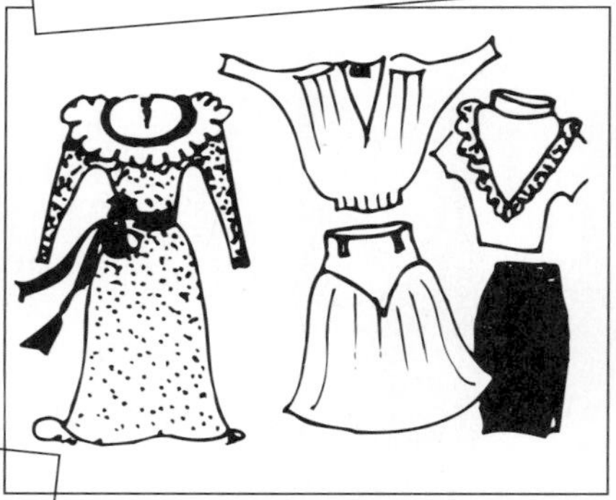

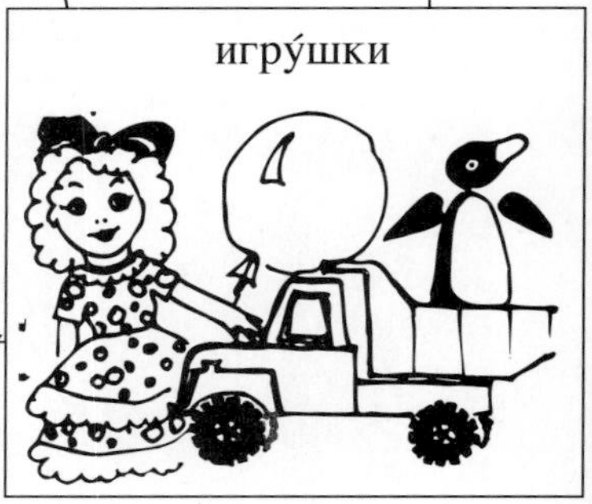

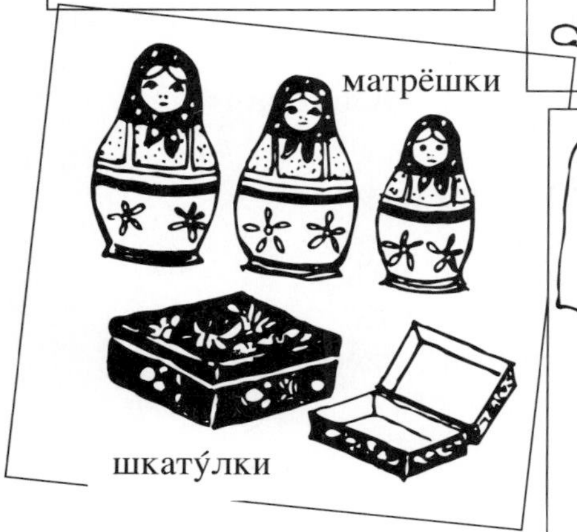

ремни́

ЧУЛКИ

шля́пы

игру́шки

матрёшки
шкату́лки

В.А. МОЦАРТ
ХОР
пласти́нки

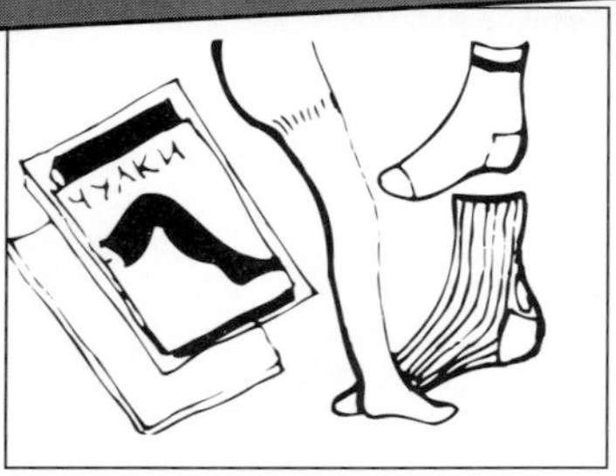

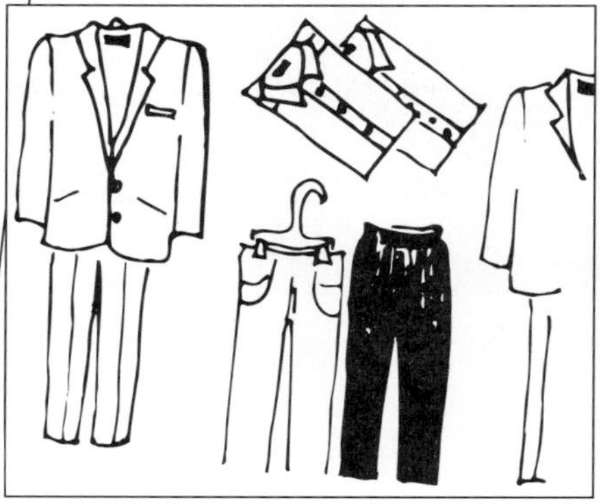

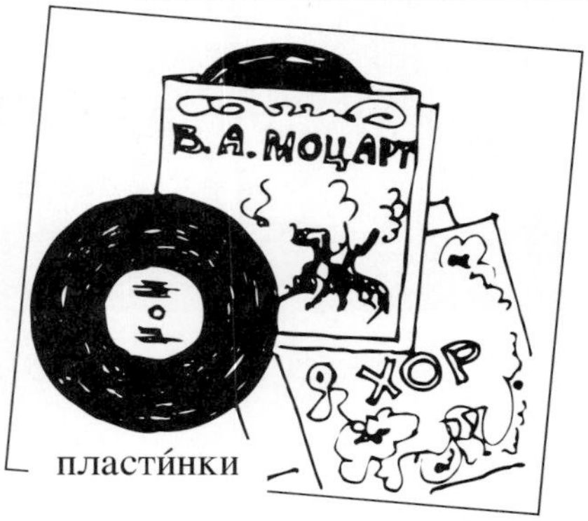

B. Make a list of gifts you could buy for the following people. Next to each item indicate the department in which you are most likely to find the gifts.

отéц   друг/подрýга
мать   бáбушка/дéдушка
брат/сестрá

C. **Что продаю́т в э́тих магази́нах?**

In what stores would you find the following items?

кни́ги, брю́ки, игру́шки, ту́фли,
матрёшки, плáтье, кáрта, блýзки, кроссóвки

D. **Разгово́ры.**

Разгово́р 1: Джим покупа́ет пода́рок.
(Разгова́ривают Валёра и Джим)

1. What does Valera advise Jim to get as a gift for Masha's birthday?
2. Jim says he has already been to the Dom knigi bookstore. Did he see anything interesting there?
3. Valera suggests that Jim go to the book mart. Will he accompany him?
4. What are the Russian equivalents of the following expressions?
   a. birthday
   b. book mart
   c. very expensive

Разгово́р 2: На кни́жном ры́нке
(Разгова́ривают Джим и продавщи́ца)

1. What kind of book does Jim ask the salesperson for?
2. How does Jim address the salesperson?
3. Are there any such books in stock?
4. Jim decides to buy Zamyatin's *We*. How much does it cost?

Разгово́р 3: С днём рожде́ния!
(Разгова́ривают Джим и Ма́ша)

1. What does Jim say to Masha as he gives her the birthday present?
2. Has Masha heard of Zamyatin?
3. What does Masha ask Jim?
4. What does Jim tell her?
5. Does Masha like the present?

Между прочим

ЕВГЕНИЙ ЗАМЯТИН

Evgeny Zamyatin (1884-1937) was an engineer, prose writer, and playwright. His antiutopian novel *We*, written in 1919 and 1920 and published in English translation in 1924, is a precursor to Aldous Huxley's *Brave New World* and George Orwell's *1984*. *We* was published in Zamyatin's homeland only in 1989.

ДИАЛОГИ 📼

1 **До́ма: Я хочу́ сде́лать Ма́ше пода́рок.**

— Пе́тя, я хочу́ сде́лать на́шей сосе́дке Ма́ше
пода́рок. У неё ведь ско́ро день рожде́ния.
— Ой, я совсе́м забы́л об э́том!
— Что ты мне посове́туешь ей купи́ть?
— Мо́жет быть, кни́гу?
— Да, мо́жно подари́ть кни́гу.
— Ты зна́ешь, я неда́вно был на кни́жном ры́нке.
Там бы́ли интере́сные ве́щи.
— А, мо́жет быть, пойдём туда́ сего́дня?
— Дава́й.

2 **В магази́не: Покажи́те, пожа́луйста …**

— Де́вушка! Покажи́те, пожа́луйста, вот
э́тот плато́к.
— Вот э́тот, зелёный?
— Нет, тот, си́ний. Ско́лько он сто́ит?
— Каки́е у вас де́ньги?
— Рубли́, каки́е же ещё?
— Молодо́й челове́к, э́то валю́тный магази́н.
— Мо́жно плати́ть до́лларами?
— Да, семь до́лларов. Плати́те в ка́ссу.

The forms of address **де́вушка**
and **молодо́й челове́к** may
sound rude to you, but they
are in fact neutral. Use them
to attract the attention of
younger service personnel,
and do not be offended if you
are addressed in this way.

3 **До́ма: Где мо́жно купи́ть ту́фли?**

— Ми́ла, где у вас мо́жно купи́ть ту́фли?
— В универма́ге и́ли в магази́не «Обувь».
— А мо́жет быть, мы пойдём туда́ вме́сте? Мне
на́до купи́ть но́вые ту́фли.
— Разме́р ты зна́ешь?
— Да, зна́ю. А ещё мне на́до купи́ть носки́
и перча́тки.
— Хорошо́. Пойдём в «Гости́ный двор». Там вы́бор
неплохо́й. Одну́ мину́точку. Я забы́ла: я там
была́ вчера́. Отде́л был закры́т. Пойдём лу́чше
в «ДЛТ».

РУССКИЕ МАГАЗИНЫ

Универмáг (an abbreviation for **универсáльный магазúн**) is usually translated as *department store,* although most **универмáги** bear little resemblance to their Western counterparts. Most **универмáги** are made up of lines of stalls in which goods are displayed behind a counter. **Светлáна, ДЛТ (Дом Ленингрáдской торгóвли)** and **Гостúный двор** are the names of some St. Petersburg **универмáги.** The famous **ГУМ (Госудáрственный универсáльный магазúн)** is on Red Square in Moscow. Many stores have no name other than that of the product sold there: **Обувь**—*Shoes,* **Одéжда**—*Clothing,* **Молокó**—*Milk.*

Few Russian stores feature self-service. Customers look at selections kept behind a sales counter and ask the salesperson **Покажúте, пожáлуйста … (кнúгу, перчáтки, кассéту,** etc.). Having made their selection, they are directed to the **кácca,** a few meters away. There they pay and get a receipt **(чек),** which they take to the original counter and exchange for the item.

A **ры́нок** is a free market where prices are set by supply and demand. Every major city has at least one **ры́нок** for produce. In the 1990s open-air markets for other goods started appearing as well.

Many shops in large Russian cities cater to customers with convertible Western currency (dollars, pounds, francs, marks, etc.) — such a store is called a **валю́тный магазúн.** Foreign currency stores, modest in selection by European or American standards, are usually stocked with Western goods: cosmetics, jewelry, liquor, electronics, and occasionally food.

Размéр. Russian clothing sizes follow the metric system. If you do not already know the metric system, you should strive to gain an approximate feel for it.

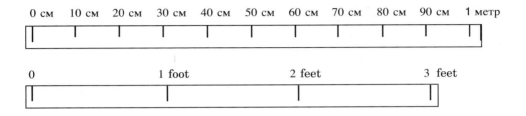

Here are some sample adult clothing sizes. All measurements are in centimeters.

Item	How to measure	Sample sizes
most clothing (shirts, blouses, dresses, coats)	chest measurement divided by 2	44-56 (even numbers only)
hats	circumference of head at mid-forehead	53-62
shoes	length of foot times 1.5	33-42 (women) 38-47 (men)
gloves	same sizes all over world	6-12

4 Дом кни́ги

— Ко́ля, ты зна́ешь, куда́ я сего́дня ходи́ла?
— Куда́?
— В «Дом кни́ги».
— Мне сказа́ли, что там откры́ли но́вый
отде́л. Ты была́?
— Да, и да́же купи́ла вот э́ту но́вую кни́гу по иску́сству.
— Ава́нгарди́сты? Интере́сно. А ско́лько она́ сто́ила?
— Девятьсо́т рубле́й.
— Э́то совсе́м не до́рого! А импрессиони́сты бы́ли?
— Они́ бы́ли ра́ньше, а тепе́рь их уже́ нет.

> The word **тепе́рь** (*now*) always implies a contrast with some other time. The other word for *now*, **сейча́с,** is neutral. It is common to see sentences that contrast a former time with the present: **ра́ньше ..., а тепе́рь ...**

5 С днём рожде́ния!

— Ма́ша, с днём рожде́ния! Я купи́л тебе́
ма́ленький пода́рок.
— Ой, Замя́тин! Я уже́ давно́ хоте́ла его́
почита́ть. Как ты узна́л?
— Ми́ша мне посове́товал купи́ть тебе́ кни́гу.
— Но как ты узна́л, что я люблю́ Замя́тина?
— Ты же неда́вно сама́ говори́ла о Замя́тине.
— Како́й ты молоде́ц! Спаси́бо тебе́ огро́мное.

> The word **сам** (*-self*) is marked for gender and number. When using **вы** to one person say **вы са́ми.** When using **ты,** say **ты сам** to a man, **ты сама́** to a woman.

A. **Что здесь продаю́т?** What is being sold in this department store?

Образе́ц: — Здесь продаю́т самова́р и ...

B. **Ско́лько сто́ит ...?** Ask how much the following items cost.

Образе́ц: — Ско́лько сто́ит чемода́н?

C. **В каком отделе?** In which department of a store do you think the following items are sold? Verify your answers by asking your teacher where these items can be bought.

ОТДЕЛ	ЭТАЖ	ОТДЕЛ	ЭТАЖ
товары для детей	3	мужская одежда	3
парфюмерия	1	игрушки	1
фототовары	4	обувь	3
мебель	2	головной убор	2
электротовары	4	подарки	1
женская одежда	3	грампластинки	4

Образец:

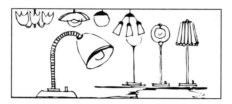

— Где можно купить лампу?

купить: to buy

я хочу купить: I want to buy.

1.

2.

3.

4.

5.

6.

7.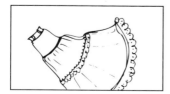

8.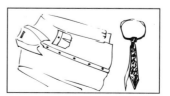

D. **Где мóжно купи́ть ...?** Match the articles with the store or shop in which they can be found.

ВЕЩИ

_____ 1. кни́га по му́зыке

_____ 2. пласти́нки и кассе́ты

_____ 3. пальто́

_____ 4. фотоаппара́т

_____ 5. сапоги́

_____ 6. игру́шки

_____ 7. шкаф

_____ 8. матрёшки

МАГАЗИН

а. «Дом о́буви»

б. «Пода́рки»

в. «Ме́бель»

г. «Де́тский мир»

д. «Мело́дия»

ж. «Дом кни́ги»

з. Же́нская и мужска́я оде́жда

е. Фототова́ры

Язык в действии

ДАВАЙТЕ ПОГОВОРИМ

A. **Подготовка к разговору.** Review the dialogs. How would you do the following?

- say you want to give your friend a present
- ask a friend to help you choose a gift for someone
- suggest that your friend go with you to the book mart
- get a salesperson's attention
- ask a salesperson to show you a scarf (book, hat)
- ask how much the scarf (book, hat) costs
- ask a friend where you can buy shoes (gloves, hats, pants)
- state that you need to buy socks (shoes, gloves)
- tell a friend to wait a minute
- wish someone a happy birthday
- ask how someone knew you love Zamyatin (Chekhov, Bunin)
- thank someone enthusiastically

B. In the third dialog Mila first proposes going to **Гостиный двор,** then changes her mind and suggests going to **ДЛТ** instead. Review the dialog to find out how she makes the second proposal. Then respond to the following suggestions with counter-proposals of your own.

- Пойдём в Дом книги.
- Пойдём на рынок.
- Пойдём в кино.

- Пойдём в Макдоналдс.
- Пойдём в парк.

C. **Давай пойдём вместе!**

1. In the first dialog the speaker invites Petya to go with him to the book mart. Review the dialog to find out how he issues the invitation. _____

2. Now look at the following possible responses. Which one(s) would you use to accept an invitation? to make a counter–proposal? to turn down an invitation?

   - Хорошо, давай.
   - Сегодня не могу. Я должен заниматься.
   - Давай лучше пойдём в кино.

3. How do you signal agreement to plans that you have made with someone?

4. In pairs, prepare and act out a dialog in which you invite a partner to do something.

D. **Игровы́е ситуа́ции.**

1. Ask a friend where you can buy a good book on
   a. art
   b. medicine
   c. biology
   d. sociology
   e. literature
   f. your field of interest

   Invite him/her to go with you to make the purchase.

2. You are in a clothing store. Ask the salesperson to let you see
   a. a shirt
   b. a dress
   c. a pair of pants
   d. a swimming suit
   e. a blouse
   f. a pair of shoes

   Specify which item you want to look at and what your size is. Find out how much it costs.

3. You want to buy a present for the 7-year-old son of your Russian teacher. Ask the salesperson for advice on what to buy.

4. Help a Russian visitor to your town decide what presents to buy for family members at home. Your friend wants to know what's available and how much it will cost.

5. Working with a partner, prepare and act out a situation of your own that deals with the topics of this unit.

E. **Устный перево́д.** You are in Russia. A friend who knows no Russian passes through on a two-week tour and asks you to help buy gifts. Serve as the interpreter in a store.

English speaker's part

1. Could I take a look at that scarf over there?
2. No, the red one.
3. How much does it cost?
4. That's awfully expensive. How much do those gloves cost?
5. Okay. I'll take the gloves then.

F. **Когда́ ты был ма́леньким …** Practice asking other members of your class as many questions as you can about what they did when they were little. Write down your partner's responses. Then reverse roles.

> *Образе́ц:* — Когда́ ты был ма́леньким, где вы жи́ли?
> — Когда́ ты была́ ма́ленькой, каку́ю му́зыку ты слу́шала?

> *When you were little …* Note that this phrase is marked for gender. Use **когда́ ты был ма́леньким …** for a man, and **когда́ ты была́ ма́ленькой** for a woman.

ДАВАЙТЕ ПОЧИТАЕМ

A. **Магази́ны.** Look through the lists of St. Petersburg stores to find answers to these questions.

1. Where would you go to look for the following items?

   children's clothing   women's clothing
   men's clothing   books
   children's books   souvenirs
   sporting goods   cosmetics
   shoes   furniture

2. If you were planning to be on Nevsky Prospekt, a main thoroughfare in St. Petersburg, what stores would you have a chance to visit?

3. What are the standard abbreviations for

   - **проспе́кт** *(avenue)?*
   - **у́лица** *(street)?*
   - **пло́щадь** *(square)?*

4. What are the Russian expressions for

   - goods for children?   • goods for men?
   - goods for women?   • goods for newlyweds?

СПЕЦИАЛИЗИРОВАННЫЕ МАГАЗИНЫ

«Болгарская роза» (косметика). Невский пр., 55

«Ванда» (косметика). Невский пр., 111

Гастроном «Центральный». Невский пр., 56

«Детский книжный мир». Лиговский пр., 105

Дом книги. Невский пр., 28

Дом мод (торговые залы). Кировский пр., 37

«Дом обуви». Пл. Брежнева, 6

«Изделия художественных промыслов». Невский пр., 51

Магазин-салон «Лавка художников». Невский пр., 8

«Мебель». Пр. Большевиков, 33

Обувной магазин №. 1. Невский пр., 11

«Подарки». Невский пр., 54

«Рапсодия». Ул. Желябова, 13

Спортивные товары. Пр. Шаумяна, 2

«Сувениры». Невский пр., 92

«Товары для новоселов». Якорная ул., 1, 2

«Фарфор». Невский пр., 147

«Цветы Болгарии». Кировский пр., 5

«Элегант» (модные товары). Большой пр., 55

«Юный техник». Краснопутиловская ул., 55

УНИВЕРМАГИ

«Выборгский». Лесной пр., 37

«Гостиный двор». Невский пр., 35

«Дом ленинградской торговли»
    (ДЛТ—товары для детей). Ул. Желябова,
    21-23

«Ждановский». Богатырский пр., 4, 5

«Калининский». Кондратьевский пр., 40

«Кировский». Пл. Стачек, 9

«Купчинский». Пр. Славы, 4, 12, 16, 30

Ленкомиссионторг. Садовая ул., 28-30

«Московский». Московский пр., 205, 220

«Нарвский». Ленинский пр., 120-136

«Невский». Ивановская ул., 6, 7

Окружной военный универмаг.
    Пр. Непокоренных, 6

«Пассаж» (товары для женщин). Невский
    пр., 48

«Ржевский». Рябовское шоссе, 101

«Светлановский». Пр. Энгельса, 21

«Северомуринский». Пр. Просвящения,
    84, 87

«Юбилей» (товары для мужчин).
    Московский пр., 60

«Юность» (товары для новобрачных и
    юбиляров, подарки). Свердловская
    наб., 60

B. **Пишу́ Вам из Влади́мира.**

1. Read through the following letter to find answers to these questions:

   a. Who wrote the letter?
   b. Where does she live?
   c. How did she get your name and address?
   d. What does she know about you?
   e. What information does she provide about herself and her family?
   f. What information does she want from you?

Здра́вствуйте!

Пишу́ Вам из стари́нного го́рода Влади́мира, кото́рый вхо́дит в „Золото́е кольцо́" Росси́и. Получи́ла Ва́ше и́мя от на́шего о́бщего знако́мого Па́вла, когда́ он был у нас на про́шлой неде́ле. Он рассказа́л немно́го о Вас и о Ва́шей семье́. Сказа́л ещё, что Вы уже́ хорошо́ понима́ете и пи́шете по-ру́сски. Э́то хорошо́, потому́ что я чита́ю по-англи́йски то́лько с больши́м трудо́м.

Немно́го о себе́. Меня́ зову́т Ла́ра. Мне 22 го́да. Рабо́таю в больни́це в на́шем го́роде. Я за́мужем. Му́жа зову́т Ди́ма (Дми́трий) — ему́ 25 лет. По профе́ссии он инжене́р. Пока́ у нас нет дете́й.

Мы с му́жем наде́емся пое́хать в Евро́пу и в Аме́рику, и мно́го говори́м о тако́й пое́здке. И́менно поэ́тому Па́вел дал нам Ваш а́дрес. Он сказа́л, что Вы смо́жете нам рассказа́ть немно́го о Ва́шей стране́ и посове́товать нам, в каки́е города́ пое́хать.

Жду отве́та.

Ва́ша
Ла́ра Па́нина

2. Go back to the letter to find Russian equivalents for the following expressions:

   a. I got your name from a mutual acquaintance
   b. with great difficulty
   c. a bit about myself
   d. I'm married (woman talking)
   e. We hope to go to Europe
   f. Write soon

> *I'm married*: a woman says **Я за́мужем**; a man says **Я жена́т.**

В магазине.

Background. The script for this exercise has three parts:
  A. A conversation on the street between two friends, Lara and Nina
  B. Nina's trip to the store
  C. Nina's retelling of her day's experience to her husband Dima.

1. Listen to the entire script once before proceeding.

2. These conversations hinge on a number of key words. Judging by the context of the conversation, what do the following words mean?

   занаве́ски
   a. curtains
   b. rings
   c. stationery
   d. pictures

   о́чередь
   a. small store or shop
   b. article or report
   c. line or waiting list
   d. balcony or veranda

3. Now read through the following bold words outloud. Be careful about the place of stress. You will hear these words in the script.

   коммуна́льная кварти́ра (коммуна́лка)—communal apartment, one in which a family lives in one or two rooms, sharing kitchen and bath facilities with others in the apartment.

   обме́ниваться/обменя́ться—to make an exchange. One of the quickest ways of getting a new apartment is by exchanging what you have for something more convenient. A typical exchange might be a small, uncomfortable apartment conveniently located downtown for a larger, but less solidly built apartment on the outskirts of town (**на окра́ине го́рода**).

   устра́ивать/устро́ить новосе́лье—to give a housewarming party.

4. Now listen to the conversation between Lara and Nina on the street (A) again, with the following questions in mind.

   a. Are these two women on familiar or formal terms?
   b. Where does Lara live now? Where did she live before?
   c. Why was Lara so eager to move out of her old place?
   d. What had Lara managed to buy?
   e. Name one other detail about this conversation.

5. Now listen to the conversations that Nina has in the store (B) with these questions in mind:

    a. What overall situation does Nina find when she gets to the store?
    b. What details can you give about the thing that Nina wants to buy?
    c. What happens when Nina is about to make her purchase?

6. Listen to the conversation between Nina and her husband Dima (C). List four things that she tells him about her experience that day.

7. Finally, listen to the entire script once again. Match each caption with the correct picture.

_____ а. Ой, какáя большáя óчередь! Вы дáвно стóйте?

_____ б. — Дáйте занавéски, одúн набóр.

         — Всё. Кóнчились.

_____ в. — Простúте, дéвушка, мне сказáли, что у вас сегóдня в продáже

         занавéски.

         — Вторóй этáж.

_____ г. Скóлько мóжно жить в однóй кóмнате?

_____ д. Я увéрена, что сосéди знáют всё, что происхóдит у нас в дóме.

1.

2.

3.

4.

5.

В ПОМОЩЬ УЧАЩИМСЯ

8.1 THE PAST TENSE—INTRODUCTION

— Что вы де́лали вчера́?	What *did* you *do* yesterday?
— Мы **чита́ли, слу́шали** ра́дио и **смотре́ли** телеви́зор.	We *read, listened to* the radio, and *watched* TV.
— А что **де́лала** Анна?	And what *did* Anna *do*?
— Она́ **ходи́ла** на фильм.	She *went* to a movie.
— А её брат?	And her brother?
— Он **занима́лся.**	He *studied*.

You already know several past tense verb forms (**Где вы родили́сь?** *Where were you born?*; **Где вы вы́росли?** *Where did you grow up?*; **Как вы сказа́ли?** *What did you say?*). In this unit you will learn to form past-tense verbs on your own.

- **Forms.** The mark of the past tense in Russian is **-л**. For most verbs, the past tense is formed by removing the **-ть** from the infinitive and adding **-л**. It is important to remember that the past tense is formed from the *infinitive*, and not from one of the conjugated forms!

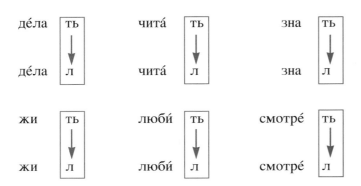

If the verb has the particle **-ся,** that particle is not dropped:

The past tense in Russian is *always* formed this way. Whereas English has several different past tenses (e.g., *We lived, We did live, We were living*), Russian has only one (**Мы жи́ли**). Unlike English, the Russian past tense never involves the use of "helping verbs."

- **Agreement.** You are already familiar with the fact that Russian past-tense verbs agree with their grammatical subjects:

When the subject is masculine and singular, the past-tense verb ends in **-л** (**де́лал, чита́л, жил**). This form is always used with the question word **кто**. For example: **Кто вчера́ был в библиоте́ке?**

When the subject is feminine and singular, the past-tense verb ends in **-ла** (**де́лала, чита́ла, жила́**).

When the subject is neuter and singular, the past-tense verb ends in **-ло** (**де́лало, чита́ло, жи́ло**). This form is always used with the question word **что**. For example: **Что бы́ло в чемода́не?**

When the subject is plural, the past-tense verb ends in **-ли** (**де́лали, чита́ли, жи́ли**). Note that the plural form of the verb is always used with **вы**, even when it refers to only one person.

If the verb has the particle **-ся**, that particle is never dropped. Remember that this particle is spelled **-ся** after consonant letters, and **-сь** after vowel letters.

> **он роди́лся, занима́лся**
> **она́ родила́сь, занима́лась**
> **оно́ родило́сь, занима́лось**
> **они́ родили́сь, занима́лись**

- **Stress.** The glossary will give the past-tense forms for which the stress is not always the same as in the infinitive:

> **роди́ться (роди́лся, родила́сь, родили́сь)**
> **жить (жил, жила́, жи́ли)**

In the absence of such a note, you may assume that the stress in the past tense is the same as the infinitive.

- **New verbs.** Some new verbs introduced in this unit will be used only in the past tense for the time being. They are:

был (была́, бы́ло, бы́ли)	was
пошёл (пошла́, пошли́)	set out (see 8.3)
ходи́л	went and returned (see 8.3)
забы́л	forgot
сказа́л	said
откры́л	opened
купи́л	bought
узна́л	found out

Упражнения

1. How would you ask these people if they did the activities listed in the box?

   Образец: Антон Па́влович, вы вчера́ отдыха́ли?

   a. your teacher
   b. a female classmate
   c. a male classmate
   d. your parents

   отдыха́ть; смотре́ть телеви́зор; ходи́ть в кино́; рабо́тать ве́чером; за́втракать в столо́вой; у́жинать в рестора́не; чита́ть газе́ту; занима́ться

   How would you indicate whether or not you did these things?

2. Construct truthful and grammatically correct sentences about what you and your acquaintances did yesterday by combining the words and phrases from the columns below. Do not change word order. Be sure to make the verb agree with the grammatical subject and to put direct objects into the accusative case.

   Образец: Вчера́ я убира́ла ко́мнату.

				газе́ты
				дом
			слу́шать	журна́л
			смотре́ть	интере́сная кни́га
вчера́	мой друзья́		убира́ть	кварти́ра
	мой това́рищ по ко́мнате	(не)	чита́ть	ко́мната
	моя́ сосе́дка по ко́мнате		купи́ть	пи́сьма
	я		писа́ть	ра́дио
				телеви́зор
				фильм
				фотогра́фии

➤ Complete Oral Drills 1–4 and Written Exercises 1–3 in the Workbook.

8.2 PAST TENSE—*БЫЛ*

As you know, Russian usually does not use a verb for *to be* in present-tense sentences. In the past tense, however, the verb *to be* is expressed. Its forms are **был**, (**была́, бы́ло, бы́ли**).

PRESENT TENSE	PAST TENSE
Джон в библиоте́ке. Ка́тя на ле́кции. Их роди́тели в рестора́не. Кто здесь? Что здесь?	Джон **был** в библиоте́ке. Ка́тя **была́** на ле́кции. Их роди́тели **бы́ли** в рестора́не. Кто здесь **был**? Что здесь **бы́ло**?

Упражнения

3. Ask and answer questions as in the example.

   Образе́ц: — Ма́ша сего́дня в библиоте́ке?
   — Нет, но она́ вчера́ была́ в библиоте́ке.

   а. Анато́лий Петро́вич сего́дня на ле́кции?
   б. Ве́ра Па́вловна сего́дня до́ма?
   в. Эрик сего́дня в па́рке?
   г. Его́ бра́тья сего́дня в кино́?
   д. Мари́на сего́дня на кни́жном ры́нке?

4. Look at Victor's daily schedule and tell where he was and what he might have done there. Remember to switch from the 24-hour clock to the 12-hour clock in your responses.

8.00	буфе́т
9.00	ле́кция
13.00	рестора́н
14.00	банк
17.00	кино́
20.00	библиоте́ка
23.00	до́ма

➤ Complete Oral Drills 5–6 and Written Exercise 5 in the Workbook.

8.3 *HAD* AND *DID NOT HAVE*—THE PAST TENSE OF *ЕСТЬ* AND *НЕТ*

- **Existence.** Russian expresses existence, presence, and "having" by using **есть** (see p.168). To express sentences with **есть** in the past, Russian uses **был (была́, бы́ло, бы́ли)**. Remember that the verb must agree with the grammatical subject of the Russian sentence, and that in Russian the thing that exists or that one has is the grammatical subject.

PRESENT TENSE	PAST TENSE
Здесь **есть** письмо́.	Здесь **бы́ло** письмо́.
Здесь **есть** библиоте́ка.	Здесь **была́** библиоте́ка.
Там **есть** кни́ги.	Там **бы́ли** кни́ги.
У меня́ **есть** компью́тер.	У меня́ **был** компью́тер.
У неё **есть** пла́тье.	У неё **бы́ло** пла́тье.
У меня́ **есть** маши́на.	У меня́ **была́** маши́на.
У меня́ **есть** де́ньги.	У меня́ **бы́ли** де́ньги.

Упражнение

5. Your friends told you they forgot to take many things on their trip last week. How would you ask if they had the following items?

   де́ньги, чемода́н, оде́жда, кни́ги,
   газе́та, джи́нсы, фотоаппара́т,
   компью́тер, ра́дио, кроссо́вки,
   слова́рь, рома́н Замя́тина

➤ Complete Oral Drill 7 in the Workbook.

- **Nonexistence.** Russian expresses nonexistence, absence, and "not having" by using **нет** plus the genitive case (see pp. 169-170). To express these negative conditions with **нет** in the past, Russian uses **не́ бы́ло**. The verb in such sentences is always **не́ бы́ло** (neuter and singular), because there is no grammatical subject in the nominative case for the verb to agree with.

PRESENT TENSE	PAST TENSE
Здесь **нет** письма́.	Здесь **не́ бы́ло** письма́.
Здесь **нет** библиоте́ки.	Здесь **не́ бы́ло** библиоте́ки.
У меня́ **нет** журна́ла.	У меня́ **не́ бы́ло** журна́ла.
У неё **нет** пла́тья.	У неё **не́ бы́ло** пла́тья.
У меня́ **нет** маши́ны.	У меня́ **не́ бы́ло** маши́ны.

Упражнения

6. Answer these questions in the negative.

Образе́ц: Здесь был институ́т?   ➡   *Нет, здесь не́ бы́ло институ́та.*

а. Здесь был универма́г?
б. Здесь была́ шко́ла?
в. Здесь бы́ло кафе́?
г. Здесь был медици́нский институ́т?
д. У Ма́ши был большо́й чемода́н?
е. У Ки́ры была́ но́вая оде́жда?
ж. У Ви́ктора бы́ло но́вое пальто́?
з. У Юры был рома́н Замя́тина?

7. Create meaningful and gramatically correct sentences by combining words from the columns below. The question marks indicate that you may substitute a word or phrase of your own in this position.

	у меня́	есть	краси́вое пла́тье
	у моего́ бра́та	был	хоро́шая маши́на
	у мое́й сестры́	была́	кни́га по иску́сству
ра́ньше	у нас	бы́ло	рома́н «Мы»
сейча́с	у роди́телей	бы́ли	хоро́шее ра́дио
	здесь	нет	но́вая библиоте́ка
	у моего́ дру́га	не́ бы́ло	большо́й университе́т
	?		?

➤ Complete Oral Drill 8 and Written Exercise 5 in the Workbook.

8.4 *WENT—ХОДИЛ* vs. *ПОШЁЛ*

The following short dialogs show that Russian differentiates between "went" in the sense of "set out" and "went" in the sense of "went and came back." within the confines of one city.

пошёл-пошла́-пошли́ *set out* ⟹	ходи́л-ходи́ла-ходи́ли *went and came back* ⟸ ⟹
— Где Вади́м? — Он **пошёл** на ле́кцию. — Где Ма́ша и Юра? — Они́ **пошли́** в кино́. — Где Алекса́ндра? — Она́ **пошла́** в библиоте́ку. Мы вста́ли в 6 часо́в, **пошли́** на рабо́ту в 7 и **пошли́** на обе́д в 12.	— Где был Вади́м? — Он **ходи́л** на ле́кцию. — Что де́лали Ма́ша и Юра вчера́? — Они́ **ходи́ли** в кино́. — Что де́лала Алекса́ндра у́тром? — Она́ **ходи́ла** в библиоте́ку. Мы вчера́ **ходи́ли** на рабо́ту.

For the time being, use a form of **пошёл** (**пошла́, пошли́**) if the people are still gone or if you are specifying the precise time they set out. Use a form of **ходи́л** otherwise — e.g., if the entire trip is over and you are not specifying the precise time of departure.

Упражнение

8. Fill in the blanks with an appropriate from of **пошёл** or **ходи́л**.

    а. — Где Анна?
        — Она́ _____ на заня́тия.

    б. — Где Ви́тя?
        — Он _____ в магази́н.

    в. — Где они́ бы́ли вчера́?
        — Они́ _____ в Дом кни́ги.

    г. — Что вы де́лали вчера́?
        — Мы _____ в центр.

    д. У Анто́на был интере́сный день. Он _____ в зоопа́рк.

    е. Оля была́ о́чень занята́ вчера́. В 9 часо́в она́ _____ на заня́тия, в 2 часа́ она́ _____ в центр и в 7 часо́в она́ _____ на конце́рт.

➤ Complete Oral Drills 9–11 and Written Exercise 6 in the Workbook.

8.5   THE DATIVE CASE

Мне два́дцать оди́н год.
Мое́й сестре́ два́дцать два го́да.
Моему́ бра́ту шестна́дцать лет.
На́шим роди́телям со́рок семь лет.

In Unit 7 you learned the forms of the personal pronouns in the dative case and the use of the dative case to express age. This unit introduces the forms of nouns and their modifiers in the dative, and some additional uses of the dative case.

The dative singular endings for masculine and neuter phrases are **-ому** for adjectives (**-ему** to avoid breaking the 5-letter spelling rule or if the adjective has a soft stem) and **-у** for nouns (**-ю** if the noun stem is soft).

The dative singular endings for feminine phrases are **-ой** for adjectives (**-ей** to avoid breaking the 5-letter spelling rule or if the adjective has a soft stem) and **е** for nouns (except for feminine **-ь** nouns and nouns ending in **-ия,** which take the ending **-и**).

The dative plural endings are **-ым** for adjectives (**-им** to avoid breaking the 7-letter spelling rule or if the adjective has a soft stem) and **-ам** for nouns (**-ям** if the noun stem is soft). The plural endings are not drilled in the exercises for this unit, but are given here so that you have a complete picture of the dative case.

The dative case of modifiers and nouns

	ADJECTIVES		NOUNS	
masculine and neuter singular	но́в - ому после́дн - ему	**-ому** **-ему**	студе́нт - у иску́сств - у писа́тел - ю общежи́ти - ю	**-у** **-ю**
feminine singular	но́в - ой после́дн - ей	**-ой** **-ей**	студе́нтк -е биоло́ги - и	**-е** **(-и)**
plural	но́в - ым после́дн - им	**-ым** **-им**	студе́нт - ам студе́нтк - ам писа́тел - ям	**-ам** **-ям**

Notes

1. Some masculine nouns have end stress whenever an ending is added:
   стол ➡ **столу́; стола́м** (*pl.*), **гара́ж** ➡ **гаражу́; гаража́м** (*pl.*).

2. Some masculine nouns with **e** or **o** in the semi-final position lose this vowel whenever an ending is added: **оте́ц** ➡ **отцу́; отца́м** (*pl*).

3. The words **мать** and **дочь** have a longer stem in every case except the nominative and accusative singular. Their dative forms are **мать** ➡ **ма́тери** (*sg.*); **матеря́м** (*pl.*) and **дочь** ➡ **до́чери** (*sg.*); **дочеря́м** (*pl.*).

4. The dative endings for the special modifiers are not irregular, but because they do involve accent shifts, soft endings, and application of the 5- and 7-letter spelling rules, you may wish simply to memorize them.

masculine and neuter singular	мо - **ему́**	ва́ш - **ему**	э́т - **ому**
	тво - **ему́**	чь - **ему́**	одн - **ому́**
	на́ш - **ему**	сво - **ему́**	тре́ть - **ему**
feminine singular	мо - **е́й**	ва́ш - **ей**	э́т - **ой**
	тво - **е́й**	чь - **ей**	одн - **о́й**
	на́ш - **ей**	сво - **е́й**	тре́ть - **ей**
plural	мо - **и́м**	ва́ш - **им**	э́т - **им**
	тво - **и́м**	чь - **им**	одн - **и́м**
	на́ш - **им**	сво - **и́м**	тре́ть - **им**

5. The possessive modifiers **его́** (*his*), **её** (*her*), and **их** (*their*) never change. Do not confuse *his* (**его́**) with the dative form *him* (**ему́**)!

Мы хоти́м сде́лать **его́ бра́ту** пода́рок.   We want to give a gift to *his brother*.

       BUT   BUT

Мы хоти́м сде́лать **ему́** пода́рок.   We want to give *him* a gift.

Упражнение

9. Ask how old these people and things are.

> *Образец:*   э́тот но́вый студе́нт   ➡   *Ско́лько лет э́тому но́вому студе́нту?*

   а. ваш интере́сный сосе́д
   б. твой профе́ссор
   в. хоро́ший учи́тель
   г. его́ ста́рое пальто́
   д. э́то ста́рое зда́ние
   е. но́вая балери́на
   ж. на́ша интере́сная сосе́дка
   з. её ку́хня
   и. э́то больша́я лаборато́рия
   й. твоя́ мать

➤ Complete Oral Drill 12 and Written Exercises 7–8 in the Workbook.

8.6   USES OF THE DATIVE CASE

Expressing age.

You already know that the dative case is used to express age:

> **Мне** два́дцать оди́н год, а **моему́ бра́ту** девятна́дцать.

Indirect objects.

The dative case is also used for indirect objects. An indirect object is the person to whom or for whom an action is done.

> Я хочу́ сде́лать **Ма́ше** пода́рок.   I want to give *Masha* a gift.

The present, the thing being given, is the direct object; Masha, the person for whom the present is intended, is the indirect object.

Упражнение

10. Identify the direct and the indirect objects in the following English text.

> Everyone bought a present for Masha. John gave Masha a book. Jenny gave her a sweater. Her mother bought her a new record. She told them "Thank you."

Now fill in the blanks in the equivalent Russian text:

> Все купи́ли пода́рки _____ . Джон подари́л _____ кни́гу. Дже́нни подари́ла _____ сви́тер. Её ма́ма купи́ла _____ но́вую пласти́нку. Она́ сказа́ла _____ «Спаси́бо».

➤ Complete Oral Drill 13 and Written Exercise 9 in the Workbook.

The preposition *по*.

The dative case is used after the preposition **по**. You have seen several examples of this:

> Кто **по национа́льности** ва́ши роди́тели?
> Кто **по профе́ссии** ва́ша сестра́?
> У вас есть сосе́дка (това́рищ) **по ко́мнате**?
> У вас есть кни́ги **по иску́сству**?

> Use the structure
> **кни́ги по** + *dative*
> only for fields of study.

Упражнение

11. How would you express the following in Russian?

   a. Do you have any music books?
   b. Do you have any philosophy books?
   c. Do you have any books on medicine?
   d. Do you have any books on [fill in *your* field of special interest]?

➤ Complete Oral Drill 14 and Written Exercise 10 in the Workbook.

Expressing necessity and possibility.

The dative case is used with the words **на́до** and **ну́жно** to express necessity and with **мо́жно** to express possibility. For your purposes at present, you may think of **на́до** and **ну́жно** as synonyms.

Э́тому студе́нту ну́жно (на́до) рабо́тать.	*This student* has to work.
Где **мне** мо́жно купи́ть пода́рок?	Where can *I* buy a present?

Note the structure used for these sentences:

кому́	на́до	
(person in dative case)	ну́жно	*+ infinitive*
	мо́жно	

Упражнения

12. Create truthful and grammatically correct sentences by combining the elements from the columns, or substituting words of your own choosing in the columns with the question mark.

    Образе́ц: Мне всегда́ на́до занима́ться.

я	сейча́с		занима́ться
мой това́рищ по ко́мнате	ча́сто	мо́жно	рабо́тать
моя́ сосе́дка по ко́мнате	ре́дко	на́до	купи́ть пода́рок
наш преподава́тель	всегда́	ну́жно	отдыха́ть
на́ши роди́тели			смотре́ть но́вости
?			?

13. In the following paragraph, find the words that are in the dative case and explain why the dative is used in each instance. Then answer the question at the end in Russian.

У нас больша́я семья́—тро́е дете́й! Ста́ршего сы́на зову́т Кири́лл. Ему́ во́семь лет, он уже́ хо́дит в шко́лу. Мла́дшему сы́ну Макси́му пять лет. А до́чери три го́да. Её зову́т Ната́ша. Ско́ро у Ната́ши бу́дет день рожде́ния. Её бра́тья хотя́т ей сде́лать пода́рок. Когда́ у меня́ был день рожде́ния, они́ мне купи́ли кни́гу. Но Ната́ша ещё не чита́ет. Что вы им посове́туете ей купи́ть?

➤ Complete Oral Drills 15–17 and Written Exercise 11 in the Workbook.

8.7 QUESTION WORDS AND PRONOUNS

Several oral drills and written exercises in this unit give you a chance to practice the pronouns and question words in the different cases you already know. This table summarizes the forms of the pronouns and question words.

	QUESTION WORDS		PRONOUNS						
nom.	кто	что	я	ты	он/оно́	она́	мы	вы	они́
acc.	кого́	что	меня́	тебя́	его́ *него́*	её *неё*	нас	вас	их *них*
gen.	кого́	чего́	меня́	тебя́	его́ *него́*	её *неё*	нас	вас	их *них*
prep.	о ком	о чём	обо мне́	о тебе́	о нём	о ней	о нас	о вас	о них
dat.	кому́	чему́	мне	тебе́	ему́ *нему́*	ей *ней*	нам	вам	им *ним*

* The forms of **он, оно́, она́,** and **они́** have an initial **н** only when they immediately follow a preposition: *У него́ есть кни́га.*
but
Его́ нет.

Упражнения

14. Ask questions about the words in boldface.

   Образе́ц: **Моего́ бра́та** зову́т Алёша. ➡ *Кого́* зову́т Алёша?

Моего́ бра́та зову́т Алёша. **Ему́** 16 лет. **Он** хорошо́ у́чится. Он изуча́ет **хи́мию и матема́тику.** Ещё он о́чень лю́бит **теа́тр.** Он ча́сто говори́т об **э́том.** На день рожде́ния я хочу́ сде́лать **ему́** пода́рок. Я ду́маю купи́ть ему́ **кни́гу.** Он о́чень лю́бит **Шекспи́ра и Пу́шкина.** У **него́** есть Пу́шкин. Но у него́ нет ни одно́й **кни́ги** Шекспи́ра.

15. **Answer yes to the questions. Use complete sentences and replace the nouns with pronouns.**

 а. Алёша лю́бит Пу́шкина?
 б. Вы чита́ли о Пу́шкине?
 в. Пу́шкин писа́л о Росси́и?
 г. Ру́сские студе́нты чита́ют интере́сные кни́ги?
 д. Вы хоти́те чита́ть ру́сскую литерату́ру?

➤ Complete Oral Drills 17–21 and Written Exercises 12–14 in the Workbook.

ОБЗОРНЫЕ УПРАЖНЕНИЯ

🔊 А. **Разгово́ры.**

Разгово́р 1: *Где мо́жно купи́ть шля́пу?*
(Разгова́ривают Ди́на и Нэ́нси)

1. Nancy is talking to Dina about a hat. What does she ask?
2. Who gave Nancy the idea to buy a hat?
3. Two stores are mentioned in this conversation. Name one.
4. What is the Russian word for *hat*?

Разгово́р 2: *В магази́не «Светла́на»*
(Разгова́ривают Ди́на, Нэ́нси и продавщи́ца)

1. Does Nancy want to look at the yellow hat or the red hat?
2. What is Nancy's hat size?
3. How much does the hat cost?

Разгово́р 3: *В валю́тном магази́не*
(Разгова́ривают Джефф и продавщи́ца)

1. Does Jeff want to see the red scarf or the white one?
2. Can Jeff pay for his purchases with rubles in this store?
3. What form of payment does he end up using?
4. How much does the scarf cost?

B. Посоветуй мне. A Russian friend wants your advice on what gifts to buy for three family members. Listen to the descriptions, and select the most appropriate gift for each person.

1. джинсы	шапка	телевизор	книга по искусству
2. телевизор	телефон	пластинка	радио
3. игрушка	книга	телевизор	магнитофон

C. Сувениры. Imagine that you are going to Russia next week.

1. List five family members and/or friends. Next to each name indicate what present you would like to buy for that person.

2. Ask a Russian friend in St. Petersburg where you can buy the presents on your list.

3. On the lists of stores on pages 228-229, circle the location of the store(s) suggested.

4. Act out the scene in which you make one or more of your intended purchases.

5. After your shopping spree, tell a Russian friend what you bought for whom.

D. Записка другу. Tomorrow is your last shopping day in Moscow. You would like to buy gifts for a relative, but don't know what to get. You won't see your Russian friends today, but you know if you leave them a note, they'll call you later with suggesions. Write a note asking for advice.

НОВЫЕ СЛОВА И ВЫРАЖЕНИЯ

NOUNS

авангарди́ст	avant-garde artist
вещь (*fem.*)	thing
вы́бор	selection
галантере́я	men's accessories (*store or department*)
головно́й убо́р	hat
граммпласти́нки	records (*store or department*)
де́вушка	(young) woman
д(е)нь рожде́ния	birthday (*lit.* day of birth)
де́ньги (*always plural*)	money
до́ллар (5-20 до́лларов)	dollar
игру́шки	toys
импрессиони́ст	impressionist
иску́сство	art
ка́рта	map
ка́сса	cash register
копе́йка (5-20 копе́ек)	kopeck
матрёшка	Russian nested doll
метр	metre
молодо́й челове́к	young man
о́бувь (*fem.*)	footwear
отде́л	department
парфюме́рия	cosmetics (*store or department*)
перча́тки	gloves
пласти́нка	record
плат(о́)к (*endings always stressed*)	(hand)kerchief
разме́р	size
рем(е́)нь (*endings always stressed*)	belt (man's)
рубль (2-4 рубля́, 5-20 рубле́й) (*endings always stressed*)	ruble
ры́н(о)к (на)	market
кни́жный ры́н(о)к	book mart
сантиме́тр	centimetre
сувени́р	souvenir
това́р	goods
универма́г	department store
цент (5-20 це́нтов)	cent
чек	check, receipt
челове́к (*pl.* лю́ди)	person
чулки́	stockings
ша́пка	cap, fur hat, knit hat
шкату́лка	painted or carved wooden box (*souvenir*)
шля́па	hat (e.g., business hat)

ADJECTIVES

валю́тный	hard currency
же́нский	women's
закры́т (-а,-о,-ы)	closed
кни́жный	book(ish)
мужско́й	men's
неплохо́й	pretty good
огро́мный	huge

VERBS

плати́ть (плачу́, пла́тишь, пла́тят)	to pay
покупа́ть (покупа́ю, покупа́ешь, покупа́ют)	to buy
продава́ть (продаю́, продаёшь, продаю́т)	to sell

For now, use the following verbs only in the forms given
Infinitives and Past Tense:

быть (был, была́, бы́ли)	to be
забы́ть (забы́л, забы́ла, забы́ли)	to forget
закры́ть (закры́л, закры́ла, закры́ли)	to close
купи́ть (купи́л, купи́ла, купи́ли)	to buy
откры́ть (откры́л, откры́ла, откры́ли)	to open
подари́ть (подари́л, подари́ла, подари́ли)	to give a present
посове́товать (посове́товал, посове́товала, посове́товали)	to advise
сказа́ть (сказа́л, сказа́ла, сказа́ли)	to say
узна́ть (узна́л, узна́ла, узна́ли)	to find out
ходи́ть (ходи́л, ходи́ла, ходи́ли)	to go (and come back) on foot

Third-person forms:

сто́ить (сто́ит, сто́ят) (сто́ил, сто́ила, сто́ило, сто́или)	to cost

ADVERBS

давно́	for a long time
да́же	even
наприме́р	for instance
неда́вно	recently
ра́ньше	previously
ско́ро	soon
тепе́рь	now (*as opposed to some other time*)
туда́	there (*answers* **куда́**)

SUBJECTLESS CONSTRUCTIONS

(*кому́*) мо́жно + *infinitive*	it is possible
(*кому́*) на́до + *infinitive*	it is necessary
(*кому́*) ну́жно + *infinitive*	it is necessary

QUESTION WORD

Ско́лько …?	How much?

PHRASES AND OTHER WORDS

ведь	you know, after all (*filler word, never stressed*)
Дава́й(те)	Let's
Де́вушка!	Excuse me, miss!
Мне сказа́ли, что …	I was told that …
Мо́жно плати́ть до́лларами?	Can I pay in dollars?
Молоде́ц! (Како́й ты (он, она́, etc.) молоде́ц!)	Good show! (*lit.* Good fellow, *but used for both sexes*)
Молодо́й челове́к!	Excuse me, sir!
Огро́мное спаси́бо!	Thank you very much!
Одну́ мину́точку!	Just a moment!
Плати́те в ка́ссу.	Pay the cashier.
Пойдём!	Let's go!
Пойдём лу́чше …	Let's go to … instead.
Покажи́(те)!	Show!
сам (сама́, са́ми)	-self
С днём рожде́ния!	Happy birthday!
Ско́лько сто́ит?	How much does it cost?
Что вы посове́туете нам взять?	What do you advise us to take?
Это (совсе́м не) до́рого!	That's (not at all) expensive!
Я хочу́ сде́лать *кому́* пода́рок.	I want to give *someone* a present.

PERSONALIZED VOCABULARY

_____

_____

_____

_____

УРОК

9

ЧТО МЫ БУДЕМ ЕСТЬ?

▼ **КОММУНИКАТИВНЫЕ ЗАДАНИЯ**

Reading menus
Making plans to go to a restaurant
Ordering meals in a restaurant
Making plans to cook dinner
Interviews about food stores

▼ **В ПОМОЩЬ УЧАЩИМСЯ**

Conjugation of the verbs **есть** and **пить**
Specifying quantity: portions, rubles,
    kopecks
Subjectless expressions: **нельзя́,**
    невозмо́жно, легко́, тру́дно
The future tense
Introduction to verbal aspect

Workbook: Vowel reduction:
    о, а, ы

▼ **МЕЖДУ ПРОЧИМ**

Russian food stores
Russian restaurants, cafes
    and cafeterias
The metric system: pounds
    vs. kilograms
    measurements of liquids
Kopecks

Точка отсчёта

О ЧЁМ ИДЁТ РЕЧЬ?

Which of the following foods would you eat for breakfast, lunch or dinner?

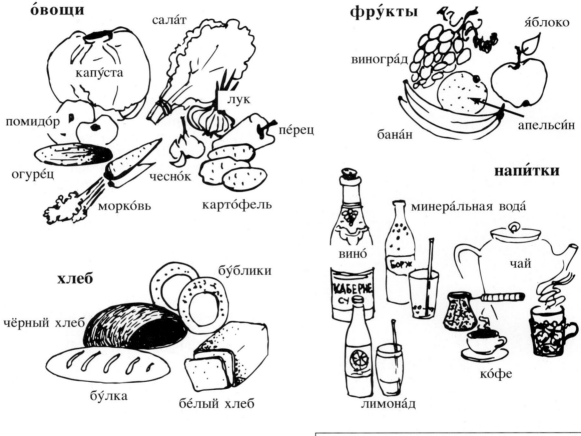

óвощи

салáт

капýста

лук

помидóр

пéрец

огурéц

чеснóк

моркóвь

картóфель

фрýкты

виногрáд

я́блоко

банáн

апельси́н

напи́тки

минерáльная водá

вино́

чай

хлеб

бýблики

чёрный хлеб

бýлка

бéлый хлеб

кóфе

лимонáд

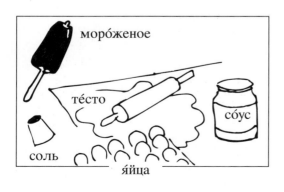

морóженое

тéсто

сóус

соль

я́йца

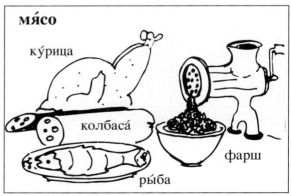

мя́со

кýрица

колбасá

фарш

ры́ба

супы́

щи

бульо́н

борщ

рассо́льник

горя́чие блю́да

ланге́т

га́мбургер

котле́ты по-ки́евски

моло́чное

молоко́

ма́сло

сыр

заку́ски

мясно́й сала́т

икра́

мясно́е ассорти́

бутербро́д

сала́т из помидо́ров

сала́т из огурцо́в

пи́цца

A. List your most and least favorite foods.

_____   _____

_____   _____

_____   _____

_____   _____

_____   _____

B. List the ingredients you would need for the following dishes.

пицца	гамбургер	салат

C. Identify the foods being sold in each of these stores.

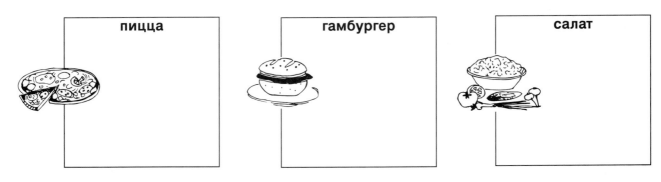

МАГАЗИНЫ

Food stores in Russia tend to specialize in one or two types of items. *Гастроном* usually specializes in **колбаса** and **сыр.** *Булочная* and *бакалея* sell fresh bread, pastries, and baking goods. *Кулинария* sells ready-to-bake items, such as pre-made dough and ground beef as well as other prepared food items. *Молочный магазин* offers dairy products. *Продовольственный магазин* is a generic grocery store. *Универсам* is a self-service grocery store, found in large cities.

Metric System: Weight and Volume

Most food sold in Russian stores is not pre-packaged. When you buy an item you need to specify how much you want. When you buy drinks by the bottle, they are measured in liters. When you order individual servings, in a restaurant for example, they are measured in grams. The following conversion information should help you with the metric system.

стака́нчик моро́женого: 100 г.

3 помидо́ра: 500 г. (полкило́)

буты́лка шампа́нского: 0,75 л.
небольшо́й стака́н воды́: 200 г. (0,2 л.)

Он роди́лся сего́дня! 3,5 кг.

18-ле́тняя де́вушка (1,6 м.): 52 кг.
баскетболи́ст (2 м.): 80 кг.

Автомоби́ль берёт 40 л. бензи́на.

D. **Разгово́ры.**

Разгово́р 1: Ты уже́ обе́дала?

(Разгова́ривают Вади́м и Кэ́рен)

1. Where do Vadim and Karen decide to go?
2. What street is it located on?
3. What time of day is it easiest to get in?

Разгово́р 2: В кафе́

(Разгова́ривают Вади́м , Кэ́рен и официа́нт)

1. What kind of soup does the waiter recommend?
2. What does Vadim order to drink?
3. Does Karen get dessert?

Разгово́р 3: В кафе́

1. How much does the meal cost?

Между прочим

The English *restaurant* applies to almost any eatery. The Russian **рестора́н** is a full-service restaurant featuring a three-course meal, live entertainment, and dancing. A bit less formal is a **кафе́,** which can range from a few tables in a small room to something quite elaborate. A **кафете́рий** is a first-class self-service establishment, while a **столо́вая** is a cafeteria, often at school or work.

In many restaurants a menu is provided only after you have asked for one (**Принеси́те меню́, пожа́луйста.**), and often only one menu is provided for a table. Not everything listed on the menu may be available, however. Prices are customarily written in only for the available items. It is thus not unusual for a customer to ask the waiter what is available (**Что у вас есть сего́дня?**) or to ask for a recommendation (**Что вы посове́туете взять?**).

Tips (**чаевы́е**) in Russian restaurants are normally about five percent.

ДИАЛОГИ

1 **Мо́жет быть, пойдём в кафе́?**

— Кэ́рен, ты уже́ обе́дала?
— Нет, но уже́ стра́шно хочу́ есть.
— А мо́жет быть, пойдём в кафе́? Я слы́шал, что на Большо́й у́лице то́лько что откры́лось но́вое кафе́ «Мину́тка».
— А я слы́шала, что попа́сть туда́ про́сто невозмо́жно.
— Ве́чером попа́сть тру́дно, а днём мо́жно. Я ду́маю, что сейча́с мы то́чно попадём.
— Хорошо́, пошли́.

Между прочим

While **за́втрак** is indisputably *breakfast,* one can argue about **обе́д** and **у́жин.** Traditionally **обе́д** is the largest meal of the day (*dinner*), whereas **у́жин** is the evening meal (*supper*). In the past, the largest meal was taken at midday. Now **обе́д** is usually lunch, regardless of size. However, you may hear any large meal taken in the afternoon or early evening referred to as **обе́д.**

Обе́д usually consists of two, three, or even four courses. **Заку́ски** are appetizers. The first course (**пе́рвое**) is **борщ, бульо́н, щи,** or some other kind of **суп.** The main course (**второ́е**) follows, and the meal is rounded off by **сла́дкое** (dessert and/or coffee). Dessert is ordered at the same time as the rest of the meal.

2 **Что вы бу́дете зака́зывать?**

— Что вы бу́дете зака́зывать?
— А что вы нам посове́туете взять?
— На пе́рвое я вам посове́тую взять борщ украи́нский. На второ́е—цыпля́та табака́.
— Хорошо́. Две по́рции, пожа́луйста.
— А пить что вы бу́дете? Есть лимона́д, минера́льная вода́.
— Два лимона́да, пожа́луйста.
— Моро́женое бу́дете?
— Да.
— А я возьму́ ко́фе с молоко́м.

Настроение = mood.

③ Рассчита́йте нас!

— Де́вушка! Бу́дьте добры́, рассчита́йте нас!
— Зна́чит так: борщ, цыпля́та табака́, лимона́д,
   одно́ моро́женое, оди́н ко́фе. С вас 1250 рубле́й.
— Вот. Получи́те, пожа́луйста.

РЕСТОРАН "МОСКВА"

Борщ	2	350-60
Цыплята табака	2	600-00
Лимонад	2	49-40
Мороженое	1	150-00
Кофе	1	100-00

Итого 1250-00

④ Хо́чешь, я тебе́ пригото́влю пи́ццу?

— Оля, хо́чешь, я тебе́ пригото́влю пи́ццу?
— Да, коне́чно. Что на́до купи́ть?
— Сейча́с поду́маю. На́до сде́лать тома́тный со́ус.
— Хорошо́. Зна́чит, мы ку́пим помидо́ры,
   лук и чесно́к.
— Мне нельзя́ есть чесно́к. У меня́ аллерги́я.
— Тогда́ сде́лаем без чеснока́. Что ещё ну́жно?
— Ну, ещё сыр, фарш мясно́й, пе́рец и те́сто.
— Ну, те́сто мо́жно купи́ть в кулина́рии. Овощи
   и фарш мы ку́пим на ры́нке. А сыр у нас
   уже́ есть.
— Отли́чно!

1. Помидоры
2. Лук, чеснок
3. Перец
4. Тесто
5. Фарш
6. Сыр

⑤ Хо́чешь, я тебе́ пригото́влю бутербро́ды?

— Хо́чешь, я тебе́ пригото́влю бутербро́ды?
— Да, коне́чно!
— Мне то́лько на́до купи́ть хлеб.
— Слу́шай, хлеб куплю́ я. Бу́лочная недалеко́.
— Хорошо́, а я пока́ сде́лаю тома́тный со́ус.
— Что ещё ну́жно? Соль у нас есть?
— Есть. Купи́ то́лько хлеб. Чёрный и бе́лый.

> **А бутербро́д** (an *open face sand-wich*) usually consists of a piece of cheese or meat on a small piece of white or black bread.

Девятый урок

ГОЛОСА **259**

A. **Что вы бу́дете есть?** If you were in this restaurant, what would you order? Choose something from each of the following category.

заку́ски   **пе́рвые блю́да**   **вторы́е блю́да**   **сла́дкое**   **напи́тки**

П Р А Г А

ФИРМЕННЫЕ БЛЮДА

Салат «Прага»	285-00
Бифштекс «Прага»	226-00
Шампиньоны в сметане	196-00
Пломбир «Прага»	196-00
Торт «Прага»	195-00

ХОЛОДНЫЕ ЗАКУСКИ

Икра зернистая	698-00
Икра кетовая	537-00
Севрюга копченая	400-00
Осетрина под майонезом	352-00
Осетрина с хреном	330-00
Ростбиф с гарниром	349-00
Ветчина с гарниром	227-00
Ассорти мясное	---------
Сардины	120-00
Грибы маринованные	125-00
Салат из огурцов	175-00
Салат из помидоров	189-00
Маслины	150-00
Салат «Столичный»	273-00
Сыр	102-00
Масло сливочное	50-00

ГОРЯЧИЕ ЗАКУСКИ

Жульен из дичи	336-00
Шампиньоны кокот	---------
Шницель «Ленинград»	375-00

СУПЫ

Борщ «Московский»	195-00
Солянка мясная	337-00
Солянка рыбная	374-00
Суп-лапша с курицей	285-00
Суп-пюре из кур	267-00
Бульон с гренками	187-00
Бульон с яйцом	148-00
Бульон с пирожком	284-00
Щи кислые	101-00

ГОРЯЧИЕ РЫБНЫЕ БЛЮДА

Осетрина паровая	437-00
Осетрина по-московски	453-00
Судак по-польски	271-00

ГОРЯЧИЕ МЯСНЫЕ БЛЮДА

Бефстроганов с картофелем	337-00
Бифштекс натуральный	300-00
Филе в соусе мадера	--------
Лангет натуральный	309-00
Котлеты бараньи натуральные	258-00
Эскалоп из свинины с гарниром	411-00
Шашлык по-кавказски	375-00
Шницель «Ленинград»	375-00
Сосиски	178-00

БЛЮДА ИЗ ПТИЦЫ И ДИЧИ

Куры жареные с картофелем	380-00
Котлеты из кур по-киевски	356-00
Цыпленок табака	462-00
Индейка жареная	555-00
Гусь жареный	490-00
Утка жареная	436-00

БЛЮДА ИЗ ЯИЦ

Яичница натуральная	183-00
Омлет с ветчиной	224-00

СЛАДКИЕ БЛЮДА

Пломбир с шоколадом	156-00
Компот из фруктов	151-00
Блинчики с вареньем	205-00

НАПИТКИ

Чай	22-00
Чай с лимоном	29-00
Кофе черный	36-00
Кофе по восточному	38-00
Вода минеральная	30-00
Кофе гляссе	55-00

ОБСЛУЖИВАНИЕ 5%

B. **Что на́до купи́ть?** You have agreed to make hamburgers, salad, and french fries for your Russian friends for dinner. They have to do all the shopping. Make a list of all the things you will need.

Язык в действии

ДАВАЙТЕ ПОГОВОРИМ

A. **Подготовка к разговору**. Review the dialogs. How would you do the following?

- ask if someone has had lunch
- say you are (very) hungry
- suggest going out to eat
- say that a new cafe (store, theater) opened recently
- say that it is impossible to get into a new restaurant
- ask a waiter for suggestions on what to order
- order a complete meal (soup, main course, dessert, drinks) in a restaurant
- order two (three, four, etc.) servings of borsch
- tell the waiter to bring you the check
- pay the check
- offer to make someone pizza (sandwiches, dinner)
- ask what you need to buy
- tell someone you need to buy meat (milk)

B. **Как вы думаете?** A number of assertions reflecting common Russian views of life in the West are listed below. Working in pairs, use your own experience to respond to each assertion. The following expressions will help you organize your responses.

Я ду́маю, что …	
Это так.	
Это не совсе́м так.	
Это совсе́м не так.	
Если говори́ть о себе́, то …	*If I use myself as an example, then …*
С одно́й стороны́ …	*On the one hand …*
А с друго́й стороны́ …	*On the other hand …*
Во-пе́рвых …	*First of all …*
Во-вторы́х …	*Second of all …*

1. Я слы́шал(а), что америка́нцы (кана́дцы, англича́не) о́чень лю́бят есть в Макдо́налдсе.
2. Говоря́т, что америка́нская (кана́дская, англи́йская) ку́хня совсе́м не интере́сная.
3. Америка́нцы до́ма не гото́вят. Они́ покупа́ют гото́вые проду́кты в магази́не.

C. **Игровы́е ситуа́ции.** Imagine that you are in Russia. Act out the following situations.

1. In a cafe, order yourself and a friend a meal. Find out if your friend wants an appetizer or soup. Use the menu on pages 260-261.

2. At a restaurant you ordered borsch, Chicken Kiev, and coffee, but the waiter brought a different soup and some kind of beef, and completely forgot the coffee. Complain.

3. You are in a restaurant. Order a complete meal for yourself and a friend who is a vegetarian.

4. A Russian friend would like to try hamburgers. Offer to make them and explain what ingredients are needed. Decide who will buy what.

5. To celebrate a Russian friend's birthday, invite her to a new restaurant that you have heard is really good. Agree on a time.

6. Working with a partner, prepare and act out a situation of your own that deals with the topics of this unit.

D. **Устный перево́д.** In Moscow, you are in a restaurant with a friend who doesn't know Russian. Help him order a meal.

English speaker's part

1. Can we get a menu?
2. I don't understand a thing. Do they have any salads?
3. I'll get the tomatoes, I guess.
4. I don't want any soup.
5. Do they have any chicken dishes?
6. Okay. And I'd like to get a Pepsi.
7. How about coffee? Do they have coffee?
8. I'll take coffee then.
9. Yes.
10. No, that's it for me.

ДАВАЙТЕ ПОЧИТАЕМ

Меню.

1. Scan the menu to see which dishes are available.

   - Лю́ля-кеба́б
   - Шашлы́к
   - Котле́ты по-ки́евски
   - Ку́рица

2. Now look at the menu again to find out which drinks are available.

   - Во́дка
   - Пепси-ко́ла
   - Минера́льная вода́
   - Пи́во

3. How much do the following cost?

   - Grilled chicken
   - Black coffee
   - Bottle of Stolichnaya vodka
   - 100 grams of Stolichnaya vodka
   - Bottle of Zhigulevskoe beer
   - A glass of fruit punch

4. What kinds of mineral water were available?

5. What kinds of wine are available in this restaurant?

6. This menu contains a number of words you do not yet know. What strategies would you use to order a meal if you were in this restaurant, alone and hungry, and no one else in the restaurant knew English?

М Е Н Ю

Вино-водочные изделия	Стакан	Бутылка
Водка «Русская»	70-00	700-00
Водка «Столичная»	72-00	720-00
Водка «Экстра»	61-00	610-00
Вино «Цинандали»	29-00	260-00
Рислинг	30-00	270-00
Минеральная вода «Боржоми»	5-00	50-00
Минеральная вода «Эвиан»	98-00	890-00
Пиво «Жигулевское»	35-00	320-00
Пиво «Невское»	28-00	280-00

Горячие блюда

Осетрина жареная на решетке	351-00
Курица жареная на гриле	278-00
Бастурма	189-00
Шашлык из свинины	187-00
Шашлык из баранины	262-00

Сладкие блюда и напитки

Напиток фруктовый	5-80
Кофе чёрный	3-40
Пломбир с джемом	5-50

ДАВАЙТЕ ПОСЛУШАЕМ 📼

Интервью. You will hear street interviews with some of the first customers at a new cooperative food store named **За ваше здоровье** (To Your Health), and an interview with the store's manager.

1. Background. The early 1990s saw an explosion of small private enterprise in Russia. Leading the way were cooperative food stores and restaurants. Cooperative stores often had things not available in state-run stores. On the other hand, prices were often higher.

2. Predict what will happen. You already know a bit about the difference between cooperative and state stores.

   - Pick out two things that you think customers are likely to say.

      a. The new store has empty shelves. Why did they bother opening this store to begin with?
      b. The new store sure has a lot, but the prices are outrageous!
      c. The service in government-run stores is much nicer.
      d. There isn't much available in state-run stores, so people end up coming here.
      e. Cooperative stores don't have enough meat.

   - Pick out one thing that the manager is likely to say.

      a. We have to keep prices low or else we won't be able to compete with the state-run stores.
      b. State stores are no competition for us—either in the variety of things available or in terms of customer service.
      c. Other cooperative stores should be closed.

3. **Словарь.** Before listening to the interviews, read the following list of expressions aloud, paying close attention to stress.

   государственный магазин—state store
   закон—law
   он(а) готов(а) платить—s/he is willing to pay
   полкило—half a kilo (**пол** = half)
   свежий—fresh
   цена—price; **высокие цены**—high prices
   церковь—church

4. Now listen to the interviews and see if your predictions were correct.

5. Listen to the interviews again. Which food items are mentioned? What other foods are named?

апельси́н—orange
виногра́д—grapes
гру́ша—pear
карто́шка—potatoes
колбаса́—sausage
лимо́н—lemon
смета́на—sour cream
творо́г—cottage cheese
я́блоко—apple

6. There is a lot of talk about **высо́кие це́ны**. Here are some typical prices in state stores at the time of the interview. How do the prices discussed here compare?

Наименования	Количество	Цена
молоко́	1 л.	70к.
колбаса́	1 кг.	3р.50к.
сыр росси́йский	1 кг.	4р.50к.
смета́на	1 кг.	5р.

7. Listen to the interviews one more time. Which of the following best describes the attitude of the manager? After you make your choice, listen to the interview again. Jot down the Russian words that correspond to the key portions (indicated in bold) of the utterance you chose:

a. Perhaps I should **apologize for our prices,** but the **law** makes operating expenses very high.

b. We only charge **high prices** for **meat, potatoes, and milk**. All of our other prices match those of the **state stores.**

c. We compromise with those who **cannot pay** what we charge **for our produce**. I believe that's the only way **to do business.**

d. We operate by the natural **law of the market**. If you think **we have high prices, don't buy!**

В ПОМОЩЬ УЧАЩИМСЯ

9.1 VERB CONJUGATION—*ЕСТЬ, ПИТЬ*

The verb **есть** (*to eat*) is one of only four truly irregular verbs in Russian. Use it to talk about eating a certain food. To express *eat breakfast, eat lunch,* and *eat dinner,* use the verbs **за́втракать, обе́дать,** and **у́жинать.**

The verb **пить** (*to drink*) has regular first-conjugation endings. But note the **-ь** throughout the present-tense conjugation.

есть	
я	ем
ты	ешь
он/она́	ест
мы	еди́м
вы	еди́те
они́	едя́т
past tense	ел, е́ла, е́ли
	to eat

пить	
я	пью
ты	пьёшь
он/она́	пьёт
мы	пьём
вы	пьёте
они́	пьют
past tense	пил, пила́, пи́ли
	to drink

Упражнение

1. Make sentences by combining words from the columns below. Use the appropriate present-tense form of **есть** or **пить.**

я			мя́со
ты			ко́фе
мы	всегда́ *Always*		чай
америка́нцы	никогда́ не *Never*	есть	суп
кто	ча́сто *often*	пить	кра́сное вино́
де́ти	ре́дко *rarely*		бе́лое вино́
ру́сские	ка́ждый день *every day*		о́вощи
вы			фру́кты
ма́ма			сала́т

➤ Complete Oral Drills 1–3 and Written Exercises 1–3 in the Workbook.

9.2 SPECIFYING QUANTITY

You already know that after the numbers 2, 3, and 4 nouns are in the genitive singular (see Unit 6). You also know that after the words **ско́лько** and **мно́го**, and the numbers 5-20 a genitive plural noun is used. You know the genitive plural form for a number of words (see Unit 7). Here are the forms for *rubles* and *kopecks*.

1, 21, 31, 41, 1561 ...	рубль	копе́йка
2, 3, 4, 22, 53, 74, ...	рубля́	копе́йки
5-20, 27, 55, 129 ...	рубле́й	копе́ек

Между прочим

For most of the latter half of the twentieth century the **копе́йка** (=1/100 of a ruble) was officially worth between a cent and a cent and a half in U.S. currency. In the early 1990s, inflation ate up the value of Russian currency, and kopecks became virtually worthless (1/500 of a cent). By 1992-1993 the kopeck was not in common use.

When ordering more than one portion in a restaurant, you don't need to use the genitive case of the food you are ordering. Learn the genitive forms for the word **по́рция (две, три, четы́ре по́рции; пять по́рций)**, and use them after rather than before the noun:

Борщ, две по́рции.   *Borshch, two orders.*

Упражнение

2. How would you express the following in Russian?

   "Bouillon, two orders, and chicken Kiev, five orders, please."
   "How much do we owe?"
   "750 rubles."

➤ Complete Oral Drill 4 and Written Exercise 4 in the Workbook.

9.3 ADDITIONAL SUBJECTLESS EXPRESSIONS:
НЕЛЬЗЯ, НЕВОЗМОЖНО, ТРУДНО, ЛЕГКО

In Unit 8 you learned how to express necessity and possibility with the words **на́до, ну́жно,** and **мо́жно.** Sentences with these words do not have a grammatical subject, and they are therefore called subjectless expressions. (In English, these expressions have grammatical subjects, because English sentences must always have grammatical subjects.) Here are examples of the subjectless expressions introduced in this unit:

— Я слы́шала, что попа́сть туда́ про́сто **невозмо́жно.**	"I heard that *it's* simply *impossible* to get in."
— Ве́чером попа́сть о́чень **тру́дно,** а днём **мо́жно.**	"In the evening *it's* very *difficult* to get in, but in the afternoon *it's possible.*"
Легко́ пригото́вить бутербро́д, а пригото́вить пельме́ни **тру́дно.**	*It's easy* to make a sandwich, but *hard* to make pelmeni (Ukrainian dumplings).
У него́ аллерги́я, **ему́ нельзя́** есть шокола́д.	He has an allergy, *he's not allowed* to eat chocolate.

The person is expressed in the dative case. The subjectless expression is followed by an infinitive:

$$(кому́) \quad + \quad \begin{matrix} легко́ \\ мо́жно \\ на́до \\ ну́жно \\ невозмо́жно \\ нельзя́ \\ тру́дно \end{matrix} \quad + \quad infinitive$$

Упражнение

3. Make truthful and grammatically correct sentences by combining elements from the columns below. Be sure to put the person in the dative case. The question mark at the bottom of two of the columns indicates that you may substitute your own words.

мы	- легко́	- говори́ть по-ру́сски
ма́ма и па́па	· мо́жно	- чита́ть по-ру́сски
наш преподава́тель	- на́до	чита́ть ру́сское меню́
?	ну́жно	гото́вить пи́ццу
	невозмо́жно	занима́ться в библиоте́ке
	нельзя́	- у́жинать в рестора́не
	трудно	?

➤ Complete Oral Drills 5–6 and Written Exercises 5–6 in the Workbook.

9.4 FUTURE TENSE OF *БЫТЬ*

— Вы бы́ли до́ма вчера́? "Were you at home yesterday?"
— Нет, но мы **бу́дем** до́ма за́втра. "No, but we *will be* home tomorrow."

Although Russian does not express the verb *to be* in the present tense, it does so in the past and future tenses. As with many Russian verbs, the stem of the conjugated verb differs from the stem of the infinitive, but the endings are regular, first-conjugation endings.

быть	
я	**бу́ду**
ты	**бу́дешь**
он/она́	**бу́дет**
мы	**бу́дем**
вы	**бу́дете**
они́	**бу́дут**

Упражнения

4. Anna wrote this postcard during her vacation. What words have been obliterated by the ink marks?

Здравствуй!
Наша экскурсия очень интересная. Вчера наша группа ▆▆▆ во Владимире. Сегодня мы в Санкт-Петербурге. Завтра мы ▆▆▆ в Москве. Там ▆▆▆ экскурсия по Кремлю и центру города. Я ▆▆▆ дома в субботу.
Целую. Анна

5. Say where the following people will be tomorrow.

Образе́ц: моя́ сестра́ — шко́ла   ➡   ***Моя́ сестра́ бу́дет в шко́ле.***

   а. наш друг—рестора́н   г. на́ши сосе́ди—ры́нок
   б. вы—кафете́рий   д. мы—дом
   в. ты—гастроно́м   е. я—?

➤ Complete Oral Drill 7 and Written Exercises 7–8 in the Workbook.

9.5 THE FUTURE TENSE

— Что вы **бу́дете де́лать** сего́дня?
— Я **бу́ду занима́ться.**

For all of the verbs you learned in Units 1 through 7, the future tense is formed by combining the conjugated form of **быть** with the infinitive.

Упражнения

6. Make two-line dialogs as in the model.

Образе́ц: Со́ня—чита́ть   ➡   — Что Со́ня **бу́дет де́лать** за́втра?
                               — Она́ **бу́дет чита́ть.**

   а. Григо́рий Ви́кторович—писа́ть пи́сьма
   б. мы—смотре́ть телеви́зор
   в. на́ши друзья́—отдыха́ть
   г. Анна Никола́евна—рабо́тать
   д. студе́нты—занима́ться в библиоте́ке
   е. вы—?
   ж. ты—?

7. Answer the following questions.

   а. Кто бу́дет отдыха́ть за́втра?
   б. Кто не бу́дет занима́ться за́втра?
   в. Кто бу́дет у́жинать в рестора́не в пя́тницу?
   г. Кто бу́дет убира́ть кварти́ру за́втра?
   д. Кто бу́дет смотре́ть телеви́зор сего́дня ве́чером?
   е. Кто не бу́дет гото́вить у́жин за́втра?
   ж. Кто в суббо́ту не бу́дет за́втракать?

➤ Complete Oral Drills 8-9 and Written Exercise 9 in the Workbook.

9.6   VERBAL ASPECT—INTRODUCTION

Unlike English, Russian verbs encode both tense and aspect. Aspect tells something about *how* an action takes place. It is not to be confused with tense, which indicates *when* an action takes place. Almost all Russian verbs belong either to the imperfective or perfective aspect. In most cases imperfective and perfective verbs come in pairs where their meaning is the same, or very close, but they differ in aspect.

Perfective verbs are used to refer to complete, one-time actions, normally of short duration or with a result that is being emphasized. Perfective verbs have only two tenses: past and future.

Imperfective verbs are used in other circumstances. For instance, they refer to repetitive actions, or to one-time actions in situations where the focus is not on the result but on the process or duration. Imperfective verbs have present, past, and future tense.

Imperfective/perfective pairs

Up until this unit, you have learned primarily verbs in the imperfective aspect. That's because your Russian has largely been limited to the present tense, which is expressed only in the imperfective. Now, more and more, you will see verbs listed in their aspectual pairs. The difference between perfective and imperfective is seen everywhere except the present tense: in the infinitive (**гото́вить/пригото́вить**), the future tense (**бу́ду гото́вить/пригото́влю**), the past tense (**гото́вил/пригото́вил**) and the imperative (**гото́вь/пригото́вь**).

Formation of the future tense

The **imperfective future** is a compound form: **бу́дем гото́вить.** The perfective future is formed by conjugating a perfective verb. When conjugated, perfective verbs have the same conjugation pattern as imperfective verbs. **Прочита́ть** is conjugated exactly like **чита́ть**. But conjugated perfective verbs have future meaning.

	PRESENT	FUTURE
imperfective	чита́ю я гото́влю я ем	я бу́ду чита́ть я бу́ду гото́вить я бу́ду есть
perfective		я прочита́ю я пригото́влю я съем

imperfective aspect	*perfective aspect*

готóвить

Мы **бýдем готóвить** пи́ццу весь вéчер.
We *will make* pizza all evening.

we'll go to the movies.

приготóвить

Вéчером мы **приготóвим** пи́ццу,
а потóм мы пойдём в кинó.
Tonight we *will make* pizza and then

покупáть

Когдá я бýду в Росси́и, я **бýду покупáть**
газéту кáждый день.
When I'm in Russia, I *will buy*
a newspaper every day.

купи́ть

Я обы́чно не покупáю газéту,
но зáвтра я её **куплю́.**
I don't usually buy a newspaper,
but tomorrow I *will buy* one.

Use

The perfective is used to emphasize the *result* of a *one-time* action:
Мы **приготóвим** пи́ццу (*We'll get the pizza made*).

In other instances, the imperfective is used. For example, when the amount
of time the action will last is mentioned (*We will make pizza all evening*), the
focus is on duration rather than result and the imperfective must be used:
Мы **бýдем готóвить** пи́ццу весь вéчер. When the action is repeated (*We will
make pizza every day*), the imperfective must also be used (Мы **бýдем
готóвить** пи́ццу кáждый день).

Since perfective verbs emphasize the result of a one-time action, some sentences with perfective verbs do not make sense without a direct object. Just
as the English phrase "I will buy..." begs for a direct object, so do the Russian
phrases **Я куплю́... (хлеб), Я прочитáю... (кни́гу), я приготóвлю... (ýжин), я
съем... (бутербрóд), я вы́пью... (молокó).**

Formation of imperfective/perfective pairs

As you can see from the examples, perfective verbs differ from imperfective
verbs in several ways. There are three patterns for aspectual pairs:

1. Prefixation:
   готóвить/приготóвить
   совéтовать/посовéтовать
   дéлать/сдéлать
   читáть/прочитáть
   писáть/написáть

Prefixed verbs are listed in the vocabulary like this: **готóвить/при- .**

2. Change in the verb stem:
покупа́ть/купи́ть

3. Separate verbs:
брать (беру́, берёшь, беру́т) / взять (возьму́, возьмёшь, возьму́т)
говори́ть / сказа́ть (скажу́, ска́жешь, ска́жут)

The formation of aspectual pairs is not uniform, and in the initial stages of your study of Russian you will have to memorize each pair individually.

The glossaries in this textbook list the imperfective verb first. If only one verb rather than a pair is given, its aspect will be noted.

Упражнение

8. Which aspect would you use to express the italicized verbs in the following sentences?

   a. I *will fix* the pizza tomorrow night. (**бу́ду гото́вить/пригото́влю**)
   b. I *will fix* pizza often. After all, I always fix pizza. (**бу́ду гото́вить/ пригото́влю**)

   c. We *will read* all evening. (**бу́дем чита́ть/прочита́ем**)
   d. We *will read* through the paper now. (**бу́дем чита́ть/прочита́ем**)

   e. Tomorrow evening I *will eat* and drink. (**бу́ду есть/съем**)
   f. I *will eat* a hamburger. I always eat hamburgers. (**бу́ду есть/съем**)

   g. We *will buy* milk here every week. (**бу́дем покупа́ть/ку́пим**)
   h. We *will buy* the milk here. (**бу́дем покупа́ть/ку́пим**)

➤ Complete Oral Drills 10–14 and Written Exercises 10–11 in the Workbook.

ОБЗОРНЫЕ УПРАЖНЕНИЯ

🔲 **A. Разговóры.**

Разговóр 1: Пойдём в ресторáн.
(Разговáривают Áлла, Тóля и Кéвин)

1. For what occasion do Alla and Tolya invite Kevin to dinner?
2. What is Kevin's reaction?

Разговóр 2: В рестоpáне
(Разговáривают Áлла, Кéвин и официáнт)

1. What do Kevin and his friends order to drink?
2. In the list below, circle the foods that Kevin and his friends order.

закýски	пéрвое	вторóе
мяснóй салáт	борщ украúнский	рóстбиф
икрá	бульóн	котлéты по-кúевски
мяснóе ассортú	щи	лангéт
салáт из огурцóв	овощнóй суп	кýрица
салáт из помидóров	рассóльник	цыплáта табакá

3. Why are Kevin and his friends dissatisfied with the meal?

Разговóр 3: Бýдем готóвить шашлы́к.
(Разговáривают Олéг и Элúзабет)

1. Where does Oleg invite Elizabeth?
2. Oleg asks Elizabeth if she's ever tried shishkebab. What is the Russian word for shishkebab?
3. Name some of the things they must buy.
4. Where will they go to buy these things?
5. When and where will they meet to go to the dacha?

B. **Запи́ска.** Write a note inviting a Russian friend to your place for dinner tomorrow at 7:00 pm.

C. **Письмо́.** Your Russian pen pal has asked you about your eating habits: do you like to cook, what foods do you like, where do you usually eat, etc. Write a short letter answering these questions and asking about your pen pal's eating habits. Use the letter below as a guide.

Здравствуй, Маша!
Получил (а) твоё письмо вчера. Ты спрашиваешь, люблю ли я готовить...

Ну, пока всё. Жду твоего письма.
Твой/ Твоя

D. **Интервью́.** Imagine that you will be interviewing a Russian visitor about Russian cuisine.

1. In preparation for the interview, write ten interesting questions about food. Find out who prepares the meals in the visitor's home, what are the favorite dishes, what ingredients are needed for one of the dishes, and whatever else interests you.

2. Using your prepared questions, conduct a class interview in Russian with a visitor, or with your teacher. Be sure to listen to other students' questions and to all the answers. Take notes so that you can reconstruct the information afterwards.

3. Compare your notes with two or three other students. Did you understand the same things? Check with your teacher if you have questions.

4. Work with the others in your small group to write one to two paragraphs in Russian about the information you learned during the interview.

НОВЫЕ СЛОВА И ВЫРАЖЕНИЯ

Memorize Again!

NOUNS

пи́ща	food
апельси́н	orange
бана́н	banana
борщ	borsch
бу́блик	bagel
бу́лка	small white loaf of bread; roll
бульо́н	bouillon
бутербро́д	(open-faced) sandwich
виногра́д	grapes
заку́ски	appetizers
икра́	caviar
капу́ста	cabbage
карто́фель (карто́шка)	potato
колбаса́	sausage
котле́ты по-ки́евски	Kiev cutlet
ко́фе (*masc., indecl.*)	coffee
ку́рица	chicken
ланге́т	fried steak
лимона́д	soft drink
лук	onion(s)
ма́сло	butter
минера́льная вода́	mineral water
молоко́	milk
моро́женое (*adj. decl.*)	ice cream
морко́вь (*fem.*)	carrot
мя́со	meat
мясно́е ассорти́	cold cuts assortment
напи́т(о)к	drink
о́вощи	vegetables
огур(е́)ц	cucumber
пельме́ни	pelmeni (Ukrainian dumplings)
пер(е)ц	pepper
пи́цца	pizza
помидо́р	tomato
рассо́льник	fish (or meat) and cucumber soup
рис	rice
ро́стбиф	roast beef
сала́т	salad; lettuce
сала́т из огурцо́в	cucumber salad
сала́т из помидо́ров	tomato salad
сла́дкое (*adj. decl.*)	dessert
соль (*fem.*)	salt
со́ус	sauce

суп	soup
сыр	cheese
тéсто	dough
томáтный сóус	tomato sauce
фарш	chopped meat
фрýкты	fruit
хлеб	bread
цыпля́та табакá	a chicken dish from the Caucasus
чай	tea
чеснóк	garlic
шашлы́к	shishkebab
шоколáд	chocolate
щи	cabbage soup
я́блоко	apple
яйцó (*pl.* я́йца)	egg

магази́ны/рестора́ны	stores/restaurants
бакалéя	baking goods store
бýлочная (*adj. decl.*)	bakery
гастронóм	grocery store
кафé [кафэ́] (*masc.; indecl.*)	cafe
кафетéрий	restaurant-cafeteria
кулинáрия	store that sells **полуфабрика́ты,** products such as ground beef, tomato sauce, or dough—ready to cook
универсáм	self-service grocery store

други́е существи́тельные	other nouns
аллерги́я	allergy
блю́до	dish (food, not the physical plate)
вторóе (*adj. decl.*)	main course; entree
зáвтрак	breakfast
кýхня	cuisine, style of cooking
меню́ (*neuter; indecl.*)	menu
обéд	lunch
пéрвое (*adj. decl.*)	first course (always soup)
пóрция	portion, order
продýкты (*pl.*)	groceries
ýжин	supper
чаевы́е (*pl.; adj. decl.*)	tip

ADJECTIVES

вкýсный	good, tasty
готóвый	prepared
минерáльный	mineral
молóчный	milk; dairy
мяснóй	meat
овощнóй	vegetable
продовóльственный (магази́н)	grocery store
томáтный	tomato

Memorize Again!

VERBS

быть (бу́ду, бу́дешь, бу́дут) (был)	to be—*future tense conj.*
брать/взять	to take
(беру́, берёшь, беру́т)	
(возьму́, возьмёшь, возьму́т)	
гото́вить/при-	to prepare
(гото́влю, гото́вишь, гото́вят)	
де́лать/с- (де́лаю, де́лаешь, де́лают)	to do, to make
ду́мать/по- (ду́маю, ду́маешь, ду́мают)	to think
е́хать/по- (е́ду, е́дешь, е́дут)	to go (*by vehicle*)
есть/съ-	to eat
(ем, ешь, ест, еди́м, еди́те, едя́т)	
за́втракать/по-	to have breakfast
(за́втракаю, за́втракаешь, за́втракают)	
зака́зывать (*imperf.*)	to order
(зака́зываю, зака́зываешь, зака́зывают)	
идти́/пойти́	to go (*on foot, or within city*)
(иду́, идёшь, иду́т)	
(пойду́, пойдёшь, пойду́т)	
обе́дать/по-	to have lunch, dinner
(обе́даю, обе́даешь, обе́дают)	
откры́ться (*perf.*)	to open up
(откры́лся, откры́лась, откры́лось,	
откры́лись) (*past*)	
писа́ть/на- (пишу́, пи́шешь, пи́шут)	to write
пить/вы́пить	to drink
(пью, пьёшь, пьют; пил, пила́, пи́ли)	
(вы́пью, вы́пьешь, вы́пьют)	
покупа́ть/купи́ть	to buy
(покупа́ю, покупа́ешь, покупа́ют)	
(куплю́, ку́пишь, ку́пят)	
попа́сть (*perf.*)	to manage to get in, *also hitting a target*
(попаду́, попадёшь, попаду́т; попа́л, -а, -и)	
слу́шать/про-	to listen
(слу́шаю, слу́шаешь, слу́шают)	
слы́шать/у- (слы́шу, слы́шишь, слы́шат)	to hear
смотре́ть/по-	to watch
(смотрю́, смо́тришь, смо́трят)	
сове́товать/по- (*кому́*)	to advise
(сове́тую, сове́туешь, сове́туют)	
у́жинать/по-	to have supper
(у́жинаю, у́жинаешь, у́жинают)	

ADVERBS

недалеко́	not far
пока́	meanwhile
про́сто	simply
стра́шно	terribly
то́лько что	just

SUBJECTLESS CONSTRUCTIONS

легко́ (*кому́*)	easy
невозмо́жно (*кому́*)	impossible
нельзя́ (*кому́*)	forbidden, not allowed
тру́дно (*кому́*)	difficult

PREPOSITION

без (*чего́*)	without

PHRASES AND OTHER WORDS

Бу́дьте добры́!	Could you please …?
Во-пе́рвых …, во-вторы́х …	In the first place …, in the second place …
Е́сли говори́ть о себе́, то…	If I use myself as an example, then …
Как называ́ется (называ́ются) …?	What is (are) … called? (*said of things, not people*)
ко́фе с молоко́м	coffee with milk
Получи́те!	Take it! (*said when paying*)
Мы то́чно попадём.	We'll get in for sure.
Пошли́!	Let's go!
Принеси́те, пожа́луйста, меню́.	Please bring a menu.
Рассчита́йте (нас, меня́)!	Please give (us, me) the check.
С (*кого́*) …	Someone owes …
С одно́й стороны́ …, с друго́й стороны́ …	On the one hand …, on the other hand …
Что ещё ну́жно?	What else is needed?
Что вы (нам, мне) посове́туете взять?	What do you advise (us, me) to order?

PERSONALIZED VOCABULARY

_____

_____

_____

_____

УРОК 10

БИОГРАФИЯ

▼ **КОММУНИКАТИВНЫЕ ЗАДАНИЯ**

Talking more about yourself and
your family
Telling where your city is located
Reading and listening to short
biographies
Giving an oral presentation
on a Russian cultural figure

▼ **В ПОМОЩЬ УЧАЩИМСЯ**

Expressing resemblance: **похо́ж (-а, -и)
на кого́,**
Comparing ages: **моло́же/ста́рше кого́
на ско́лько лет**
Expressing location: **на ю́ге (се́вере,
восто́ке, за́паде) (от) чего́**
Entering and graduating from school:
**поступа́ть/поступи́ть
око́нчить**
Time expressions: **В како́м году́,
че́рез, наза́д**
Verbal aspect: past tense
Е́здил vs. **пое́хал**
Present tense in "have been doing"
constructions

Workbook: IC–4 in questions
asking for additional
information

▼ **МЕЖДУ ПРОЧИМ**

Location of some major Russian cities
Russian educational system
Andrei Dmitrievich Sakharov

Точка отсчёта

О ЧЁМ ИДЁТ РЕЧЬ?

In previous units, you learned to talk about yourself, your family, and where you live. In this unit, you will review these topics and learn to talk in more detail about your background and family relationships.

A. **На кого́ вы похо́жи?**

— Это моя́ сестра́.
— Слу́шай, ты **о́чень похо́ж на сестру́.**

— Это мой оте́ц.
— Слу́шай, ты **о́чень похо́жа на отца́.**

— Это на́ша мать.
— Слу́шайте, вы **о́чень похо́жи на мать.**

Practice telling your partner who resembles whom in your family by combining elements from the columns below. Then switch roles. Note that the nouns in the righthand column are in the accusative case.

	ба́бушку
Я похо́ж(а) на …	де́душку
Сестра́ похо́жа на …	мать
Брат похо́ж на …	отца́
Оте́ц похо́ж на …	бра́та
Мать похо́жа на …	сестру́
	дя́дю
	тётю

В. Моло́же и́ли ста́рше?

Это мой мла́дший брат.
Он моло́же меня́ на́ год.

А э́то моя́ мла́дшая сестра́.
Она́ моло́же меня́ на два го́да.

Вот э́то мой ста́рший брат.
Он ста́рше меня́ на три го́да.

И наконе́ц, это моя́ ста́ршая сестра́.
Она́ ста́рше меня́ на пять лет.

With a partner, practice comparing the ages of people in your family by combining elements from the columns below. Note that **моло́же** and **ста́рше** do not change their form to agree with the subject, and that the person mentioned second is in the genitive case.

я		меня́		год
брат		его́		два го́да
сестра́	ста́рше	её		три го́да
мать	моло́же	бра́та	на	четы́ре го́да
оте́ц		сестры́		пять лет
		ма́тери		два́дцать лет
		отца́		два́дцать оди́н год

Разгово́р 1: У Ча́рлза в гостя́х
(Разгова́ривают Же́ня, Лю́да и Чарлз)

1. Luda says that she is from Irkutsk. Charles is not sure where Irkutsk is located. What is his guess?
2. According to Luda, in what part of Russia is Irkutsk in fact located?
3. Where was Luda born?
4. Where did she go to college?
5. How long did she work after graduating from college?
6. At what university will she be doing graduate work?

Ме́жду про́чим

УЧЁНЫЕ СТЕПЕНИ

Competition for entrance into Russian institutions of higher learning is intense. One who has graduated (**око́нчил университе́т, институ́т**) receives a **дипло́м**. Admission to graduate school (**аспиранту́ра**) is even more limited. To be eligible for the next degree (**кандида́тская сте́пень**), one must pass exams and write a dissertation. The highest degree (**до́кторская сте́пень**) requires years of research experience, published works, and a published dissertation.

Law and medical degrees are taken at the undergraduate, not graduate, level.

Разгово́р 2: По́сле обе́да
(Разгова́ривают Чарлз и Лю́да)

1. How old is Charles' sister?
2. Where does she go to college?
3. How much older than Charles is his brother?
4. Where does Charles' brother work?

Разгово́р 3: Америка́нцы ча́сто переезжа́ют.
(Разгова́ривают Чарлз и Лю́да)

1. How old was Charles when his family moved to Denver?
2. In what state did his family live before that?
3. Where did his family move after five years in Denver?
4. Based on this conversation, what do you think the verb **переезжа́ть/перее́хать** means?

ДИАЛОГИ

study... Friday they will be graded.

1 Я поступа́ла в аспиранту́ру, но не поступи́ла.

— Здра́вствуй, Дэн! Познако́мься, э́то моя́ знако́мая Ка́тя.

— Очень прия́тно, Ка́тя!

— Ка́тя прие́хала из Перми́. Это на восто́ке от Москвы́.

— Как интере́сно! А вы роди́лись в Перми́?

— Нет, я вы́росла в Смоле́нске. Но учи́лась в Перми́.
Три го́да наза́д я око́нчила университе́т. Я поступа́ла
в аспиранту́ру, но не поступи́ла.

— Да. Я слы́шал, что у вас о́чень тру́дно попа́сть
в аспиранту́ру.

— Ну вот. И я пошла́ рабо́тать. Рабо́тала два го́да,
а пото́м поступи́ла в Моско́вский университе́т.

2 Дава́й перейдём на «ты»!

— Дэн, я ви́жу, что у тебя́ на столе́ фотогра́фии лежа́т.
Это семья́?

— Да. Хоти́те, покажу́?

— Дэн, дава́й перейдём на «ты».

— Хорошо́, дава́й! Вот э́то фотогра́фия сестры́.

— Она́ о́чень похо́жа на тебя́. Ско́лько ей лет?

— Два́дцать. Она́ моло́же меня́ на два го́да.

— Она́ у́чится?

— Да, в Калифорни́йском университе́те. Она́ око́нчит
университе́т че́рез год.

> When referring to one's own family there is no need to use possessive pronouns.

3 Кто э́то на фотогра́фии?

— Кто э́то на фотогра́фии?

— Это я три го́да наза́д.

— Не мо́жет быть!

— Пра́вда, пра́вда. Мы тогда́ жи́ли
в Теха́се.

— Ты тогда́ учи́лся в шко́ле?

— Да, в деся́том кла́ссе.

— Вы до́лго жи́ли в Теха́се?

— Нет, всего́ два го́да. Мы перее́хали,
когда́ я был в оди́ннадцатом кла́ссе.

> ### ОБРАЗОВАНИЕ
>
> Remember that Russian universities and institutes have 5, not 4, classes (**ку́рсы**). The students are called **студе́нт/студе́нтка**. Russian schools have 11, not 12, grades (**кла́ссы**). The pupils are called **шко́льник/шко́льница** or **учени́к/учени́ца**. Graduate school is **аспиранту́ра**. Graduate students are called **аспира́нт/аспира́нтка**.

4 **Американцы ча́сто переезжа́ют?**

— Ребе́кка, а э́то пра́вда, что америка́нцы ча́сто переезжа́ют?
— Да. Мы, наприме́р, переезжа́ли ча́сто. Когда́ мне бы́ло 10 лет, мы перее́хали в Кли́вленд.
— А до э́того?
— До э́того мы жи́ли в Чика́го.
— А пото́м?
— А пото́м че́рез пять лет мы перее́хали из Кли́вленда в Да́ллас.
— А у нас переезжа́ют ре́дко. Вот я роди́лся, вы́рос и учи́лся в Москве́.

5 **Отку́да вы?**

— Здра́вствуйте! Дава́йте познако́мимся. Меня́ зову́т Наза́рова Наде́жда Анато́льевна. Пожа́луйста, расскажи́те о себе́. Как вас зову́т? Отку́да вы?
— Меня́ зову́т Мише́ль. Я из Нью-Хэ́мпшира.
— Нью-Хэ́мпшир, ка́жется, на за́паде Аме́рики?
— Нет, на восто́ке.
— А вы живёте у роди́телей?
— Нет, ма́ма и па́па живу́т в друго́м шта́те, во Флори́де, на ю́ге страны́.

А. **Немно́го о семье́.**

1. In five minutes, find out as much as you can from your classmates about who resembles whom in their families, by asking questions such as the following in Russian. Jot down what you learn, and be prepared to report several facts to the entire class.

Ты похо́ж(а) на ма́му и́ли на па́пу?
Твои́ бра́тья и сёстры похо́жи
　　на роди́телей?
Кто похо́ж на твоего́ де́душку?
Кто похо́ж на тебя́?

◄ Here are four accusative animate plurals you might find helpful as you discuss your family:

Он похо́ж на **бра́тьев.**
Она́ похо́жа на **сестёр.**
Кто похо́ж на **дете́й?**
Де́ти похо́жи на **роди́телей.**

2. Find out from your classmates how old they and their siblings are and what year of school they are in. Be ready to report your findings to the class. Be sure to use **в (-ом) кла́ссе** for grades in grade school and high school, and **на (-ом) ку́рсе** for year in college or university.

B. **Отку́да вы?**

— Са́ра, отку́да вы?
— **Я из Ло́ндона.**

— Джим, отку́да вы?
— **Я из Та́мпы.**

— Ребя́та, отку́да вы?
— **Мы из Торо́нто.**

How would you ask the following people where they are from?

1. преподава́тель
2. большо́й друг
3. мать подру́ги
4. делега́ция Моско́вского университе́та

Find out where your classmates are from and jot down their answers. Everyone asks and answers at the same time. The first person to be able to tell where everyone is from wins. Note that the word following **из** is in the genitive case.

C. **Родно́й го́род.** Just as most Europeans and Americans would not know the location of **Хи́мки,** a major Moscow suburb familiar to many Russians, Russians may not know the location of your hometown. If you are not from a major city like New York, London, or Montreal, you will need to provide more than the name of your hometown. Here are some ways to do this.

Я из Са́нта-Мо́ники.

Это го́род **в шта́те Калифо́рния.**
Это го́род **на ю́ге Калифо́рнии.**
Это **при́город Лос-Анджелеса.**
Это го́род **на за́паде от Лос-Анджелеса.**

It is important to provide a context for references to points of the compass. **На за́паде США (Аме́рики)** = in the western part of the U.S. (America); **на за́паде от Кли́вленда** = west of Cleveland. If you leave out the context, most Russian listeners will assume you are speaking about the concepts "the West" or "the East" in broad general terms.

1. Practice telling in what states the following cities are located.

   Олбани, Ли́тл-Рок, Атла́нта, Та́мпа, Сан-Анто́нио, Балтимо́р, Анн-Арбор, Сэнт-Лу́ис

2. Using the model below, say where the following U.S. states are located.

   Образе́ц: Калифо́рния на за́паде Аме́рики.

   Орего́н, Мэн, Нева́да, Флори́да, Миннесо́та, Мэ́риленд, Вермо́нт, Теха́с, Виско́нсин

3. Using the model below, indicate where the following cities are in relation to Moscow. Consult the map if necessary.

   Образе́ц: — Где Яросла́вль?   — Он на се́вере от Москвы́.

   Ки́ев, Санкт-Петербу́рг, Калинингра́д,
   Арха́нгельск, Тбили́си, Ри́га, Ерева́н,
   Ирку́тск, Смоле́нск

4. Now, working in small groups, practice telling where you are from. Choose one or more of the alternative structures given in the examples to provide more exact information.

Язык в действии

ДАВАЙТЕ ПОГОВОРИМ

A. **Подготóвка к разговóру.** Review the dialogs. How would you do the following?

- introduce someone
- say where you were born (grew up)
- ask where someone was born (grew up, went to college)
- say you applied to college
- say you entered college
- say that you graduated from college one (two, four) years ago
- say that you worked (lived) somewhere for two (three, five) years
- suggest switching to **ты** with someone
- say that someone's sister resembles him/her
- say that your sister (brother) is two years younger (older) than you
- say that you will graduate in one (three) years
- say that your family moved somewhere (e.g., New York)
- say that you moved somewhere (e.g., Texas) when you were ten (thirteen)
- say that your family moved often (seldom)
- say that you moved from New York to Boston

B. **Игровы́е ситуа́ции.**

1. You are in Russia on an exchange program and your group has been invited to a let's-get-acquainted meeting with Russian students. To get things started, everyone has been asked to say a little bit about themselves.

2. You are at a party in Russia and are anxious to meet new people. Strike up a conversation with someone at the party and make as much small talk as you can.

3. You were at a Russian friend's house and met someone who spoke English extremely well. Ask your friend about that person's background to find out how s/he learned English so well.

4. At a school in Russia, you have been asked to talk to students about getting into college in your country. Tell about your own experience.

5. Working with a partner, prepare and act out a situation of your own that deals with the topics of this unit.

C. **Устный перевод.** A Russian friend has come to visit your family. Everyone is interested in your friend's background. Serve as the interpreter.

English speaker's part

1. Sasha, are you from Moscow?
2. Vladivostok is in the north, isn't it?
3. Were you born there?
4. And you're in Moscow now? Where do you go to school?
5. Where did you stay?
6. When will you graduate?
7. So in two years, right?

D. **О семье.** With a partner, have a conversation in Russian in which you find out the following information about each other's families.

- names, ages, and birthplaces of family members
- where family members went to college
- whether the family has moved often
- where the family has lived

E. **О себе.** With a new partner, take turns telling each other as much as you can about yourself and your family in two minutes. Then, to work on fluency, repeat the exercise and try to condense the same information into a minute.

F. **Двадцать вопросов.** One person in the group thinks of a famous contemporary person. The others ask up to twenty yes-no questions to figure out the person's identity. For example, one might ask: **Вы мужчи́на?** (*man*)? **Вы же́нщина** (*woman*)? **Вы роди́лись в Росси́и? Вы америка́нец? Вы писа́тель?**

ДАВАЙТЕ ПОЧИТАЕМ

A. **На́ши а́вторы.** Here is a reference listing of famous Russian authors. Read through it and find answers to the following questions:

1. What is the purpose of this article?
2. Complete the following chart with information from the passage.

Author	Birth place and year	Education (if given)	Place of residence

3. How many of the authors listed are women?
4. How many of the authors listed are still alive?
5. Which author has a famous father?
6. Which authors have a scientific background?
7. Two of the authors are also translators (**перево́дчики**). Can you identify them and indicate what languages they translate from?
8. **СП= Сою́з писа́телей,** Union of Writers. From context, what do you think **член** means?

НАШИ АВТОРЫ

ПАНОВА ВЕРА ФЁДОРОВНА. Родилась в 1905 году в Ростове-на-Дону. Начинала как драматург. Среди самых известных произведений—повесть «Серёжа», романы «Времена года», «Сентиментальный роман», кинофильмы «Поезд милосердия». Лауреат государственных и международных премий. Скончалась в 1973 в Ленинграде.

ЧУКОВСКАЯ ЛИДИЯ КОРНЕЕВНА— дочь известного писателя и литературоведа Корнея Ивановича Чуковского — родилась в Петербурге. Автор книг: «Декабристы — исследователи Сибири», «Борис Житков», «В лаборатории редактора» и других произведений. Живет в Москве.

СОЛОУХИН ВЛАДИМИР АЛЕКСЕЕВИЧ. Родился в 1924 году в Ставровском районе Владимирской области. Окончил Литаратурный институт им. Горького. Автор многих книг прозы и поэзии. Главная тема Солоухина—Родина и родная природа. Награжден орденом «Знак почета» и другими премиями. Член СП. Живет в Москве.

АБРАМОВ ФЕДОР АЛЕКСАНДРОВИЧ. Родился в 1920 в Ленинграде. Окончил филологический факультет ЛГУ. В 50-е годы служил заведующим кафедрой советской литературы ЛГУ. Автор тетралогии «Пряслины», сборника «Деревянные кони» и других произведений. Лауреат Государственной премии. Член СП. Скончался в 1983 году.

АМУСИН МАРК ФОМИЧ. Родился в 1948 году в Ленинграде. Окончил Ленинградский электротехнический институт связи имени Бонч-Бруевича. Литературно-критические статьи публикует с 1979 года. Живет в Ленинграде.

ЧЕЖЕГОВА ИННА МИХАЙЛОВНА. Родилась в Ленинграде. В 1954 году окончила филологический факультет ЛГУ. Поэт-переводчик с английского, французского, испанского и португальского языков, автор исследований в области латино-американской литературы. Член СП. Живет в Ленинграде.

ДОНСКОЙ МИХАИЛ АЛЕКСАНДРОВИЧ. Родился в 1913 году в Петербурге. Окончил математико-механический факультет ЛГУ в 1937 году. Кандидат физико-математических наук. Переводчик поэзии и драматургии с английского, французского, испанского языков, автор работ по теории художественного перевода. Член СП. Живет в Ленинграде.

You are about to hear two short biographies. The first is about Dr. Martin Luther King, and the other is about Andrei Dmitrievich Sakharov.

You probably know that both became famous for their defense of human rights. How much more do you know? Most Russians have heard about King, but are unfamiliar with the details of his life. Similarly, many Americans have a vague notion of who Sakharov was, but know little more.

You are not expected to understand either of the passages word for word. However, keeping in mind the background knowledge you already possess and listening for key phrases will allow you to get the main ideas.

For both passages you will need these new words:

> права—rights:
> защи́та гражда́нских прав—defense of civil rights
> защи́та прав челове́ка—defense of human rights
> расшире́ние экономи́ческих прав—expansion of economic rights
> вопро́с прав челове́ка—problem of human rights
> де́ятельность—activity
> обще́ственная де́ятельность—public activity
> полити́ческая де́ятельность—political activity

A. **Ма́ртин Лю́тер Кинг**

1. List five things you know about King. Then check to see whether any of them are mentioned in the biography.

2. Listen to the passage again. Pay special attention to the cognates below. Can you identify them? (Note the words in this list are given in the nominative singular. They may appear in other forms in the passage. Do not let the unfamiliar endings throw you off!)

> семина́рия
> бойко́т городско́го тра́нспорта
> бапти́стский па́стор
> ра́совая гармо́ния

3. Listen to the passage once again, paying special attention to the following phrases. Then use context to figure out the meanings of the underlined words.

> филосо́фия ненаси́льственности Га́нди
> Но́белевская пре́мия Ми́ра
> война́ во Вьетна́ме
> «У меня́ есть мечта́».

B. **Андре́й Дми́триевич Са́харов**

1. Before listening to the passage, read the following new words aloud.

   ми́рное сосуществова́ние—peaceful coexistence
   свобо́да—freedom
   свобо́да мышле́ния—freedom of thought
   он был лишён конта́кта—he was deprived of contact
   Съезд наро́дных депута́тов—Congress of People's Deputies
   у́мер—he died (Note: он у́мер, она́ умерла́, они́ у́мерли.)

2. How much do you already know about Sakharov? If the name is unfamiliar, look up Sakharov in a recent encyclopedia. Then, armed with that background knowledge, listen to the passage with these questions in mind.

   a. When was Sakharov born?
   b. What sort of work did he do when he was young?
   c. What sorts of questions did Sakharov become concerned with later?
   d. What award did Sakharov receive in 1975?
   e. Sakharov was exiled from his home in Moscow to the city of Gorky (now called Nizhniy Novgorod) for seven years. Name one of the things he managed to do while in exile.
   f. In what year was Sakharov elected as a delegate to the Congress of People's Deputies?
   g. When did Sakharov die?

3. Use context to figure out the meaning of the underlined words.

   Он защити́л кандида́тскую диссерта́цию.
   термоя́дерная реа́кция
   конта́кт с за́падными корреспонде́нтами

В ПОМОЩЬ УЧАЩИМСЯ

10.1 GRAMMATICAL ENVIRONMENT

Learning a language means not only learning words, because just stringing words together does not always produce sentences. You must also learn how the words are related to one another in sentences. Many Russian words are always used with a particular preposition and/or a particular case; that is, they always have a particular environment. When learning such words, you must learn their environment as well.

In this textbook, as in many Russian dictionaries, the environment for such words is shown by listing the prepositions and the question words **кто** and **что** in the required case. If you do not know the various forms of the question words, consult the table on page 245.

Expressing resemblance: похо́ж на кого́

The word **похо́ж (похо́жа, похо́жи)** is always used with the preposition **на** followed by the accusative case.

Сын похо́ж **на отца́.**   Дочь похо́жа **на ба́бушку.**   Де́ти похо́жи **на мать.**

Упражнения

1. Use the correct form of the words in parentheses.

а. — На (кто) похо́ж Анто́н?
— Он похо́ж на (брат).

б. — На (кто) похо́жа Анна?
— Она́ похо́жа на (оте́ц).

в. — На (кто) похо́ж Гри́ша?
— Он похо́ж на (ма́ма).

г. — На (кто) похо́жи твои́ бра́тья?
— Они́ похо́жи на (па́па).

д. — На (кто) похо́жа Со́ня?
— Она́ похо́жа на (сестра́).

е. — На (кто) похо́ж Ви́тя?
— Он похо́ж на (сёстры).

ж. — На (кто) похо́жа Ла́ра?
— Она́ похо́жа на (бра́тья).

з. — На (кто) похо́жи де́ти?
— Они́ похо́жи на (роди́тели).

2. How would you express the following in Russian? Don't translate the words in brackets.

   a. Vanya looks like [his] brother.
   b. Katya and Tanya look like [their] parents. That means Katya looks like Tanya.
   c. "Whom do you look like?"
      "My mother thinks I look like her, but my father thinks I look like him."

➤ Complete Oral Drills 1–2 and Written Exercise 1 in the Workbook.

Comparing ages: ста́рше/моло́же кого́ на ско́лько лет

Whereas English uses the preposition *than* in comparisons, Russian uses the genitive case. To indicate the age difference, use **на** followed by the time expression (1 год, 2-4 го́да, 5-20 лет).

Оте́ц ста́рше ма́тери на пять лет.	My father is five years older than my mother.
Сестра́ моло́же бра́та на три го́да.	My sister is three years younger than my brother.

Упражнение

3. Make truthful and grammatically correct sentences by combining words from the columns below. Do not change word order, but remember to put the nouns after **моло́же** and **ста́рше** in the genitive case. Use the proper form of **год** after the numbers.

па́па		я	1	год
ма́ма		па́па		
сестра́		ма́ма	2	
брат		сестра́	3	го́да
ба́бушка		брат	4	
де́душка	моло́же	ба́бушка	на	
сосе́д	ста́рше	де́душка	5	
сосе́дка		сосе́д	10	лет
друг		сосе́дка	50	
двою́родный брат		дя́дя		

➤ Complete Oral Drills 3–4 and Written Exercise 2 in the Workbook.

Expressing location: на ю́ге/се́вере/восто́ке/за́паде (от) чего́

The points of the compass are **на** words. To provide a context, use either **от** + the genitive case, or the genitive case alone. The above illustrations show the difference in meaning between these two structures.

Упражнения

4. Make truthful and grammatically accurate sentences by combining words from the columns below. Do not change word order or add extra words, but do put the words in the last column in the genitive case. (The genitive case of **США** looks and sounds the same as the nominative case. Like all abbreviations that are pronounced as letters, it is indeclinable.)

Атла́нта			
Владивосто́к		се́вере	Кана́да
Ванку́вер		ю́ге	Росси́я
Монреа́ль	на	за́паде	США
Санкт-Петербу́рг		восто́ке	
Сан-Франци́ско			

5. Make truthful and grammatically accurate sentences by combining words from the columns below. Do not change word order or add extra words, but do put the words following the preposition **от** in the genitive case.

Берли́н				Берли́н
Бонн		се́вере		Бонн
Ло́ндон		ю́ге		Ло́ндон
Мадри́д	на	за́паде	от	Мадри́д
Осло		восто́ке		Осло
Пари́ж				Пари́ж
Хе́льсинки				Хе́льсинки

➤ Complete Written Exercise 3 in the Workbook.

10.2 ENTERING AND GRADUATING FROM SCHOOL: *ПОСТУПА́ТЬ/ ПОСТУПИ́ТЬ, ОКО́НЧИТЬ*

Ка́тя говори́т: «Три го́да наза́д я **око́нчила университе́т. Я поступа́ла в** аспиранту́ру, но не **поступи́ла**».

As with many Russian verbs, it is important to learn the grammatical environment for **око́нчить** and **поступа́ть/поступи́ть,** because the Russian structures differ from their English equivalents.

поступа́ть/поступи́ть $\left\{\begin{array}{l}\text{в институ́т} \\ \text{в университе́т} \\ \text{в аспиранту́ру}\end{array}\right.$

око́нчить $\left\{\begin{array}{l}\text{шко́лу} \\ \text{институ́т} \\ \text{университе́т} \\ \text{аспиранту́ру}\end{array}\right.$

Упражне́ния

6. Fill in the blanks with the preposition **в** where needed.

   а. Ма́ша уже́ око́нчила _____ шко́лу.
   б. Когда́ она́ посту́пит _____ университе́т?
   в. Когда́ Са́ша око́нчит _____ университе́т, он посту́пит _____ аспиранту́ру?
   г. Вы не зна́ете, когда́ он око́нчит _____ аспиранту́ру?

7. How would you express the following in Russian?

   a. Masha graduated from school and entered the university.
   b. When did she finish high school?
   c. When will she graduate from college?
   d. Will she go to graduate school?

➤ Complete Oral Drills 7–9 and Written Exercise 4.

10.3 INDICATING THE YEAR IN WHICH AN EVENT TAKES (TOOK) PLACE: *В КАКОМ ГОДУ?*

To answer the question **В како́м году́?** (*In what year?*), Russian uses **в** followed by the prepositional case of the ordinal number, plus **году́** (which is a special prepositional case form of **год**).

> — **В како́м году́** вы бы́ли в Евро́пе?
> — Мы там бы́ли **в се́мьдесят тре́тьем году́.**

If the year is a compound number, only the last word in the number will have the prepositional (**-ом**) adjective ending. If context makes the century clear, the "19" or "18" may be omitted.

в	(ты́сяча девятьсо́т) (ты́сяча восемьсо́т)	два́дцать три́дцать со́рок пятьдеся́т шестьдеся́т се́мьдесят во́семьдесят девяно́сто	пе́рвом второ́м тре́тьем четвёртом пя́том шесто́м седьмо́м восьмо́м девя́том	году́

If the year is not a compound but rather one of the "tens," it may have a different stress and/or an additional syllable not present in the cardinal number.

в	(ты́сяча девятьсо́т) (ты́сяча восемьсо́т)	деся́том двадца́том тридца́том сороково́м пятидеся́том шестидеся́том семидеся́том восьмидеся́том девяно́стом	году́

What you need to be able to do:

LISTENING. You should be able to understand the years when they are spoken at normal speed.

WRITING. Only rarely are years written out as words. It is more common to abbreviate as follows: **Мы бы́ли в Евро́пе в 74-ом году́.** Note that the prepositional ending and either the abbreviation **г.** or the word **году́** are written, even when the year is written as numerals rather than as words. You should be able to do this.

SPEAKING. You should learn to pronounce with confidence the correct answers to the following questions:

> В како́м году́ вы родили́сь?
> В како́м году́ родили́сь ва́ши роди́тели?
> В како́м году́ родили́сь ва́ши бра́тья и сёстры?
> В како́м году́ родила́сь ва́ша жена́ (роди́лся ваш муж)?
> В како́м году́ родили́сь ва́ши де́ти?

Strategy: If you are asked other **Когда́?** or **В како́м году́?** questions, you will probably find it easier to answer them using **че́рез** or **наза́д** (See 10.4).

Упражнение

8. Read the following sentences aloud.

   а. Пе́тя роди́лся в 1989-ом г.
   б. А́ля родила́сь в 1972-ом г.
   в. И́ра родила́сь в 1990-ом г.
   г. Ва́ня роди́лся в 1980-ом г.
   д. Вади́м поступи́л в университе́т в 1993-ем г.
   е. Кса́на око́нчила университе́т в 1994-ом г.

➤ Review *Числительные* in the Workbook; Complete Oral Drill 10 and Written Exercise 7 in the Workbook.

10.4 TIME EXPRESSIONS WITH *ЧЕРЕЗ* AND *НАЗАД*

To indicate that something took place (or will take place) after a certain amount of time, use **чéрез** followed by the time expression.

Оля сказáла, что онá приготóвит обéд в 6 часóв. Сейчáс 4 часá. Знáчит онá приготóвит обéд **чéрез** 2 часá.

чéрез	час 2-4 часá 5-20 часóв (зáвтра) 2-4 дня 5-20 дней недéлю 2-4 недéли 5-20 недéль мéсяц 2-4 мéсяца 5-20 мéсяцев год 2-4 гóда 5-20 лет

> однá недéля=семь дней
> одúн мéсяц=четы́ре недéли

To indicate that something took place a certain amount of time ago, use the time expression followed by **назáд**.

Сейчáс 6 часóв. Пéтя пришёл в 4 часá. Знáчит он пришёл 2 часá **назáд**.

час 2-4 часá 5-20 часóв (вчерá) 2-4 дня 5-20 дней недéлю 2-4 недéли 5-20 недéль мéсяц 2-4 мéсяца 5-20 мéсяцев год 2-4 гóда 5-20 лет	**назáд**

Упражнения

9. How would you express the following in Russian?

Alla graduated from high school a week ago. In three months she'll start university. *Алла окончила школу*

10. Answer the following questions truthfully, using time expressions from the table on the previous page. Pay attention to the tense of the verbs.

    а. Когда́ вы поступи́ли в университе́т?
    б. Когда́ вы око́нчите университе́т?
    в. Когда́ вы посту́пите в аспиранту́ру?
    г. Когда́ ва́ши бра́тья и сёстры око́нчили шко́лу?
    д. Когда́ вы е́дете в Росси́ю?
    е. Когда́ вы е́здили в Нью-Йо́рк?
    ж. Когда́ вы ходи́ли в кино́?

➤ Complete Oral Drill 11 and Written Exercise 8 in the Workbook.

10.5 VERBAL ASPECT—PAST TENSE

The difference in meaning between imperfective and perfective verbs in the future applies to the past tense as well. Perfective verbs refer to complete one-time actions, normally of short duration or with a result that is being emphasized. Imperfective verbs, on the other hand, are used when the action itself, and not its completion or end result is emphasized. Imperfective verbs are also used to describe actions in progress, or actions that are repeated frequently. All verbs, perfective and imperfective, take the usual past tense endings: **-л, -ла, -ло, -ли.**

REPEATED ACTIONS: *imperfective verbs*

If the action described took place more than once, it is expressed with an imperfective verb. Often the repetitive nature of the action is signalled by an adverb such as **всегда, всё время, обычно, часто, редко, каждый день,** or **раньше.**

> Когда Ваня был в Америке, он каждый день **читал** газету.
> Когда я училась в институте, я редко **отдыхала.** Я всё время **занималась.**

Note

Sometimes English signals repetition by *used to*: *used to read, used to rest*, etc. Such *used to* expressions are always imperfective in Russian.

Упражнение

11. Which of these sentences requires an imperfective verb because the action is repeated?

    а. Когда Женя училась в Вашингтоне, она каждый день
       (**слушала/послушала**) радио.
    б. Мы раньше (**покупали/купили**) газеты на русском языке.
    в. Серафима Денисовна, вы уже (**писали/написали**) письмо директору?
    г. Мама всё время (**говорила/сказала**) ребёнку, что не надо опаздывать.
    д. Извините, что вы (**говорили/сказали**)? Я вас не расслышала.
    е. Ваня, почему ты сегодня (**опаздывал/опоздал**) на урок? Ты ведь раньше
       не (**опаздывал/опоздал**).

ONE-TIME ACTIONS

Both perfective and imperfective verbs can be used to convey one-time actions. However, as you will see below, perfective verbs are used to emphasize the *result* of an action.

a. Emphasis on result: *perfective verbs*

The people answering the questions in the captioned pictures below emphasize that they have completed the one-time actions by using perfective verbs.

— Мо́жно? Или вы ещё
пи́шете?
— Нет, уже́ всё **написа́л.**
Пожа́луйста.

— Яи́чницу бу́дешь?
— Нет, спаси́бо. Я уже́
поза́втракала.

— Вы ещё чита́ете газе́ту?
— Я её уже́ **прочита́л.**
Бери́те.

b. Lack of emphasis on result: *imperfective verbs*

Sometimes an action is complete and has a result, but the speaker does not emphasize its completion or result. In such cases, imperfective verbs are used. This is most common with verbs denoting extended activities, such as **чита́ть, слу́шать, смотре́ть, де́лать,** etc.

— Что ты вчера́ де́лал?
— Я **отдыха́л, смотре́л** телеви́зор.

> The question "What did so-and-so do?" is always imperfective.

— Ты чита́ла «Отцо́в и дете́й»?
— Да, чита́ла в про́шлом году́.

> The speaker is interested in whether this activity has ever taken place, not whether it was completed.

Упражнение

12. Are the boldfaced verbs perfective or imperfective? Why?

а. — Та́ня, ты хо́чешь есть?
— Нет, спаси́бо. Я уже́ **пообе́дала.**

б. — Ви́тя, где ты был вчера́ ве́чером?
— Я был в це́нтре. **Обе́дал** в но́вом рестора́не.

в. — Что вы **де́лали** вчера́?
— Мы **занима́лись.**

г. — Воло́дя ещё **пока́зывает** сла́йды?
— Нет, уже́ всё **показа́л.** Мо́жет быть, он тебе́ пока́жет их за́втра.

д. — Ты **чита́ла** «Анну Каре́нину»?
— Да, я её **чита́ла,** когда́ ещё учи́лась в институ́те.

е. В сре́ду Анна **купи́ла** но́вое пла́тье.

ж. Мы до́лго **чита́ли** э́тот рома́н. Наконе́ц мы его́ **прочита́ли.**

з. — Что вы **де́лали** в суббо́ту?

Duration. Imperfective verbs are used when the speaker focuses on the length of time an action took place. Often this is conveyed through the use of time expressions such as **весь день, всё у́тро, три часа́.** English allows speakers to focus on process through the use of the past progressive (for example, *was buying, were doing*). Such expressions in the past progressive are always imperfective in Russian.

Мы весь день **покупа́ли** проду́кты.

Студе́нты **де́лали** уро́ки всю ночь.

Упражнение

13. Pick the best Russian equivalent for the verbs in the sentences below.

   а. Some students *were playing cards* all night. (**игра́ли в ка́рты/ сыгра́ли в ка́рты**)
   Others *read* their assignments for the next day. (**чита́ли/прочита́ли**)

   б. Do you want to get something to eat? Or have you already *had lunch*? (**обе́дали/пообе́дали**)

   в. Some students spent the hour *eating lunch.* (**обе́дали/пообе́дали**)

   г. "Did your parents *manage to order* the plane tickets yesterday?" (**зака́зывали/заказа́ли**)
   "Yes, they spent all morning *ordering* those tickets." (**зака́зывали/заказа́ли**)

   д. "Did you *manage to write* your term paper?" (**писа́ли/написа́ли**)
   "Yes, but I *wrote* all night." (**писа́л(а)/написа́л(а)**)

   е. We spent four hours *fixing* dinner. (**гото́вили/пригото́вили**)

c. Consecutive vs. simultaneous events

Мы **прочита́ли** газе́ту и **поза́втракали.**

We read the paper and then had breakfast.

Мы **чита́ли** газе́ту и **за́втракали.**

We were reading the paper while we were having breakfast.

Since one action must be finished before the next can begin in a series of events, perfective verbs are usually used to describe a series of complete, one-time actions that took place one after the other.

Two or more actions occurring simultaneously are normally described with imperfective verbs.

---

14. For each sentence, indicate whether the events occurred at the same time or one after the other.

    а. Мы поýжинали, пошли́ в кино́ и посмотре́ли фильм.

    б. Когда́ мы поýжинали, мы пошли́ в кино́.

    в. Мы ýжинали и смотре́ли фильм.

    г. Когда́ мы ýжинали, мы смотре́ли фильм.

    д. Когда́ мы поýжинали, мы посмотре́ли фильм.

    е. Мы купи́ли проду́кты, пошли́ домо́й и пригото́вили обе́д.

    ж. Когда́ мы купи́ли проду́кты, мы пошли́ домо́й.

    з. Когда́ мы покупа́ли проду́кты, мы говори́ли о фи́льме.

d. Different meanings

In some instances imperfective and perfective Russian verb partners have different English equivalents.

Анна **поступа́ла** в аспиранту́ру, но не **поступи́ла.**
Anna *applied* to graduate school, but *did not enroll (get in).*

Анна и Вади́м до́лго **реша́ли**, что де́лать, и наконец **реши́ли.**
Anna and Vadim *considered* what to do for a long time, and finally *decided.*

The oral and written exercises in this unit give you a chance to learn and practice the perfective partners of a number of verbs you already know in the imperfective, as well as of a number of new verbs. Refer to the vocabulary list at the end of the unit.

15. Read Masha's description of what she did last night. Then help her complete it by selecting the most neutral verb choice for each pair of past tense verbs given. Pay attention to context.

Вчера́ ве́чером я (смотре́ла - посмотре́ла) телеви́зор. Я (смотре́ла - посмотре́ла) одну́ переда́чу, а пото́м пошла́ в центр. Там я до́лга (реша́ла - реши́ла) что де́лать. Наконе́ц я (реша́ла - реши́ла) пойти́ в кафе́. Там сиде́ли мои́ друзья́ Со́ня и Ко́стя. Ра́ньше мы ча́сто (обе́дали - пообе́дали) вме́сте, а тепе́рь мы ре́дко ви́дим друг дру́га. Мы до́лго (сиде́ли - посиде́ли) в кафе́, (обе́дали - пообе́дали), (спра́шивали - спроси́ли) друг дру́га об университе́те и о рабо́те, и (расска́зывали - рассказа́ли) о се́мьях. Когда́ мы обо всём уже́ (расска́зывали - рассказа́ли), мы (говори́ли - сказа́ли) «До свида́ния» и пошли́ домо́й. Я о́чень по́здно пришла́ домо́й.

➤ Complete Oral Drill 12 and Written Exercises 9–12 in the Workbook.

10.6   WENT—*ЕЗДИЛ* vs. *ПОЕХАЛ*

In references to a single trip that went beyond the borders of one city, *went* is normally expressed by **éздил** or **поéхал.**

In describing an entire trip that is already over, a form of **éздил** is used:

— Где былá Мáша?
— Онá **éздила** в Москвý.

В прóшлом годý Мáша **éздила** в Москвý.

A form of **поéхал** is used when the motion being described is in one direction, for example:

- the person has set out for a destination but has not returned:

    — Где Мáша?
    — Онá **поéхала** в Москвý.

- the speaker is focusing on the point of departure rather than on the entire trip:

    В суббóту мы **поéхали** в Москвý. Там мы вúдели интерéсные местá.

- the speaker mentions a trip in one direction as an element in a series of one-time actions:

    Мы купúли продýкты и **поéхали** на дáчу.

In Unit 8 we showed similar uses of **ходúл** and **пошёл,** which are normally used for trips within the confines of one city.

Упражнения

16. Pick the correct form of the verb based on the context of the sentence.

а. — Где родúтели?
    — Их нет. Онú (éздили-поéхали) на дáчу. Онú бýдут дóма вéчером.

б. — Анна былá в Сибúри?
    — Да, онá (éздила-поéхала) в Сибúрь мéсяц назáд. Хóчешь, онá тебé всё расскáжет.

в. — Где вы бы́ли год назáд?
    — Мы (éздили-поéхали) на юг отдыхáть.
    — Какúе местá вы вúдели?
    — Из Москвы́ мы (éздили-поéхали) в Сóчи. А из Сóчи мы (éздили-поéхали) в Волгогрáд. Потóм из Волгогрáда мы (éздили-поéхали) в Астрахань.

17. How would you express the following in Russian?

    a. "Where did you go last year?"
       "We went to New York."

    b. "Where is Pavel?"
       "He's gone to St. Petersburg."

    c. "Where was Anya this morning?"
       "She went to a lecture."

    d. "The students had dinner at a restaurant and went home."

Как давно = Сколько времени.

➤ Complete Written Exercise 13 in the Workbook.

10.7 *HAVE BEEN DOING*—PRESENT TENSE

Russian normally uses present-tense verbs for actions that began in the past and continue into the present:

Мы давно́ **живём** в Нью-Йо́рке.	*We have been living in New York for a long time.*
А мы здесь **живём** то́лько четы́ре ме́сяца.	*We've been living here for only four months.*

Сколько времени

Do not be tricked by your knowledge of English into using a past-tense verb for these constructions!

Упражнение

18. How would you express the following questions in Russian? How would you answer them?

Where do you live?
How long (ско́лько вре́мени) have you lived there?
How long have you been a student at this university?
How long have you been studying Russian?
What other foreign languages do you know?
How long have you studied … language?

➤ Complete Written Exercises 14–15 in the Workbook.

ОБЗОРНЫЕ УПРАЖНЕНИЯ

A. Разгово́р.

Дава́йте познако́мимся!
(Разгова́ривают Наде́жда Анато́льевна и её студе́нты).

1. Where does Jonathan go to school?
2. Where does Nadezhda Anatolievna think Indiana is?
3. Where do Jonathan's parents live now?
4. Where did they live before?

B. Интервью́. You have been asked to write a feature article for your local newspaper about a visiting Russian musician.

1. In preparation for the interview, write out the questions you plan to ask. The musician knows only Russian.

2. Compare your questions with those of at least one other class member. Help each other determine the appropriateness and accuracy of your questions.

3. Conduct the interview. Your teacher or a visitor will play the role of the musician. Be sure to take notes!

4. On the basis of your interview notes, write the newspaper article in English. This will allow you and your teacher to evaluate how much of the interview you were able to understand.

C. Выступле́ние. Consult a Russian encyclopedia.

1. Find basic information on one of the people listed below (e.g., where s/he was born, grew up, lived, and worked).

Никола́й Бердя́ев, Юрий Гага́рин, Алекса́ндр Ге́рцен, Ольга Кни́ппер, Алекса́ндра Коллонта́й, Наде́жда Кру́пская, Ве́ра Пано́ва, Ма́йя Плисе́цкая, Валенти́на Терешко́ва Лев Толсто́й, Пётр Чайко́вский Анто́н Че́хов

2. Present your findings to the class. Remember to use what you know, not what you don't.

3. Take notes as your classmates give their presentations.

D. **Перепи́ска.** Read the following letter to find answers to these questions.

1. To whom is this letter written?
2. In what newspaper did Larisa Ivanovna find out that the organization Carol heads was looking for Russian penpals?
3. What is Larisa Ivanovna's nationality?
4. Where does she live?
5. She mentions two things she loves. What are they?
6. What did she study at the university?
7. What is her daughter studying?
8. In what language does she want to correspond?

Дорогая Кэрол!

Из моей любимой газеты „Известия" я узнала, что члены Вашей организации хотят переписываться с русскими женщинами.

Несколько слов о себе: зовут меня Лариса, я грузинка, живу в Тбилиси, столице Грузии. Очень люблю свою родину - Грузию.

Мне 47 лет, окончила Тбилисский государственный университет, филологический факультет, замужем, дочь - студентка первого курса медицинского института.

К сожалению, я не владею английским языком. Если кто-либо из членов Вашей организации владеет русским, я бы хотела переписываться на русском языке. Если нет, то я найду себе переводчика. Главное, чтобы разборчиво писали.

С уважением,
Лариса Ивановна.

Answer Larisa Ivanovna's letter. Include as much information as you can about yourself and your family, as well as two or three questions about her.

НОВЫЕ СЛОВА И ВЫРАЖЕНИЯ

NOUNS

аспиранту́ра	graduate school
восто́к (на)	east
за́пад (на)	west
ка́ждый	every
класс (в)	class, year of study in grade school or high school
курс (на)	class, year of study in institution of higher education
ме́сяц (2-4 ме́сяца, 5 ме́сяцев)	month
неде́ля (2-4 неде́ли, 5 неде́ль)	week
при́город	suburb
се́вер (на)	north
страна́	country, nation
юг (на)	south

ADJECTIVES

друго́й	other, another
знако́мый	acquaintance, friend
моло́же *кого́ на … лет*	younger than someone by x years
похо́ж (-а, -и) *на кого́*	resemble, look like
ста́рше *кого́ на … лет*	older than someone by x years

VERBS

вы́расти (*perfective*) вы́рос, вы́росла, вы́росли (*past tense*)	to grow up
за́втракать/по- (за́втракаю, за́втракаешь, за́втракают)	to eat breakfast

зака́зывать/заказа́ть
    (зака́зываю, зака́зываешь, зака́зывают)
    (закажу́, зака́жешь, зака́жут)
	to order

обе́дать/по- (обе́даю, обе́даешь, обе́дают)	to have lunch
око́нчить (*perfective*) (око́нчу, око́нчишь, око́нчат)	to graduate from (*requires direct object*)

переезжа́ть/перее́хать *куда́*
    (переезжа́ю, переезжа́ешь, переезжа́ют)
    (перее́ду, перее́дешь, перее́дут)
	to move, to take up a new living place

писа́ть/на- (пишу́, пи́шешь, пи́шут)	to write
пойти́ рабо́тать *куда́* (*perfective*) (пойду́, пойдёшь, пойду́т)	to begin to work, to begin a job

пока́зывать/показа́ть
    (пока́зываю, пока́зываешь, пока́зывают)
    (покажу́, пока́жешь, пока́жут)
	to show

поступа́ть/поступи́ть *куда́*	to apply to, to enroll in
(поступа́ю, поступа́ешь, поступа́ют)	
(поступлю́, посту́пишь, посту́пят)	
приезжа́ть/прие́хать	to arrive (*by vehicle*)
(приезжа́ю, приезжа́ешь, приезжа́ют)	
(прие́ду, прие́дешь, прие́дут)	
расска́зывать/рассказа́ть	to tell, narrate
(расска́зываю, расска́зываешь, расска́зывают)	
(расскажу́, расска́жешь, расска́жут)	
реша́ть/реши́ть	to decide
(реша́ю, реша́ешь, реша́ют)	
(решу́, реши́шь, реша́т)	
слу́шать/про- *кого́/что*	to listen to
(слу́шаю, слу́шаешь, слу́шают)	
смотре́ть/по- (смотрю́, смо́тришь, смо́трят)	to watch
у́жинать/по- (у́жинаю, у́жинаешь, у́жинают)	to have dinner
чита́ть/про- (чита́ю, чита́ешь, чита́ют)	to read

ADVERBS

давно́ (+ *present tense verb*)	for a long time
до́лго (+ *past tense verb*)	for a long time
пото́м	then, afterwards
ре́дко	rarely
тогда́	then, at that time
ча́сто	frequently

PREPOSITIONS

из *чего́*	from
наза́д	ago
че́рез	in, after

PHRASES AND OTHER WORDS

В про́шлом году́	last year
Дава́й перейдём на ты.	Let's switch to **ты.**
до э́того	before that
ка́жется	it seems
на ю́ге (на се́вере, на восто́ке, на за́паде) страны́	in the south (north, east, west) of the country
Отку́да вы?	Where are you from?
Ребя́та!	Guys (*conversational term of address*)
у роди́телей	at (one's) parents' (house)

PERSONALIZED VOCABULARY

_____

_____

_____

_____

APPENDIX A

SPELLING RULES

The spelling rules account for the endings to be added to stems that end in "gagging sounds," or velars (**г, к, х**), and "choo-choo sounds," or obstruents (**ш, щ, ж, ч, ц**).

For words whose stem ends in one of these letters, do not worry about whether the stem is hard or soft. Rather, always attempt to add the basic ending, then apply the spelling rule if necessary.

Never break a spelling rule when adding endings to Russian verbs or nouns!

THE 8-LETTER SPELLING RULE

After the letters   **г к х   ш щ ж ч   ц**   do not write **-ю**, write **-у** instead
do not write **-я,** write **-а** instead

THE 7-LETTER SPELLING RULE

After the letters   **г к х   ш щ ж ч**   do not write **-ы**, write **-и** instead

THE 5-LETTER SPELLING RULE

After the letters   **ш щ ж ч   ц**   do not write **unaccented -о,**
write **-е** instead

Use

The 8-letter spelling rule is used in second-conjugation verbs.

The 7- and 5-letter spelling rules are used in the declension of modifiers and nouns.

APPENDIX B

NOUNS AND MODIFIERS: HARD VS. SOFT STEMS

Every Russian noun and modifier has either a *hard* (nonpalatalized) or a *soft* (palatalized) stem. When adding endings to hard-stem nouns and modifiers, always add the basic (hard) ending. When adding endings to soft-stem nouns and modifiers, always add the soft variant of the ending.

However, if the stem of a modifier or noun ends in one of the "gagging sounds" or velars (**г, к, х**), or one of the "choo-choo sounds" or obstruents (**ш, щ, ж, ч, ц**), do not worry about whether the stem is hard or soft. Rather, always attempt to add the basic ending, then apply the spelling rule if necessary (see Appendix A).

One can determine whether a noun or modifier stem is hard or soft by looking at the first letter in the word's ending. For the purposes of this discussion, **й** and **ь** are considered to be endings.

Hard Stems Have one of these letters or nothing as the first letter in the ending	Soft Stems Have one of these letters as the first letter in the ending
а	**я**
(э)* **о**	**е** **ё**
у	**ю**
ы	**и**
	ь **й**

*The letter **э** does not play a role in grammatical endings in Russian. In grammatical endings, the soft variants of **о** are **ё** (when accented) and **е** (when not accented).

APPENDIX C: DECLENSIONS

NOUNS

Masculine Singular

	Hard	Soft	
N	стол Ø	портфе́ль	музе́й
A	Inanimate like nominative; animate like genitive		
	стол Ø	музе́й	
	студе́нта	преподава́теля	
G	стола́	преподава́теля	музе́я
P	столе́	преподава́теле	музе́е
			кафете́рии[1]
D	столу́	преподава́телю	музе́ю
I	столо́м[2]	преподава́телем[3]	музе́ем

1. The prepositional case does not permit nouns ending in **-ие.** Use **-ии** instead.
2. The 5-letter spelling rule applies to words ending **ш, щ, ж, ч,** and **ц** followed by unstressed endings.
3. When stressed the soft instrumental ending is **-ём: секретарём, ремлём.**

Masculine plural

	Hard	Soft	
N	столы́[1]	преподава́тели	музе́и
A	Inanimate like nominative; animate like genitive		
	столы́[1]	музе́и	
	студе́нтов	преподава́телей	
G	столо́в[2]	преподава́телей[2]	музе́ев[2]
P	стола́х	преподава́телях	музе́ях
D	стола́м	преподава́телям	музе́ям
I	стола́ми	преподава́телями	музе́ями

1. The 7-letter spelling rule requires **и** for words whose stems end **к, г, х, ж, ч, ш,** and **щ:** па́рк**и**, гараж**и́**, карандаш**и́**, etc.
2. The genitive plural is treated fully in Book 2.

Feminine Singular

	Hard	Soft -я	Soft ...ия	Soft -ь
N	газе́та	неде́ля	пе́нсия	дверь
A	газе́ту	неде́лю	пе́нсию	дверь
G	газе́ты[1]	неде́ли	пе́нсии	две́ри
P	газе́те	неде́ле	пе́нсии[2]	две́ри
D	газе́те	неде́ле	пе́нсии[2]	две́ри
I	газе́той	неде́лей[3]	пе́нсией	две́рью

1. The 7-letter spelling rule requires **и** for words whose stems end **к, г, х, ж, ч, ш,** and **щ**: кни́ги, студе́нтки, ру́чки, etc.
2. Dative and prepositional case forms do not permit nouns ending in **-ие**. Use **-ии** instead.
3. When stressed the soft instrumental ending is **-ёй: семьёй.**

Feminine Plural

	Hard	Soft -я	Soft ...ия	Soft -ь
N	газе́ты[1]	неде́ли	пе́нсии	две́ри
A	Inanimates like nominative; animates like genitive			
	газе́ты[1] жён - Ø	неде́ли	пе́нсии	две́ри
G	газе́т Ø[2]	неде́ль[2]	пе́нсий[2]	двере́й[2]
P	газе́там	неде́лях	пе́нсиях	дверя́х
D	газе́там	неде́лям	пе́нсиям	дверя́м
I	газе́тами	неде́лями	пе́нсиями	дверя́ми дверьми́

1. The 7-letter spelling rule requires **и** for words whose stems end **к, г, х, ж, ч, ш,** and **щ**: кни́ги, студе́нтки, ру́чки, etc.
2. The genitive plural is treated fully in Book 2.

Neuter Singular

	Hard	Soft -е	Soft ...ие
N	окно́	мо́ре	общежи́тие
A	окно́	мо́ре	общежи́тие
G	окна́	мо́ря	общежи́тия
P	окне́	мо́ре	общежи́тии[1]
D	окну́	мо́рю	общежи́тию
I	окно́м	мо́рем	общежи́тием

Neuter Plural

	Hard	Soft -е	Soft ...ие
N	о́кна[1]	моря́[1]	общежи́тия
A	о́кна	моря́	общежи́тия
G	о́к(о)н Ø[2]	море́й[2]	общежи́тий[2]
P	о́кнах	моря́х	общежи́тиях
D	о́кнам	моря́м	общежи́тиям
I	о́кнами	моря́ми	общежи́тиями

1. Stress in neuter nouns consisting of two syllables almost always shifts in the plural: окно́ ➡ о́кна; мо́ре ➡ моря́.
2. The genitive plural is treated fully in Volume 2.

IRREGULAR NOUNS

Singular

N	и́мя	вре́мя	мать	дочь
A	и́мя	вре́мени	мать	дочь
G	и́мени	вре́мени	ма́тери	до́чери
D	и́мени	вре́мени	ма́тери	до́чери
P	и́мени	вре́мени	ма́тери	до́чери
I	и́менем	вре́менем	ма́терью	до́черью

Plural

N	имена́	времена́	ма́тери	до́чери
A	имена́	времена́	матере́й	дочере́й
G	имён	времён	матере́й	дочере́й
D	имена́м	времена́м	матеря́м	дочеря́м
P	имена́х	времена́х	матеря́х	дочеря́х
I	имена́ми	времена́ми	матеря́ми	дочеря́ми дочерьми́

NOUNS WITH IRREGULAR PLURALS

N	друг друзья́	сосе́д сосе́ди	сын сыновья́	брат бра́тья	сестра́ сёстры
A	друзе́й	сосе́дей	сынове́й	бра́тьев	сестёр
G	друзе́й	сосе́дей	сынове́й	бра́тьев	сестёр
P	друзья́х	сосе́дях	сыновья́х	бра́тьях	сёстрах
D	друзья́м	сосе́дям	сыновья́м	бра́тьям	сёстрам
I	друзья́ми	сосе́дями	сыновья́ми	бра́тьями	сёстрами

DECLENSION OF ADJECTIVES

Hard-stem adjectives

	Masculine, Neuter	Feminine	Plural
N	нóвый нóвое молодóй[1] молодóе	нóвая молодáя	нóвые молодьíе
A	Modifying inan. noun—like nom.; animate noun—like gen.	нóвую	Modifying inan. noun—like nom.; animate noun—like gen.
G	нóвого	нóвой	нóвых
P	нóвом	нóвой	нóвых
D	нóвому	нóвой	нóвым
I	нóвым	нóвой	нóвыми

1. Adjectives whose masculine singular form end in **-ой** always have stress on the ending.

Soft-stem adjectives

	Masculine, Neuter	Feminine	Plural
N	сúний сúнее	сúняя	сúние
A	Modifying inan. noun —like nom.; animate noun—like gen.	сúнюю	Modifying inan. noun—like nom.; animate noun—like gen.
G	сúнего	сúней	сúних
P	сúнем	сúней	сúних
D	сúнему	сúней	сúним
I	сúним	сúней	сúними

ADJECTIVES INVOLVING THE FIVE- AND SEVEN-LETTER SPELLING RULES

(Figures indicate which rule is involved.)

	Masculine, Neuter	Feminine	Plural
N	хоро́ший[7] хоро́шее[5] большо́й большо́е ру́сский[7] ру́сское	хоро́шая[5] больша́я ру́сская	хоро́шие[7] больши́е[7] ру́сские[7]
A	Modifying inan. noun—like nom.; animate noun—like gen.	хоро́шую большу́ю ру́сскую	Modifying inan. noun—like nom.; animate noun—like gen.
G	хоро́шего[5] большо́го ру́сского	хоро́шей[5] большо́й ру́сской	хоро́ших[7] больши́х[7] ру́сских[7]
P	хоро́шем[5] большо́м ру́сском	хоро́шей[5] большо́й ру́сской	хоро́ших[7] больши́х[7] ру́сских[7]
D	хоро́шему[5] большо́му ру́сскому	хоро́шей[5] большо́й ру́сской	хоро́шим[7] больши́м[7] ру́сским[7]
I	хоро́шим[7] больши́м[7] ру́сским[7]	хоро́шей[5] большо́й ру́сской	хоро́шими[7] больши́ми[7] ру́сскими[7]

SPECIAL MODIFIERS

	Masc., Neuter	Fem.	Plural
N	мой моё	моя́	мои́
A	inan./anim.	мою́	nom./gen.
G	моего́	мое́й	мои́х
P	моём	мое́й	мои́х
D	моему́	мое́й	мои́м
I	мои́м	мое́й	мои́ми

	Masc., Neuter	Fem.	Plural
N	твой твоё	твоя́	твои́
A	inan./anim.	твою́	nom./gen.
G	твоего́	твое́й	твои́х
P	твоём	твое́й	твои́х
D	твоему́	твое́й	твои́м
I	твои́м	твое́й	твои́ми

	Masc., Neuter	Fem.	Plural
N	наш на́ше	на́ша	на́ши
A	inan./anim.	на́шу	nom./gen.
G	на́шего	на́шей	на́ших
P	на́шем	на́шей	на́ших
D	на́шему	на́шей	на́шим
I	на́шим	на́шей	на́шими

	Masc., Neuter	Fem.	Plural
N	ваш ва́ше	ва́ша	ва́ши
A	inan./anim.	ва́шу	nom./gen.
G	ва́шего	ва́шей	ва́ших
P	ва́шем	ва́шей	ва́ших
D	ва́шему	ва́шей	ва́шим
I	ва́шим	ва́шей	ва́шими

	Masc., Neuter	Fem.	Plural
N	чей чьё	чья	чьи
A	inan./anim.	чью	nom./gen.
G	чьего́	чьей	чьих
P	чьём	чьей	чьих
D	чьему́	чьей	чьим
I	чьим	чьей	чьи́ми

	Masc., Neuter	Fem.	Plural
N	э́тот э́то	э́та	э́ти
A	inan./anim.	э́ту	nom./gen.
G	э́того	э́той	э́тих
P	э́том	э́той	э́тих
D	э́тому	э́той	э́тим
I	э́тим	э́той	э́тими

	Masc., Neuter	Fem.	Plural
N	весь всё	вся	все
A	inan./anim.	всю	nom./gen.
G	всего́	всей	всех
P	всём	всей	всех
D	всему́	всей	всем
I	всем	всей	все́ми

	Masc., Neuter	Fem.	Plural
N	один одно́	одна́	одни́
A	inan./anim.	одну́	nom./gen.
G	одного́	одно́й	одни́х
P	одно́м	одно́й	одни́х
D	одному́	одно́й	одни́м
I	одни́м	одно́й	одни́ми

	Masc., Neuter	Fem.	Plural
N	тре́тий тре́тье	тре́тья	тре́тьи
A	inan./anim.	тре́тью	nom./gen.
G	тре́тьего	тре́тьей	тре́тьих
P	тре́тьем	тре́тьей	тре́тьих
D	тре́тьему	тре́тьей	тре́тьим
I	тре́тьим	тре́тьей	тре́тьими

QUESTION WORDS AND PERSONAL PRONOUNS

N	кто	что	я	ты	мы	вы	он, оно́	она́	они́
A	кого́	что	меня́	тебя́	нас	вас	(н)его́	(н)её	(н)их
G	кого́	чего́	меня́	тебя́	нас	вас	(н)его́	(н)её	(н)их
P	ком	чём	мне	тебе́	нас	вас	нём	ней	них
D	кому́	чему́	мне	тебе́	нам	вам	(н)ему́	(н)ей	(н)им
I	кем	чем	мной	тобо́й	на́ми	ва́ми	(н)им	(н)ей	(н)их

1. Forms for **он, она́, оно́,** and **они́** take an initial **н** if preceded by a preposition. For example, in the genitive case, the initial **н** is required in the following sentence:

   У неё есть кни́га.

   But not in the sentence:

   Её здесь нет.

СЛОВАРЬ

РУССКО-АНГЛИЙСКИЙ

А

а - and (*often used to begin question or statement in continuting conversation; implies slight contrast; see 3.8*)

авангарди́ст - avant-garde artist

аллерги́я - allergy

алло́ - Hello (*on the telephone only*)

Аме́рика - America (the U.S.)

америка́н(е)ц/америка́нка - American (*See 3.6*)

америка́нский - American

англи́йский - English (*See 3.5, 3.6*)

англича́нин (*pl.* англича́не)/англича́нка - English person (*See 3.6*)

Англия - England

антрополо́гия - anthropology

апельси́н - orange

ара́б/ара́бка - Arab (*See 3.6*)

ара́бский - Arabic (*See 3.5, 3.6*)

армяни́н (*pl.* армя́не)/армя́нка - Armenian (*See 3.6*)

архите́ктор - architect

архитекту́ра - architecture

аспиранту́ра - graduate school

аудито́рия - classroom

Б

ба́бушка - grandmother

бакале́я - baking goods store

бана́н - banana

банк - bank

бассе́йн - swimming pool

без (+ *genitive*) - without

бе́лый - white

библиоте́ка - library

библиоте́карь - librarian

бизнесме́н/бизнесме́нка - businessperson

биоло́гия - biology

блу́зка - blouse

блю́до - dish (*food, not the physical plate*)

борщ - borshch (*ending always stressed*)

больни́ца - hospital

большо́й - large

большо́е спаси́бо - thank you very much

брат (*pl.* бра́тья) - brother

    двою́родный брат - (male) cousin

брать (бер-у́, -ёшь, -у́т; брала́, бра́ли)/взять (возьм-у́, -ёшь, -у́т; взяла́, взя́ли) - to take

брю́ки (*pl.*) - pants

бу́блик - bagel

Бу́дьте добры́! - Could you please...?

бу́лка - small white bread loaf; roll

бу́лочная (*adj. decl.*) - bakery

бульо́н - bouillon

бухга́лтер - accountant

бутербро́д - (open-faced) sandwich

бы́стро - quickly

быть (бу́д-у, -ешь, -ут; был, была́, бы́ли) - to be (*Used to form imperfective future; See 9.4-9.6*)

бюро́ (*indecl.*) - bureau; agency

бюро́ недви́жимости - real estate agency

В

в (+ *prep.*) - in; at (*See 3.2, 4.2*)

в (+ *accusative case for direction*) - to (*See 5.4*)

в (+ *accusative case of days of week*) - on

в (+ *hour*) - at ... o'clock

в час - at one o'clock; в два часа́ - at two o'clock; в пять часо́в - at five o'clock

    в па́спорте стои́т ... - in my passport it says...

    в по́мощь уча́щимся - to help students

    в про́шлом году́ - last year

валю́тный - hard currency (*adj.*)

ва́нная (*declines like adj.*) - bathroom (bath/shower; no toilet)

ва́режки (*pl.*) - mittens

ваш (ва́ша, ва́ше, ва́ши) - your (*formal or plural*) (*See 2.4*)

ведь - after all (*filler word, never stressed*)

ве́рующий (*declines like adj.*) - believer

весёлый (не-) - cheerful (un-)

весь день - all day

ве́чером - in the evening

вещь (*fem.*) - thing

видеокассе́та - video cassette

видеомагнитофо́н - video cassette recorder

ви́за - visa

виногра́д (*sing. and pl.*) - grape(s)

висе́ть (вишу́, -и́шь, -я́т) - hang (be hanging)

вку́сный - tasty

вме́сте - together

внук - grandson

вну́чка - granddaughter

во - in (*variant of* в *often seen preceding certain consonant clusters as in* во Фра́нции 'in France'; *See* в)

во ско́лько? - at what time?

вода́ (*pl.* во́ды) - water

во-пе́рвых ..., во-вторы́х ... - in the first place ..., in the second place ...

воскресе́нье - Sunday

восто́к (на) - east

вот ... - here is ...

    Вот как?! - Really?!

врач (*all endings stressed*) - physician
    зубно́й врач - dentist
все - everybody; everyone
всё - everything
всегда́ - always
встава́ть (вста-ю́, -ёшь, -ю́т) - to get up
вто́рник - Tuesday
второ́й - second
второ́е (*adj. decl.*) - main course; entree
вы - you (*formal and plural; See 1.1*)
вы́бор - selection
вы́расти (*perf. past:* вы́рос, вы́росла, вы́росли) - to grow up
    (*See 7.3*)
вы́сшее образова́ние - higher education
вычисли́тельная те́хника - computer science

Г

газ - natural gas
газе́та - newspaper
галантере́я - men's accessories shop; haberdashery
га́лстук - tie
гара́ж (*ending always stressed*) - garage
гастроно́м - grocery store
где - where (*at; See 5.4*)
говори́ть (говор-ю́, -и́шь, -я́т)/сказа́ть (скажу́, ска́жешь,
    ска́жут) - to speak, to say
    Говори́те ме́дленнее. - Speak more slowly.
    Говоря́т, что... - They say that...; It is said that..
    Как вы сказа́ли / ты сказа́л/а? - What did you say?
    Мне сказа́ли, что... - I was told that...
год - year
    два, три, четы́ре го́да; 5-20 лет (*with dative*) - year(s)
    [old] *See 7.4.*; в про́шлом году́ - last year
головно́й убо́р - headwear
го́лос (*pl.* голоса́) - voice
голубо́й - light blue
горя́чий - hot (*of things, not weather*)
госуда́рственный - state (*adj.*); government-owned
гости́ная (*declines like adj.*) - living room
гото́вить/при- (гото́в-лю, -ишь, -ят) - to prepare
гото́вый - prepared
грамаласти́нка - phonograph record

Д

да - yes
да - *unstressed conjunction particle as in* Да как сказа́ть? -
    Well, how should I put it?
дава́й(те) (+ *future tense of* мы) - Let's...
Дава́й перейдём на ты. - Let's switch to ты.
Дава́й(те) пое́дем ... - Let's go... (*by vehicle*)
Дава́й(те) познако́мимся! - Let's get acquainted.
Дава́й(те) пойдём ... - Let's go... (*on foot*)
давно́ (+ *present tense verb*) - for a long time
да́же - even
да́льше - further; next
дари́ть/по- (дарю́, да́ришь, -ят) - to give a present
да́ча (на) - dacha; country home
дверь (*fem.*) - door
дво́е (дете́й) - two (children; *collective number; See 7.4*)
двою́родная сестра́ - female cousin

двою́родный брат - male cousin
де́вочка - (little) girl
де́вушка - (young) woman
    Де́вушка! - Excuse me, miss!
де́душка - grandfather
деклара́ция - customs declaration
де́лать/с- (де́ла-ю, -ешь, -ют) - to do; to make
д(е)нь (*pl.* дни) - day
    весь день - all day
    д(е)нь рожде́ния - birthday (lit. day of birth): С днём
    рожде́ния! - Happy birthday!
    Како́й сего́дня день? - What day is it?
де́ньги (*always plural*) - money
де́ти (оди́н ребёнок, дво́е дете́й, тро́е дете́й, че́тверо
    дете́й, пять дете́й) - children (*See 7.5*)
джи́нсы (*pl.*) - jeans
дива́н - couch
днём - in the afternoon
До свида́ния. - Good bye.
до э́того - before that
До́брое у́тро! - Good morning!
До́брый ве́чер! - Good evening!
До́брый день! - Good afternon!
дово́льно - quite; rather
договори́лись. - okay, (we've agreed)
докуме́нт - document; identification
до́лжен (должна́, должны́) + *infinitive* - must (*See 5.6*)
до́лго (+ *past tense verb*) - for a long time
до́ллар (5-20 до́лларов) - dollar
дом (*pl.* дома́) - home; apartment building
до́ма - at home (*answers* где; *see 5.5*)
домо́й - (to) home (*answers* куда́; *see 5.5*)
домохозя́йка - housewife
дочь (*gen. and prep. sg.* до́чери; *nom. pl.* до́чери) - daughter
друг (*pl.* друзья́) - friend
ду́мать/по- (ду́ма-ю, -ешь, -ют) - to think
    поду́маю - I'll think about it; Let me think about it
дя́дя - uncle

Е, Ё

европе́йский - European
его́ - his
еди́нственный - only (*adj.*)
    еди́нственный ребёнок - only child
её - her(s)
е́здить (е́зжу, е́здишь, е́здят) - to go and come back (*by
    vehicle; see 10.6*)
Ерева́н - Yerevan (*city in Armenia*)
е́сли - if
    Если говори́ть о себе́, то ... - If I use myself as an
    example ,then ...
есть (+ *nominative*) - there is (*See 6.3.*)
Есть литерату́ра? - Is there literature? Есть пода́рки - Are
    there gifts?
есть/съ- (ем, ешь, есть, еди́м, еди́те, едя́т; ел, е́ла, е́ли) -
    to eat
е́хать/по- (е́д-у, -ешь, -ут) - to go; to set out (*by vehicle; see
    5.3, 10.6*);
    Пое́дем! - Let's go! (*by vehicle*)
ещё - still

Ж

Жду письма́. - Write! (I'm awaiting your letter)
жёлтый - yellow
жена́ (*pl.* жёны) - wife
же́нский - women's; feminine
жили́щные усло́вия - living conditions
жить (живу́, живёшь, живу́т) - to live
журна́л - magazine
журнали́ст - journalist
жунали́стика - journalism

З

забы́ть (*perf.:* забу́д-у, -ешь, ут) - to forget
заво́д (на) - factory
за́втра - tomorrow
за́втрак - breakfast
за́втракать/по- (за́втрака-ю, -ешь, -ют) - to eat breakfast
зака́зывать (зака́зыва-ю, -ешь, -ют)/заказа́ть (закажу́, зака́жешь, -ут) - to order
зака́нчивать (зака́нчива-ю, -ешь, -ют)/око́нчить (око́нч-у, -ишь, -ат) (+ *accusative; see 10.2*) - to graduate from (*requires direct object*)
закры́т (-а,-о,-ы) - closed
    Закро́й(те)! - Close!
закры́ть perf. - to close (*something; must take a direct object*)
    Мы закры́ли дверь. - We closed the door
закры́ться *perf. past* (закры́лся, закры́лась, закры́лось, закры́лись). - to be closed;
    Дверь закры́лась. - The door closed.
заку́ски - appetizers
занима́ться (занима́-юсь, -ешься, -ются) - to study; to do homework (*See 5.2*)
заня́тие (на) - class
за́пад (на) - west
за́пись (fem.) - recording
здесь - here
здоро́вый (не-) - healthy (un-)
Здра́вствуй(те)! - Hello.
зелёный - green
знако́мый - acquaintance; friend
знать (зна́-ю, -ешь, -ют) - to know
зна́чит... - so... (*lit.* it means); Зна́чит так... - Let's see...
зубно́й врач - dentist

И

и - and (*See 4.5*)
игру́шка - toy
идти́ (ид-у́, -ёшь, -у́т)/пойти́ (пойд-у́, -ёшь, -у́т; пошёл, пошла́, пошли́) - to go (*on foot, or within city; see 5.3, 8.4, 10.6*)
    Иди́(те) - Go! (*imperative*); Пойдём! - Let's go!
    Пойдём лу́чше... - Let's go to ... instead.
    пойти́ рабо́тать (пойд-у́, ёшь, ут) (куда́) (*perf.*) - to begin to work; to begin a job
    Пошли́! - Let's go!
из (+ *genitive*) - from (a place)
из Москвы́ - from Moscow
Извини́те! - Excuse me!
изуча́ть (изуча́-ю, -ешь, -ют) *что* - to study; to take (*a subject in school or college; requires direct object; See 4.3, 5.2*)

ико́на - icon
икра́ - caviar
и́ли - or
импрессиони́ст - impressionist
и́мя (*pl.* имена́) (*neut.*) - first name (*See 1.2*)
    Как ва́ше и́мя - What's your first name?
инжене́р - engineer
иногда́ - sometimes
иностра́нный - foreign
институ́т - institute (*institution of post-secondary education*)
    Институ́т иностра́нных языко́в - Institute of Foreign Languages
интере́сно... - I wonder...; it's interesting...
интере́сный - interesting
Ирку́тск - Irkutsk (*a city in Siberia*)
иску́сство - art
испа́н(е)ц/испа́нка - Spanish (*See 3.6*)
испа́нский - Spanish (*See 3.5, 3.6*)
исто́рия - history
италья́н(е)ц/италья́нка - Italian (*See 3.6*)
италья́нский - Italian (*See 3.5, 3.6*)
их - their(s)

К

кабине́т - office
ка́ждый - each; every
ка́ждый день - every day
ка́жется - it seems
как - how (*See 4.5*)
    Как вас (тебя́) зову́т? - What's your name?
    Как ва́ше о́тчество? - What's your patronymic?
    Как вы сказа́ли? (formal/plural) - What did you say?
    Как зову́т (+ *accusative*)? - What is ...'s name? (*See 7.7.*)
    Как называ́ется (называ́ются)...? - What is (are) ... called? (*said of things, not people*)
    Как по-ру́сски...? - How do you say ... in Russian?
    Как ты сказа́л/а? - What did you say? (*informal*)
    Как ты? - How are you? (*informal*)
како́й (кака́я, како́е, каки́е) - What; which
    Како́й сего́дня день? - What day is it?
    Како́й ты (он, она́, etc.) молоде́ц! - Good going! (*used for both sexes*)
Кана́да - Canada
кана́д(е)ц/кана́дка - Canadian (*See 3.6*)
капу́ста - cabbage
ка́рта - map
карто́фель - potato
карто́шка - potato (*conversational*)
ка́сса - cash register
кассе́та - cassette
кассе́тный магнитофо́н (кассе́тник) - cassette player
кафе́ [кафэ́] (*neuter; indecl.*) - café
ка́федра (на) - department (*in a university, college, or institute*)
    ка́федра ру́сского языка́ - Russian department
кафете́рий - restaurant-cafeteria
кварти́ра - apartment
Квебе́к - Quebec
кино́ (*indecl.*) - movies; movie theater
кинотеа́тр - movie theater
класс (в) - grade level (*in elementary or high school: first, second, third, etc.*)

кита́(е)ц (*pl.* кита́йцы)/китая́нка - Chinese (*See 3.6*)
кита́йский - Chinese (*See 3.5, 3.6*)
кни́га - book
кни́жный - book(ish); кни́жный ры́н(о)к - book mart
ков(ё)р (*ending always stressed*) - rug
когда́ - when (*See 4.5*)
колбаса́ - sausage
колго́тки (*pl.*) - pantyhose
копе́йка (5-20 копе́ек) - kopeck (*See 9.2*)
коне́чно - of course
коммерса́нт - businessperson
комме́рческий - commercial
    комме́рческая фи́рма - trade office; business office
компью́тер - computer
коридо́р - hallway; corridor
кори́чневый - brown
костю́м - suit
котле́ты по-киевски - Kiev cutlets
ко́фе (*masc.; indecl.*) - coffee;
    ко́фе с молоко́м - coffee with milk
краси́вый - pretty
кра́сный - red
кре́сло - armchair
крова́ть (*fem.*) - bed
кроссо́вки (*pl.*) - athletic shoes
кто - who
Кто по национа́льности (+ *nominative*)? - What is ...'s
    nationality?
    Кто вы по национа́льности? - What's your nationality?
    Кто по профе́ссии (+ *nominative*)? - What is ...'s
    profession?
    Кто вы по профе́ссии? - What's your profession?
куда́ - where (to; *see 5.4*)
кулина́рия - store that sells *полуфабрика́ты,* products such
    as ground beef, tomato sauce, or dough — ready to cook
купа́льник - woman's bathing suit
купи́ть *perf.*; *see* покупа́ть - to buy
ку́рица - chicken
курс (на) - class; year of study in institution of higher education
    на како́м ку́рсе - in what year (*in university or institute*);
    Они́ у́чатся на второ́м ку́рсе - They are sophomores.
ку́ртка - short jacket
ку́хня - cuisine; style of cooking
    Мы лю́бим ру́сскую ку́хню. - We like Russian cuisine.
ку́хня (на) - kitchen

Л

лаборато́рия - laboratory
ла́дно - it's okay
ла́мпа - lamp
ланге́т - fried steak
легко́ (+ *dative*) - easy (*See 9.3*)
лежа́ть (лежу́, -и́шь, а́т) - lie
ле́кция - lecture
ле́стница - stairway
лет (*see* год) - years (*See 7.4.*)
лимона́д - soft drink
литерату́ра - literature; Литерату́ру везёте? - Do you have
    any literature with you?
ложи́ться (спать) (ложу́сь, ложи́шься, ложа́тся) - to go to
    bed

Ло́ндон - London
Лос-Анджелес - Los Angeles
лук - onion(s)
люби́ть (люб-лю́, лю́б-ишь, -ят) - to love

М

магази́н - store
магнитофо́н - tape recorder;
    кассе́тный магнитофо́н - cassette recorder
ма́йка - tee shirt
ма́ленький - small
ма́льчик - boy
ма́ма - mom
матема́тика - mathematics
матрёшка - nested doll
мать (*gen. and prep. sg.* ма́тери; *nom. pl.* ма́тери) - mother
маши́на - car
ме́бель (*fem., always singular*) - furniture
медбра́т (*pl.* медбра́тья) - nurse (male)
медици́на - medicine (*the sudy of; not what one takes to rem-
    edy illness*)
ме́дленно - slowly
медсестра́ (*pl.* медсёстры) - nurse (female)
междунаро́дные отноше́ния - international affairs
    институ́т междунаро́дных отноше́ний - school of inter-
    national affairs
мексика́н(е)ц/мексика́нка - Mexican (*See 3.6*)
ме́неджер - manager
Меня́ зову́т ... - My name is ...
меню́ (*neuter; indecl.*) - menu
ме́сто рабо́ты - place of work
ме́сяц (2-4 ме́сяца, 5 ме́сяцев) - month
минера́льная вода́ - mineral water
мла́дший - younger
могу́ (+ *infinitive*) - I can
мо́жет быть - maybe
мо́жно: *dative* + на́до + *infinitive* - it is possible (*for someone
    to do something; see 8.6*)
    Мо́жно плати́ть до́лларами? - Can I pay in dollars?
    Мо́жно посмотре́ть кварти́ру? - May I look at the
    apartment?
мой (моя́, моё, мой) - my (*See 2.4*)
Молод(е́)ц! - Well done!; Good going! (*used with both gen-
    ders; pl.* молодцы́); Како́й ты (он, она́, etc.) молоде́ц! -
    Good going! (*used for both sexes*)
молодо́й - young
    молодо́й челове́к - young man
    Молодо́й челове́к! - Excuse me, sir!; Young man!
моло́же (+ *genitive* + на ..... лет) - younger than someone by
    x years (*See 10.1*)
молоко́ - milk; ко́фе с молоко́м - coffee with milk
моло́чный - dairy
морко́вь (*fem.*) - carrot
моро́женое (*adj. decl.*) - ice-cream
Москва́ - Moscow
моско́вский - Moscow (*adj.*)
муж (*pl.* мужья́) - husband
мужско́й - men's; masculine
музе́й - museum
му́зыка - music
музыка́нт - musician

мы - we
мя́со - meat
мясно́й - meat (adj.)
    мясно́е ассорти́ - cold cuts salad

Н

на (+ prepositional for location) - in; on; at (See 4.2);
на (+ accusative for direction) - to (See 5.4)
    На каки́х языка́х (вы говори́те, чита́ете, пи́шете) -
    What languages (do you speak, read, write; see 3.5)
    На како́м языке́ (вы говори́те, чита́ете, пи́шете) -
    What language (do you speak, read, write; see 3.5)
    На како́м ку́рсе - in what year (in university or institute)
    на пе́нсии - retired
    на ю́ге (на се́вере, на восто́ке, на за́паде) страны́ - in
    the south (north, east, west) of the country
наве́рное - probably
на́до: dative + на́до + infinitive - it is necessary (for someone
    to do something; see 8.6)
наза́д - ago (See 10.4)
наконе́ц - finally
нале́во - on the left; to the left
напи́т(о)к - drink (noun)
напра́во - on the right; to the right
наприме́р - for example
нау́ка - science
    полити́ческие нау́ки - political science
наш (на́ша, на́ше, на́ши) - our (See 2.4)
не - not; negates following word
    не́ было (+ genitive) - was not there; did not have. (See 8.3)
    Не мо́жет быть! - That's impossible!
    Не хо́чешь (хоти́те) пойти́ (пое́хать)...? - Would you
    like to go ...?
невесёлый - glum
невозмо́жно (+ dative) - impossible (See 9.3)
неда́вно - recently
недалеко́ - not far
неде́ля (2-4 неде́ли, 5 неде́ль) - week
неинтере́сный - boring
некраси́вый - ugly
нельзя́ (+ dative) - forbidden; not allowed (See 9.3)
не́м(е)ц/не́мка - German (See 3.6)
неме́цкий - German (See 3.5, 3.6)
немно́го; немно́жко - a little
    немно́го о себе́ - a bit about myself (yourself)
необыкнове́нный - unusual
непло́хо - pretty well
неплохо́й - pretty good
несерьёзный - frivolous
нет - no
нет (+ genitive) - there is not (See 6.4)
ни ... ни ... - neither ... nor ...
никогда́ (не) - never
ничего́ - nothing
    ничего́ интере́сного (+ не + verb) - nothing of interest
но - but (See 4.5)
но́вый - new
но́мер (pl. номера́) - number
норма́льно - normally
нос(о́)к (stress always on ending) - sock
но́чью - in the night

ну... - well...
ну́жно: dative + на́до + infinitive - it is necessary (for some-
    one to do something; see 8.6)
Нью-Йо́рк - New York

О

о; об (+ prepositional) - about (The form об is used before
    words beginning with vowels а, э, и, о, or у; see 7.9)
    О чём идёт речь? - What are we talking about?
обе́д - lunch; Обе́д гото́в - Lunch is ready.
обе́дать/по- (обе́да-ю, -ешь, -ют) - to eat lunch; dinner
обзо́рное упражне́ние - summary exercise; overview exercise
образова́ние (вы́сшее образова́ние) - education (higher
    education)
о́вощ - vegetable
овощно́й - vegetable (adj.)
о́бувь (fem.) - footwear
общежи́тие - dormitory
обыкнове́нный (не-) - ordinary (unusual)
обы́чно - usually
огро́мный - huge
    Огро́мное спаси́бо! - Thank you very much!
огур(е́)ц - cucumber
одева́ться (одева́-юсь, одева́-ешься, одева́-ются) - to get
    dressed
оде́жда - clothing
оди́н (одна́, одно́, одни́) - one; alone
    одно́ сло́во - one word;
    Одну́ мину́точку! - Just a moment!
ой - oh!
окно́ (pl. о́кна) - window
око́нчить perf.; see зака́нчивать - to graduate from
он - he; it (See 2.3)
она́ - she; it (See 2.3)
они́ - they (See 2.3)
оно́ - it (See 2.3)
опа́здывать (опа́здыва-ю, -ешь, -ют) - to be late
отде́л - department
отдыха́ть (отдыха́-ю, -ешь, -ют) - to relax
от(е́)ц (all endings stressed) - father
откры́ть perf. - to open (something; must take a direct object)
    Мы откры́ли дверь. - We opened the door
    Откро́йте! - Open!
откры́ться (perf. past откры́лся, откры́лась, откры́лось,
    откры́лись) - to be opened
    Дверь откры́лась. - The door opened.
отку́да - where from
    Отку́да вы зна́ете ру́сский язы́к? - How do you know
    Russian?
    Отку́да вы? - Where are you from?
отли́чно - excellent
о́тчество - patronymic (See 1.2)
    Как ва́ше о́тчество? - What's your patronymic?
о́чень - very
    О́чень прия́тно (с ва́ми, с тобо́й) (познако́миться). -
    Pleased to meet you.
очки́ (pl.) - eyeglasses

П

пальто́ - overcoat
па́па - dad

па́ра - class period
парфюме́рия - cosmetics shop
па́спорт (*pl.* паспорта́) - passport
    в па́спорте стои́т ... - in my passport it says ...
педаго́гика - education (*a subject in college*)
пе́нсия - pension; на пе́нсии - retired
пе́рвый - first
пе́рвое (*adj. decl.*) - first course (*always soup*)
переезжа́ть (переезжа́-ю, -ешь, -ют)/перее́хать (перее́д-у, -ешь, -ут) (*куда*) - to move, to take up a new living place
пе́р(е)ц - pepper
перча́тка - glove
пиджа́к - suit jacket
писа́тель - writer
писа́ть/на- (пиш-у́, пи́ш-ешь, -ут) - to write
пи́сьменный - written; writing
    пи́сьменное упражне́ние - written exercise
    пи́сьменный стол - desk
письмо́ (*pl.* пи́сьма) - letter
пить (пью, пьёшь, пьют; пил, пила́, пи́ли)/вы́пить (вы́- *prefix always stressed:* вы́пью, вы́пьешь, вы́пьют; вы́пила) - to drink
пи́цца - pizza
пи́ща - food
пла́вки - swimming trunks
пласти́нка - record (phonograph)
плати́ть/за- (плач-у́, пла́т-ишь, -ят) - to pay
    Плати́те в ка́ссу. - Pay the cashier.
плат(о́)к (*endings always stressed*) - kerchief; handkerchief
пла́тье - dress
племя́нник - nephew
племя́нница - niece
плита́ (*pl.* пли́ты) - stove
пло́хо - poorly
плохо́й - bad
по национа́льности - by nationality
    Кто вы по национа́льности
по-ара́бски - Arabic (*See 3.5*)
по-англи́йски - English (*See 3.5*)
по-ру́сски - Russian (*See 3.5*)
    Как по-ру́сски «last name»? - How do you say "last name" in Russian?
по-кита́йски - Chinese (*See 3.5*)
по-испа́нски - Spanish (*See 3.5*)
по-италья́нски - Italian (*See 3.5*)
по-неме́цки - German (*See 3.5*)
по-францу́зски - French (*See 3.5*)
по-украи́нски - Ukrainian (*See 3.5*)
по-япо́нски - Japanese (*See 3.5*)
поговори́м - We'll have a talk.
пода́р(о)к - gift
подва́л - basement
подари́ть (*perf.; see* дари́ть) - to give as a present
поду́мать (*perf.; see* ду́мать) - to think
    поду́маю - I'll think about it; Let me think about it
пое́хать (*perf.; see* е́хать) - to go by vehicle
    Пое́дем! - Let's go! (*by vehicle*)
пожа́луйста - please; you're wlcome
поза́втракать *perf.; see* за́втракать - to eat breakfast
по́здно - late
пойти́ *perf.; see* идти́ - to go by foot
    Пойдём! - Let's go!

Пойдём лу́чше... - Let's go to ... instead.
пойти́ рабо́тать (пойд-у́, ёшь, у́т) (*куда*) (*perf.*) - to begin to work; to begin a job
    Пошли́! - Let's go
пока́ - meanwhile
показа́ть *perf.; see* пока́зывать
пока́зывать (пока́зыва-ю, -ешь, -ют)/показа́ть (покаж-у́, пока́ж-ешь, -ут) - to show
    Покажи́(те)! - Show!
покупа́ть (покуп-а́ю -ешь, -ют)/купи́ть (куплю́, ку́пишь, -ят) - to buy
пол (на полу́; *ending always stressed*) - floor (*as opposed to ceiling*)
поликли́ника - health clinic
полити́ческий - political
    полити́ ческие нау́ки - political science
Получи́те! - Take it! (*Said when paying at a store, in a restaurant, etc.*)
помидо́р - tomato
понеде́льник - Monday
понима́ть (понима́ю, понима́ешь, понима́ют) - to understand
поня́тно - understood (Got it!).
пообе́дать *perf.; see* обе́дать - to eat lunch (or mid-day dinner)
попа́сть (*perf.* попад-у́,-ёшь, -у́т; попа́л, -а, -и) - to manage to get in
    Мы то́чно попадём. - We'll get in for sure.
по́рция - portion, order
после́дний - last
послу́шать *perf.; see* слу́шать - to listen to
    Послу́шай(те)! - Listen!
посмотре́ть *perf.; see* смотре́ть - to look at; to watch
    Посмо́трим... - Let's see...
посове́товать *perf.; see* сове́товать - to advise
поступа́ть (поступа́-ю, -ешь, -ют)/поступи́ть (поступл-ю́, посту́п-ишь, -ят) *куда* - to apply to; to enroll in (*See 10.2*)
поступи́ть *perf.; see* поступа́ть - to enroll in
пото́м - later; then; afterwards
потому́ что - because (*See 4.5*)
поу́жинать *perf.; see* у́жинать - to eat supper (dinner)
похо́ж (-а, -и) (на + *accusative*) - resemble; look like (*See 10.1*)
почему́ - why
Пошли́! - Let's go!
пра́вда - truth
    Пра́вда? - Really?
пра́ктика - practice
    ча́стная пра́ктика - private practice
преподава́тель - teacher (*in college*)
    преподава́тель ру́сского языка́ - Russian language teacher (*in college*)
преподава́ть (препода-ю́, ёшь, ют) - to teach
при́город - suburb
пригото́вить *perf.; see* гото́вить - to prepare
приезжа́ть (приезжа́-ю, -ешь, -ют)/прие́хать (прие́д-у, -ешь, -ут) - to arrive (*by vehicle*)
прие́хать *perf.; see* приезжа́ть - to arrive (*by vehicle*)
Принеси́те, пожа́луйста, меню́. - Please bring a menu.
принима́ть (душ) (приним-а́ю, -ешь, -ют) - to take (a shower)
при́нтер - printer
программи́ст - computer programmer
продав(е́)ц (*all endings stressed*) / продавщи́ца - salesperson
продово́льственный (магази́н) - grocery (store)

продукты - groceries
Простите! - Excuse me!
просто - simply
профессия - profession
Проходи(те). - Come in; Go on through.
психология - psychology
пятница - Friday
пятый - fifth

Р

работа (на) - work (*noun*)
работать (работа-ю, -ешь, -ют) - work
радио (радиоприёмник) - radio
размер - size
Разрешите представиться. - Allow me to introduce myself.
рано - early
раньше - previously
рассказать *perf.; see* рассказывать - to tell; to narrate
рассказывать (рассказыва-ю, -ешь, -ют)/рассказать
   (расскаж-у, расскаж-ешь, -ут) - to tell; to narrate
   Расскажи(те) (мне)... - Tell (me)... (*request for narra-tive, not just a piece of factual information*)
рассольник - fish (or) meat and cucumber soup
Рассчитайте (нас, меня)! - Give (us, me) the check.
ребён(о)к (*pl.* дети) - child(ren); (*See 7.5*)
ребята - guys (*conversational term of address*)
редко - rarely
рем(е)нь (*endings always stressed*) - belt (usually men's)
решать (реша-ю, -ешь, -ют)/решить (реш-у, -ишь, -ат) - to decide
рис - rice
родители - parents
родиться (*perf. past:* родился, родилась, родились) - to be born (*See 7.3*)
родственник - relative
Россия - Russia
ростбиф - roast beef
рубашка - shirt
рубль (*masc.;* 2-4 рубля, 5-20 рублей; *endings always stressed*) - ruble (*See 9.2*)
русский - Russian (*See 3.5, 3.6*)
русский/русская - Russian (*See 3.6*)
русское страноведение - Russian area studies
рын(о)к (на) - market
   книжный рын(о)к - book mart
рядом - alongside

С

с (+ *genitive*) ... - (*someone*) owes ...: Сколько с нас? - How much do we owe?
   С днём рождения! - Happy birthday!
   с одной стороны ..., с другой стороны ... - on the one hand ..., on the other hand ...
   С приездом! - Welcome! (*to someone from out of town*)
   с удовольствием - with pleasure
салат - salad; lettuce
   салат из огурцов - cucumber salad
   салат из помидоров - tomato salad
сам (сама, сами) - (one)self

самый + *adjective* - the most + adjective
   самый любимый - most favorite
   самый нелюбимый - least favorite
Санкт-Петербург - St. Petersburg
Санкт-Петербургский - (of) St. Petersburg
сапог (*ending always stressed*) - boot
свитер (*pl.* свитера) - sweater
свободен (свободна, свободны) - free; not busy
свободно - fluently
свой - one's own
сделать *perf.; see* делать - to do; to make
север (на) - north
сегодня - today; Какой сегодня день? - What day is it?
сейчас - now
секретарь (*masc. endings, applies to men and women; all endings stressed*) - secretary
семья (*pl.* семьи) - family
серьёзный - serious
серый - gray
сестра (*pl.* сёстры) - sister
двоюродная сестра - cousin (female)
симпатичный (не-) - nice (not...)
синий - dark blue
сказать (*perf.; see* говорить) - to say
   Как вы сказали? (*formal*) - What did you say?
   Как ты сказал/а (*familiar*) - What did you say?
   Мне сказали, что... - I was told that...
сколько - how many; how much
   Сколько (+ *dative*) лет? - How old is...? (*See 7.4*)
   Сколько сейчас времени? - What time is it?
   Сколько стоит? - How much does it cost?
   Сколько у вас комнат? - How many rooms do you have?
скоро - soon
сладкое (*adj. decl.*) - dessert
словарь (*pl.* словари) - dictionary
слово (*pl.* слова) - word
слушать/про- (*also* по-) (слуша-ю, -ешь, -ют) (+ *accusative*) - to listen to
   (По)слушай(те)! - Listen!
слышать/у- (слыш-у, -ишь, -ат) - to hear
смотреть/по- (смотр-ю, смотр-ишь, -ят) - to look at; to watch
   Посмотрим... - Let's see...
сначала - to begin with; at first
советовать/по- (совету-ю, -ешь, -ют + dative) - to advise
совсем - completely
совсем не - not at all
   Они совсем не старые. - They're not old at all.
соль (*fem.*) - salt
сосед (*pl.* соседи)/соседка - neighbor
сосед(ка) по комнате - roommate
соус - sauce
социология - sociology
спальня - bedroom
спасибо - thank you
большое спасибо - thank you very much
специальность (*fem.*) - academic major; field of concentration
спорт (*always singular*) - sports (*in general; not sport*)
спорттовары - sporting goods
среда - Wednesday
стадион (на) - stadium

стажёр - *stazher* (student on special course not leading to degree; used for foreign students doing work in Russia)
ста́рше (+ *genitive* на .... лет) - older than someone by x years (*See 10.1*)
ста́рший - elder
ста́рый - old
стена́ (*pl.* сте́ны) - wall
стол (*ending always stressed*) - table
пи́сьменный стол - desk
столо́вая (*declines like adj.*) - dining room; cafeteria
сто́ить (сто́ит, стоя́т) - to cost
стоя́ть (стою́, -и́шь, -я́т) - to stand
страна́ - country; nation
странове́дение - area studies
ру́сское странове́дение - Russian area studies
стра́шно - terribly
студе́нт/студе́нтка - student (*university, college, institute; not pre-college*)
стул (*pl.* сту́лья) - (hard) chair
суббо́та - Saturday
сувени́р - souvenir
суп - soup
сын (*pl.* сыновья́) - son
сыр - cheese
сюрпри́з - surprise

Т

так - so
тако́й - such; so (*used with noun*)
тако́й же - the same kind of
там - there
тамо́жня - customs
твой (твоя́, твоё, твои́) - your (*informal*) (*See 2.4*)
теа́тр - theater
телеви́зор - television
телеста́нция (на) - television station
тепе́рь - now (*as opposed to some other time*)
те́сто - dough
тётя - aunt
те́хника - gadgets; technology
вычисли́тельная те́хника - computer science
това́р - merchandise item
това́ры для же́нщин (мужчи́н, дете́й) - women's (men's, children's) merchandise
това́рищ по ко́мнате - roommate (male)
тогда́ - then; at that time; in that case
то́же - too
то́лько - only
то́лько что - just now
тома́тный - tomato (*adj.*)
тома́тный со́ус - tomato sauce
тот (то, та, те) - that; those (*as opposed to* э́тот)
то́чно - precisely
тради́ция - tradition
тре́тий (тре́тья, тре́тье, тре́тьи) - third
тро́е (дете́й) - three (children; *collective number; see 7.4*)
тру́дно (+ *dative*) - difficult (*See 9.3*)
тру́дный - difficult
туале́т - bathroom
туда́ - there (*answers* куда́)
туристи́ческий - tourist (*adj.*); travel (*adj.*)
туристи́ческое бюро́ - travel agency

тут - here
ту́фли (*pl.*) - shoes
ты - you (*informal*) (*See 1.1*)

У

у (+ *genitive*) - at (somebody's) house (*See 6.7*)
у роди́телей - at (one's) parents' (house)
у (+ *genitive* + есть + *nominative*) - (someone) has (something) (*See 6.2*)
У вас есть...? - Do you have ...? (*formal*) (*See 2.8*)
У меня́ есть.... - I have .... (*See 2.8*)
У тебя́ есть...? - Do you have ...? (*informal*) (*See 2.8*)
у (+ *genitive* + нет + *genitive*) - (someone) doesn't have (something) (*See 6.2*)
У меня́ не́т(у) - I don't have any of those (*See 2.8*)
убира́ть (убира́-ю, -ешь, -ют) (дом, кварти́ру, ко́мнату) - to straighten up (house, apartment, room)
уже́ - already
у́жин - supper
у́жинать/по- (у́жина-ю, -ешь, -ют) - to eat supper (dinner)
узна́ть *perf.* - to find out
украи́н(е)ц/украи́нка - Ukrainian (*See 3.6*)
украи́нский - Ukrainian (*See 3.5, 3.6*)
у́лица (на) - street
у́мный - intelligent
универма́г - department store
универса́м - self-serve grocery store
университе́т - university
упражне́ние - (training) exercise
обзо́рное упражне́ние - summary exercise; overview exercise
уро́к (на) - class; lesson (*practical*)
уро́к ру́сского языка́ - Russian class
услы́шать *perf.; see* слы́шать - to hear
у́стный - oral
у́тром - in the morning
уче́бник - textbook
учёный (*decl. like adj.; no feminine form*) - scholar; scientist
учи́тель (*pl.* учителя́) / учи́тельница - school teacher
учи́ться (учу́сь, у́чишься, у́чатся) - study; be a student (*cannot have direct object; see 4.3, 5.2*)
учрежде́ние - office
ую́тный - cozy; comfortable (*about room or house*)

Ф

факульте́т (на) - department of a college or university
фами́лия - last name (*See 1.2*)
фарш - chopped meat
фе́рма (на) - farm
фи́зика - physics
филологи́ческий - philological (*relating to the study of language and literature*)
филоло́гия - philology (*study of language and literature*)
филосо́фия - philosophy
фина́нсы - finance
фи́рма - company; firm
комме́рческая фи́рма - trade office; business office
фотоаппара́т - camera
фотогра́фия (на) - photo
францу́з/францу́женка - French (*See 3.6*)
францу́зский - French (*See 3.5, 3.6*)

фру́кты - fruit
футбо́лка - jersey

X

хи́мия - chemistry
хлеб - bread
ходи́ть (хож-у́, хо́д-ишь, -ят) - to go on foot (and come back; see 5.3, 8.4, 10.6)
холоди́льник - refrigerator
хоро́ший - good
хорошо́ - well; that's fine; that's good
хоте́ть (хочу́, хо́чешь, хо́чет, хоти́м, хоти́те, хотя́т) - to want (See 6.1)
худо́жник - artist

Ц

цвет (pl. цвета́) - color
цветно́й - color
цент (2-4 це́нта, 5-20 це́нтов) - cent
центр - downtown
цирк - circus
цыпля́та табака́ - a chicken dish from the Caucasus

Ч

чаевы́е (adj. decl. - plural) - tip
чай - tea
час (2-4 часа́, 5-12 часо́в) - o'clock
ча́стный - private (business, university, etc.)
ча́сто - frequently
часы́ (pl.) - watch
чей (чья, чьё, чьи) - whose? (See 2.4)
чек - check; receipt
челове́к (pl. лю́ди) - person
чемода́н - suitcase
черда́к (на чердаке́) (ending always stressed) - attic
че́рез (+ accusative or time expression) - in; after (See 10.4)
чёрно-бе́лый - black and white
чёрный - black
чесно́к - garlic
четве́рг - Thursday
че́тверо (дете́й) - four (children; collective number; see 7.4)
четвёртый - fourth
числи́тельное - numeral (adj. decl.)
чита́ть/про- (чита́-ю, -ешь, -ют) - to read
что - what (See 2.7, 4.5); that (See 4.5)
    О чём идёт речь? - What are we talking about?
    Что́ вы (ты)! - You can't be serious! (response to compliment)
    Что вы (нам, мне) посове́туете взять? - What do you advise (us, me) to order?
    Что ещё ну́жно? - What else is needed?
    Что э́то тако́е? - (Just) what is that?
чул(о́)к (endings always stressed) - stocking

Ш

ша́пка - cap; fur hat; knit hat
шашлы́к - shishkebab
шкаф (в шкафу́) (ending always stressed) - cabinet; wardrobe; free-standing closet
шко́ла - school (primary or secondary; not post-secondary)

шля́па - hat (e.g. business hat)
шокола́д - chocolate
штат - state

Щ

щи (always plural) - cabbage soup

Э

эконо́мика - economics
энерги́чный - energetic
эта́ж (на этаже́) (ending always stressed) - floor; storey
э́то - this is; that is; those are; these are
э́тот (э́та, э́то, э́ти) - this (See 2.7)

Ю

ю́бка - skirt
юг (на) - south
юриди́ческий - law (adj.); legal
    юриди́чкская фи́рма - law firm
юриспруде́нция - jurisprudence; (study of) law; legal system
юри́ст - lawyer

Я

я - I
язы́к (pl. языки́) - language (See 3.5)
на каки́х языка́х (вы говори́те, чита́ете, пи́шете) - What languages (do you speak, read, write)(See 3.5)
на како́м языке́ (вы говори́те, чита́ете, пи́шете) - What language (do you speak, read, write) (See 3.5)
преподава́тель ру́сского языка́ - Russian language teacher (in college)
язы́к в де́йствии - language in action
яйцо́ (pl. я́йца) - egg
япо́н(е)ц/япо́нка - Japanese (See 3.6)
япо́нский - Japanese (See 3.5, 3.6)

NUMBERS (See 6.6)

	Cardinal (one, two, three)	Ordinal (first, second, third)
1	оди́н, одна́, одно́	пе́рвый
2	два (две for feminine nouns)	второ́й
3	три	тре́тий
4	четы́ре	четвёртый
5	пять	пя́тый
6	шесть	шесто́й
7	семь	седьмо́й
8	во́семь	восьмо́й
9	де́вять	девя́тый
10	де́сять	деся́тый
11	оди́ннадцать	оди́ннадцатый
12	двена́дцать	двена́дцатый
13	трина́дцать	трина́дцатый
14	четы́рнадцать	четы́рнадцатый
15	пятна́дцать	пятна́дцатый
16	шестна́дцать	шестна́дцатый
17	семна́дцать	семна́дцатый
18	восемна́дцать	восемна́дцатый
19	девятна́дцать	девятна́дцатый
20	два́дцать	двадца́тый
21	два́дцать оди́н	два́дцать пе́рвый
30	три́дцать	тридца́тый

40	со́рок	сороково́й
50	пятьдеся́т	пятидеся́тый (пятьдеся́т пе́рвый)
60	шестьдеся́т	шестидеся́тый (шестьдеся́т пе́рвый)
70	се́мьдесят	семидеся́тый (се́мьдесят пе́рвый)
80	во́семьдесят	восьмидеся́тый (во́семьдесят пе́рвый)
90	девяно́сто	девяно́стый
100	сто	со́тый
200	две́сти	
300	три́ста	
400	четы́реста	
500	пятсо́т	
600	шестьсо́т	
700	семьсо́т	
800	восемьсо́т	
900	девятьсо́т	
1000	ты́сяча	

COLLECTIVES

дво́е, тро́е, че́тверо - 2, 3, 4 (*apply to children in a family; See 7.4*)

АНГЛО-РУССКИЙ СЛОВАРЬ

A

a bit about myself (yourself) - немно́го о себе́

about (*The form* об *is used before words beginning - о; об (+ prepositional with vowels* а, э, и, о, *or* у; *see 7.9*)

accountant - бухга́лтер

acquaintance - знако́мый

advise - сове́товать/по- (сове́ту-ю, -ешь, -ют + *dative*)
What would you advise us to get? - Что вы нам посове́туете взять?

after all - ведь (*never stressed*)

afterwards - пото́м

agency - бюро́ (*indecl.*)

ago - наза́д (*See 10.4*)

all day - весь день

allergy - аллерги́я

Allow me to introduce myself. - Разреши́те предста́виться.

alone - оди́н, одна́, одно́, одни́

alongside - ря́дом

already - уже́

always - всегда́

America (the U.S.) - Аме́рика

American - америка́н(е)ц/америка́нка; америка́нский (*See 3.6*)

and - и; а (*See 4.5*)

anthropology - антрополо́гия

apartment - кварти́ра

appetizers - заку́ски

apply to (*college, institute, etc.*) - поступа́ть (поступа́-ю, -ешь, -ют)/поступи́ть (поступл-ю́, посту́п-ишь, -ят) куда́ (*See 10.2*)

Arab - ара́б/ара́бка; (*See 3.6*)

Arabic - ара́бский; по-ара́бски (*See 3.5*)

architect - архите́ктор

architecture - архитекту́ра

area studies - странове́дение

Russian area studies - ру́сское странове́дение

armchair - кре́сло

Armenian - армяни́н (*pl.* армя́не)/армя́нка, армя́нский; по-апмя́нски (*See 3.5, 3.6*)

arrive (*by vehicle*) - приезжа́ть (приезжа́-ю, -ешь, -ют)/прие́хать (прие́д-у, -ешь, -ут)

art - иску́сство

artist - худо́жник

at - в (+ *prep.*); на (+ *prep.*) (*See 3.2, 4.2*)
at (somebody's) house (*See 6.7*) - у (+ *genitive*)
at ... o'clock - в + hour
at home - до́ма
at what time? - во ско́лько?

athletic shoes - кроссо́вки (*pl.*)

attic - черда́к (на чердаке́)(*ending always stressed*)

aunt - тётя

avant-garde artist - авангарди́ст

B

bad - плохо́й
That's bad. - Это пло́хо.

badly - пло́хо

bagel - бу́блик

bakery - бу́лочная (*adj. decl.*)

baking goods store - бакале́я

banana - бана́н

bank (financial institution) - банк

basement - подва́л

bathing suit - (women's) купа́льник; (men's) пла́вки (*always pl.*)

bathroom - туале́т (*toilet only*); ва́нная (*bath/shower only; declines like adj.*)

bathroom (bath/shower; no toilet) -

be - быть (бу́ду, бу́дешь, бу́дут; был, была́, бы́ли) (*used to form imperfective future; see 9.4-9.6*)

because - потому́ что (*See 4.5*)

bed - крова́ть (*fem.*)

bedroom - спа́льня

before that - до э́того

begin a job - пойти́ рабо́тать (пойд-у́, ёшь, у́т) (куда́) (*perf.*)

begin with; at first - снача́ла

believer - ве́рующий (*declines like adj.*)

belt (man's) - рем(е́)нь (*endings always stressed*)

big - большо́й

biology - биоло́гия

birthday (*lit.* day of birth) - д(е)нь рожде́ния

Happy birthday! - С днём рожде́ния!

bit: a little bit - немно́го; немно́жко

black - чёрный

black and white - чёрно-бе́лый

blouse - блу́зка

blue - си́ний; light blue - голубо́й

book - кни́га

book(ish) - кни́жный

book mart - кни́жный ры́н(о)к

boot - сапо́г (*ending always stressed*)

boring - неинтере́сный

born (to be born) - роди́ться (*perf. past:* роди́лся, родила́сь, родили́сь) (*See 7.3*)

borshch - борщ

boullion - бульо́н

boy - ма́льчик

bread - хлеб

breakfast - за́втрак

eat breakfast - за́втракать/по-

brother - брат (*pl.* бра́тья)

brown - кори́чневый

bureau (agency) - бюро́ (*indecl.*)

businessperson - бизнесме́н/бизнесме́нка; коммерса́нт

but - но (*See 4.5*)

buy - покупа́ть (покуп-а́ю -ешь, -ют)/купи́ть (куплю́, ку́пишь, -ят)

C

cabbage - капу́ста

cabbage soup - щи (*always plural*)

cabinet - шкаф (в шкафу́)(*ending always stressed*)

café - кафе́ [кафэ́] (*neuter; indecl.*)

cafeteria - столо́вая (*declines like adj.*); кафете́рий (slightly better than a столо́вая)

camera - фотоаппара́т

can (one) - мо́жно (*with dative + infinitive; see 8.6*)

    Can I pay in dollars? - Мо́жно плати́ть до́лларами?

    I can - Я могу́ (+ *infinitive*)

Canada - Кана́да

Canadian - кана́д(е)ц/кана́дка; кана́дский (*See 3,5 3.6*)

cannot - невозмо́жно (*with dative +infinitive; see 9.3*)

cap - ша́пка

car - маши́на

carrot - морко́вь (*fem.*)

cash register - ка́сса

cassette - кассе́та

cassette recorder - кассе́тный магнитофо́н; кассе́тник

caviar - икра́

cent - цент (2-4 це́нта, 5-20 це́нтов)

chair - стул (*pl.* сту́лья)

check - чек

    The check, please... - Рассчита́йте меня́ (нас)!; Ско́лько с меня́ (с нас)?

cheerful (un-) - весёлый (не-)

cheese - сыр

chemistry - хи́мия

chicken - ку́рица

child(ren) - ребён(о)к (*pl.* де́ти: оди́н ребёнок, дво́е дете́й, тро́е дете́й, че́тверо дете́й, пять дете́й) (*See 7.5*)

Chinese - кита́(е)ц (*pl.* кита́йцы)/китая́нка;кита́йский; по-кита́йски (*See 3.5*)

chocolate - шокола́д

choice - вы́бор

chopped meat - фарш

circus - цирк

class - (*practical lesson - generic*) - уро́к (на); (*collecge class*) заня́тие (на; *usually plural*); (*90-minute class period in Russian universities*) па́ра; (*course*) курс (на); (*class-room*) аудито́рия

    They're in Russian class now - Они́ сейча́с на уро́ке ру́сского языка́.

    She's in classes now - Она́ сейча́с на заня́тиях.

    I'm taking a class in Russian - Я слу́шаю курс ру́сского языка́.

classroom - аудито́рия

close (*something; must take a direct object*) - закры́ть *perf.*

    Close! - Закро́й(те)!

close (to get closed) - закры́ться *perf. past* (закры́лся, закры́лась, закры́лось, закры́лись).

    The door closed. - Дверь закры́лась.

closed - закры́т (-а,-о,-ы)

closet (free-standing) - шкаф (в шкафу́)(*ending always stressed*)

clothing - оде́жда

coat (long overcoat) - пальто́; (jacket- or parka-length coat) - ку́ртка

coffee - ко́фе (*masc.; indecl.*)

    coffee with milk - ко́фе с молоко́м

cold cuts salad - мясно́е ассорти́

color - цвет (*pl.* цвета́); (*adj.*) цветно́й

    What color (is something)- Како́го цве́та (+ *nominative*)

Come in; Go on through. - Проходи́(те).

comfortable (*about room or house*) - ую́тный

commercial - комме́рческий

company; firm - фи́рма

completely - совсе́м

computer - компью́тер

computer programmer - программи́ст

computer science - вычисли́тельная те́хника

corridor - коридо́р

cosmetics shop - парфюме́рия

cost - сто́ить (сто́ит, сто́ят)

couch - дива́н

Could you please...? - Бу́дьте добры́!

country - страна́

course - курс (на)

    Russian course - курс ру́сского языка́

cousin - (female) двою́родная сестра́; (male) двою́родный брат

cozy - ую́тный

cucumber - огур(е́)ц;

    cucumber salad - сала́т из огурцо́в

cuisine - ку́хня
customs (at border control) - тамо́жня
customs declaration - деклара́ция

D

dacha - да́ча (на)
dad - па́па
dairy - моло́чный
daughter - дочь (*gen. and prep. sg.* до́чери; *nom. pl.* до́чери)
day - д(е)нь (*pl.* дни)
all day - весь день
decide - реша́ть (реша́-ю, -ешь, -ют)/реши́ть (реш-у́, -и́шь, -а́т)
delicious - вку́сный
dentist - зубно́й врач (*all endings stressed*)
department (of a store) - отде́л; (*in a university, college, or institute*) - ка́федра (на); факульте́т (на) (*Note: a факульте́т is bigger than a ка́федра.*)
department store - универма́г
desk - пи́сьменный стол
dessert - сла́дкое (*adj. decl.*)
dictionary - слова́рь (*pl.* словари́)
difficult - тру́дный; тру́дно (+ *dative; see 9.3*)
dining room - столо́вая (*declines like adj.*)
dish (*food, not the physical plate*) - блю́до
Do you have ...? - У вас (тебя́) есть...? У тебя́ есть...? (*See 2.8*)
Do you have any literature with you? - Литерату́ру везёте?
do - де́лать/с- (де́ла-ю, -ешь, -ют)
doctor - врач (*all endings stressed*)
document - докуме́нт
dollar - до́ллар (5-20 до́лларов)
door - дверь (*fem.*)
dormitory - общежи́тие
dough - те́сто
downtown - це́нтр
dress (*noun*) - пла́тье; (*verb*) get dressed - одева́ться (одева́юсь, одева́ешься, одева́ются)
drink (*noun*) - напи́т(о)к; (*verb*) пить (пью, пьёшь, пьют; пил, пила́, пи́ли)/вы́- (вы́пью, вы́пьешь, вы́пьют; вы́пила)

E

each - ка́ждый
early - ра́но
east - восто́к (на)
easy - легко́ (+ *dative; see 9.3*)
eat - есть/съ- (ем, ешь, есть, еди́м, еди́те, едя́т; ел, е́ла, е́ли)
eat breakfast - за́втракать/по- (за́втрака-ю, -ешь, -ют);
eat lunch (or mid-day dinner) - обе́дать/по- (обе́да-ю, -ешь, -ют);
eat supper (dinner) - у́жинать/по- (у́жина-ю, -ешь, -ют)
economics - эконо́мика
education (*a subject in college*) - педаго́гика
education - образова́ние
higher education - вы́сшее образова́ние
egg - яйцо́ (*pl.* я́йца)
elder - ста́рший
else - ещё; What else? - Что ещё?
energetic - энерги́чный
engineer - инжене́р

England - А́нглия
English - англича́нин (*pl.* англича́не)/англича́нка; англи́йский; по-англи́йски (*See 3.5, 3.6*)
English department - ка́федра англи́йского языка́
enroll in - поступа́ть (поступа́-ю,-ешь,-ют)/поступи́ть (поступл-ю́, поступ-ишь, -ят) куда́ (*See 10.2*)
entrée - второ́е (*adj. decl.*)
European - европе́ец/европе́йка; европе́йский (*See 3.5, 3.6*)
even - да́же
every - ка́ждый
every day - ка́ждый день
everybody - все
everything - всё
example: for example - наприме́р
excellent - отли́чно
exchange student (*stazher, student on special course not leading to degree; used for foreign students doing work in Russia*) - стажёр
Excuse me! - Извини́те! Прости́те!
Excuse me, miss! - Де́вушка!
Excuse me, sir! - Молодо́й челове́к!
exercise (e.g. training exercise) - упражне́ние
eyeglasses - очки́ (*always plural*)

F

factory - заво́д (на)
family - семья́ (*pl.* се́мьи)
farm - фе́рма (на)
farther - да́льше
father - от(е́)ц (*all endings stressed*)
favorite - люби́мый; least favorite - са́мый нелюби́мый
fifth - пя́тый
finally - наконе́ц
finances - фина́нсы
find out - узна́ть (*perf.*)
first - пе́рвый
first course (always soup) - пе́рвое (*adj. decl.*)
first name - и́мя (*neut.*) (*See 1.2*)
floor (storey) - эта́ж (на этаже́) (*ending always stressed*); (as opposed to ceiling) пол (на полу́) (*ending always stressed*)
fluently - свобо́дно
food - пи́ща
footwear - о́бувь (*fem.*)
for example - наприме́р
forbidden; not allowed - нельзя́ (+ *dative; see 9.3*)
foreign - иностра́нный
forget - забы́ть (*perf.*) забу́д-у, -ешь, -ут)
four (children) - че́тверо (дете́й) (*collective number; see 7.4*)
fourth - четвёртый
free (not busy) - свобо́ден (свобо́дна, свобо́дны)
French - францу́з/францу́женка; францу́зский; по-францу́зски (*See 3.5, 3.6*)
frequently - ча́сто
Friday - пя́тница
friend - друг (*pl.* друзья́); знако́мый
fried steak - ланге́т
frivolous - несерьёзный
from (a place) - из (+ *genitive*)
fruit - фру́кты
furniture - ме́бель (*fem., always singular*)
further - да́льше

G

gadgets - те́хника (*always singular*)
garage - гара́ж (*ending always stressed*)
garlic - чесно́к
German - не́м(е)ц/не́мка; неме́цкий; по-неме́цки (*See 3.5, 3.6*)
get a job - пойти́ рабо́тать (пойд-у́, -ёшь, -у́т) (*куда́*) (*perf.*)
get dressed - одева́ться (одева́-юсь, -ешься, -ются)
get in - попа́сть (*perf.*) попаду́, -ёшь, -ут) (*куда́*)
    We'll get in for sure. - Мы то́чно попадём.
get up - встава́ть (встав-ю́, -ёшь, -ю́т)
gift - пода́р(о)к
girl - (*pre-adolescent*) де́вочка; (*adolescent and /or young woman*) - де́вушка
give a present - дари́ть/по (дар-ю́, да́р-ишь, -ят)
give as a present - подари́ть (*perf.; see* дари́ть)
glove - перча́тка
glum - невесёлый
go (*set out on foot, or within city; see 5.3, 8.4, 10.6*) - идти́ (ид-у́, -ёшь, -у́т)/пойти́ (пойд-у́, -ёшь, -у́т; пошёл, пошла́, пошли́); (*go and come back by foot; see 10.6*) - ходи́ть (хож-у́, хо́д-ишь, -ят); (*set out by vehicle - see 5.3, 10.6*) - е́хать/по- (е́д-у, -ешь, -ут); (*go and come back by vehicle; see 10.6*) - е́здить (е́зжу, е́здишь, е́здят); Let's go! - (*by foot*) Пошли́!; Пойдём!; (*by vehicle*) - Пое́дем!; Let's go to ... instead. - Пойдём лу́чше...; go! (*imperative*) - иди́(те); go to bed - ложи́ться (спать) (ложу́сь, -и́шься, -а́тся); Would you like to go ...? - Не хо́чешь (хоти́те) пойти́ (пое́хать)...?
good - хоро́ший
    pretty good - неплохо́й
    good tasting - вку́сный
    Good afternoon. - До́брый день!
    Good bye. - До свида́ния.
    Good evening. - До́брый ве́чер!
    Good going! (*used for both sexes*) - Како́й ты (он, она́, etc.) молоде́ц!
    Good morning. - До́брое у́тро!
grade level (*in elementary or high school: first, second, third, etc.*) - класс (в)
graduate from - око́нчить *perf.; see* зака́нчивать
graduate from (*requires direct object*) - зака́нчивать (зака́нчива-ю, -ешь, -ют)/око́нчить (око́нч-у, -ишь, -ат) (*+ accusative; see 10.2*)
graduate school - аспиранту́ра
granddaughter - вну́чка
grandfather - де́душка
grandmother - ба́бушка
grandson - внук
grape(s) - виногра́д (*always singular*)
gray - се́рый
green - зелёный
groceries - проду́кты
grocery store - продово́льственный магази́н; гастроно́м
grow up - вы́расти (*perf. past:* вы́рос, вы́росла, вы́росли) (*See 7.3*)
guys (*conversational term of address*) - ребя́та

H

haberdashery - галантере́я
hallway - коридо́р

hand: on the one hand ..., on the other hand ... - с одно́й стороны́ ..., с друго́й стороны́ ...
handkerchief - плат(о́)к (*endings always stressed*)
hang (be hanging) - висе́ть (вишу́, -и́шь, -я́т)
Happy birthday! - С днём рожде́ния!
hard currency (*adj.*) - валю́тный
    hard currency store - валю́тный магази́н
hat (business hat or hat with a large brim) - шля́па; (fur hat or knit hat) - ша́пка
have: (someone) has (something) - у + *genitive* + есть + *nominative* (*See 6.2*)
have not: (someone) doesn't have (something) - у + *genitive* + нет + *genitive* (*See 6.2*)
he - он
headwear - головно́й убо́р
health clinic - поликли́ника
healthy (un-) - здоро́вый (не-)
hear - слы́шать/у- (слы́ш-у, -ишь, -ат)
Hello - Здра́вствуй(те)!; (*on the telephone only*) - Алло́!
her(s) - её
here - здесь; тут
here is ... - вот ...
higher education - вы́сшее образова́ние
his - его́
history - исто́рия
home - (*place of residence*) дом (*pl.* дома́); (*answers* где; *see 5.5*) - до́ма; (*answers* куда; *see 5.5*) - домо́й
homework: do homework - занима́ться (занима́-юсь, -ешься, -ются) (*See 5.2*)
hospital - больни́ца
hot (*of things, not weather*) - горя́чий
housewife - домохозя́йка
how - как (*See 4.5*)
    How are you? (*informal*) - Как ты?
    How do you know Russian? - Отку́да вы зна́ете ру́сский язы́к?
    How do you say "last name" in Russian? - Как по-ру́сски «last name»?
    How do you say ... in Russian? - Как по-ру́сски...?
    How old is...? - Ско́лько (+ *dative*) лет? (*See 7.4*)
    how many (also how much) - ско́лько
    How many rooms do you have? - Ско́лько у вас ко́мнат?
    How much does it cost? - Ско́лько сто́ит?
huge - огро́мный
husband - муж (*pl.* мужья́)

I

I - я
    I can - могу́ (+ *infinitive*)
    I don't have any of those - У меня́ не́ту (*See 2.8*)
    I have .... - У меня́ есть.... (*See 2.8*)
    I was told that... - Мне сказа́ли, что...
    I wonder...; it's interesting... - интере́сно...
    I'll think about it; Let me think about it - поду́маю
    ice-cream - моро́женое (*adj. decl.*)
icon - ико́на
identification (ID document) - докуме́нт
if - е́сли
impossible (*See 9.3*) - невозмо́жно (+ *dative*)
    That's impossible! - Не мо́жет быть!
impressionist - импрессиони́ст

in; at (*See 3.2, 4.2*) - в (+ *prep.*)
    in my passport it says ... - в па́спорте стои́т ...
    in my passport it says ... - в па́спорте стои́т ...
    in the afternoon - днём; in the evening - ве́чером
    in the first place ..., in the second place ... -
    во-пе́рвых ..., во-вторы́х ...
    in the morning - у́тром
    in the night - но́чью
    in the south (north, east, west) of the country - на ю́ге
    (на се́вере, на восто́ке, на за́паде) страны́
    in what year (*in university or institute*) - на како́м ку́рсе
    in what year (*in university or institute*) - на како́м ку́рсе
institute (*institution of post-secondary education*) - институ́т
    Institute of Foreign Languages - Институ́т иностра́нных
    языко́в
intelligent - у́мный
interesting - интере́сный
international affairs - междунаро́дные отноше́ния
Irkutsk (*a city in Siberia*) - Ирку́тск
it - он; она́; оно́ (*See 2.3*)
    it is necessary - на́до: *dative* + на́до + *infinitive (for*
    someone to do something; see 8.6)
    it is possible - мо́жно: *dative* + на́до + *infinitive (for*
    someone to do something; see 8.6)
    it seems - ка́жется
    it's okay - ла́дно
Italian - италья́н(е)ц/италья́нка; италья́нский; по-
    италья́нски (*See 3.5, 3.6*)

J, K

Japanese - япо́н(е)ц/япо́нка; япо́нский; по-япо́нски (*See 3.5,*
    3.6)
jeans - джи́нсы (*pl.*)
jersey - футбо́лка
journalism - журнали́стика
journalist - журнали́ст
just now - то́лько что
    Just a moment! - Одну́ мину́точку!
kerchief - плат(о́)к (*endings always stressed*)
Kiev cutlets - котле́ты по-ки́евски
kitchen - ку́хня (на)
kopeck - копе́йка (2-4 копе́йки, 5-20 копе́ек; *See 9.2*)

L

laboratory - лаборато́рия
lamp - ла́мпа
language - язы́к (*pl.* языки́; *endings always stressed*) (*See 3.5*)
large - большо́й
last - после́дний
last name - фами́лия (*See 1.2*)
last year - в про́шлом году́
late - по́здно
to be late - опа́здывать (опа́здыва-ю, -ешь, -ют)
later - пото́м
law - (study of law) юриспруде́нция; (*adj.: legal, having to*
    do with laws) - юриди́ческий
law firm - юриди́чкская фи́рма
lawyer - юри́ст
lecture - ле́кция
left: on the left - нале́во

let's - Дава́й(те) (+ *future tense of* мы)
    Let's get acquainted. - Дава́й(те) познако́мимся!
    Let's go! - (*by foot*) Пошли́!; Пойдём!; (*by vehicle*) -
    Пое́дем!
    Let's go to ... instead. - Пойдём лу́чше...
    Let's see. - (Let's take a look...) Посмо́трим...; (Hmm,
    let's see...) Зна́чит так...
    Let's switch to ты. - Дава́й перейдём на ты.
letter - письмо́ (*pl.* пи́сьма)
librarian - библиоте́карь
library - библиоте́ка
lie - лежа́ть (лежу́, -и́шь, -а́т)
light blue - голубо́й
listen to - слу́шать/про- (also по-) (слу́ша-ю, -ешь, -ют)
    (+ *accusative*); Listen! - (По)слу́шай(те)!
literature - литерату́ра
little - ма́ленький
a little bit - немно́го; немно́жко
live - жить (живу́, живёшь, живу́т)
living conditions - жили́щные усло́вия
living room - гости́ная (*declines like adj.*)
loaf - бу́лка
London - Ло́ндон
long time - давно́ (+ *present tense verb*); до́лго (+ *past tense*
    verb)
look at - смотре́ть/по- (смотр-ю́, смо́тр-ишь, -ят)
look like - похо́ж (-а, -и) (на + *accusative; see 10.1*)
Los Angeles - Лос-Анджелес
love - люби́ть (люб-лю́, лю́б-ишь, -ят)
lunch - обе́д
Lunch is ready. - Обе́д гото́в.

M

magazine - журна́л
main course - второ́е (*adj. decl.*)
major - (academic concentration) специа́льность (*fem.*)
make - де́лать/с- (де́ла-ю, -ешь, -ют)
manage to get in - попа́сть (*perf.* попад-у́,-ёшь, -у́т;
    попа́л, -а, -и)
manager - ме́неджер
map - ка́рта
market - ры́н(о)к (на)
mathematics - матема́тика
may (*asking permission*) - мо́жно: *dative* + на́до + *infinitive*
    (*for someone to do something; see 8.6*)
    May I look at the apartment? - Мо́жно посмотре́ть
    кварти́ру?
maybe - мо́жет быть
meanwhile - пока́
meat - мя́со; мясно́й (*adj.*)
chopped meat - фарш
medicine (*the sudy of; not remedy for illness*) - медици́на
men's accessories shop - галантере́я
men's; masculine - мужско́й
menu - меню́ (*neuter; indecl.*)
merchandise item - това́р
Mexican - мексика́н(е)ц/мексика́нка; мексика́нский (*See*
    3.5, 3.6)
milk - молоко́; (*adj.*) моло́чный
mineral water - минера́льная вода́
mittens - ва́режки (*pl.*)

mom - ма́ма
Monday - понеде́льник
money - де́ньги (*always plural*)
month - ме́сяц (2-4 ме́сяца, пять ме́сяцев)
Moscow - Москва́; - (*adj.*) моско́вский
    from Moscow - из Москвы́
most: the most + *adjective* - са́мый + *adjective*
mother - мать (*gen. and prep. sg.* ма́тери; *nom. pl.* ма́тери)
move, take up a new living place - переезжа́ть (переезжа́-ю, -ешь, -ют)/перее́хать (перее́д-у, -ешь, -ут) (*куда́*)
movie theater - кинотеа́тр; кино́ (*indecl.*)
movies - кино́ (*indecl.*)
museum - музе́й
music - му́зыка
musician - музыка́нт
must - до́лжен (должна́, должны́) + *infinitive* (*See 5.6*)
my - мой (моя́, моё, мой) (*See 2.4*)

N

name - и́мя (*neuter; pl.* имена́)
    My name is ... - Меня́ зову́т ...
    What's your first name? - Как ва́ше и́мя
    last name - фами́лия (*See 1.2*)
nationality - национа́льность (*fem.*)
    What's your nationality? - Кто вы по национа́льности?
natural gas - газ
necessary: it's necessary - на́до: *dative* + на́до + *infinitive* (*for someone to do something; see 8.6*)
neighbor - сосе́д (*pl.* сосе́ди)/сосе́дка
neither ... nor ... - ни ... ни ...
nephew - племя́нник
nested doll - матрёшка
never - никогда́ (не)
new - но́вый
New York - Нью-Йо́рк
newspaper - газе́та
next to - ря́дом
nice (not...) - симпати́чный (не-)
niece - племя́нница
no - нет
normally - норма́льно
north - се́вер (на)
not at all - совсе́м не
    Твой де́душка совсе́м не ста́рый! - Your grandfather is not old at all!
not far - недалеко́
not (*negates following word*) - не
nothing - ничего́ (не)
nothing of interest - ничего́ интере́сного (+ не + *verb*)
now - сейча́с; (*as opposed to some other time*) - тепе́рь
number - но́мер (*pl.* номера́)
numeral - числи́тельное (*adj. decl.*)
nurse (female) - медсестра́ (*pl.* медсёстры);
    (male) - медбра́т (*pl.* медбра́тья)

O

o'clock - час (2-4 часа́, 5-12 часо́в)
of course - коне́чно
office - (place of work) кабине́т; (bureau, agency) - учрежде́ние
oh! - ой

okay - ла́дно; хорошо́; (we've agreed) - договори́лись.
old - ста́рый
    How old is...? - Ско́лько (+ *dative*) лет? (*See 7.4*)
older than someone by x years - ста́рше (+ *genitive* на .... лет) (*See 10.1*)
on - на (+ *prepositional; see 3.2, 4.2*)
on (a day of the week) - в + *accusative case of days of week*
on the left; to the left - нале́во
on the one hand ..., on the other hand ... - с одно́й стороны́ ..., с друго́й стороны́ ...
on the right - напра́во
one's own - свой
one - оди́н (одна́, одно́, одни́)
oneself - сам (сама́, са́ми)
onion(s) - лук
only - то́лько (*adv.*); еди́нственный (*adj.*)
    only child - еди́нственный ребёнок
open (*something; must take a direct object*) - откры́ть *perf.*
get opened - откры́ться (*perf. past* откры́лся, откры́лась, откры́лось, откры́лись)
    Дверь откры́лась. - The door opened.
    Open! - Откро́йте!
or - и́ли
oral - у́стный
    oral exercise - у́стное упражне́ние
orange - апельси́н
order - зака́зывать (зака́зыва-ю, -ешь, -ют)/заказа́ть (закажу́, зака́жешь, зака́жут)
ordinary (unusual) - обыкнове́нный (не-)
our - наш (на́ша, на́ше, на́ши) (*See 2.4*)
owe(s) ... - с (+ *genitive*) ...
    How much do we owe? - Ско́лько с нас?
own - свой
overcoat - пальто́ (*neuter; indecl.*)

P

pants - брю́ки (*pl.*)
pantyhose - колго́тки (*pl.*)
parents - роди́тели
passport - па́спорт (*pl.* паспорта́)
patronymic - о́тчество (*See 1.2*)
pay - плати́ть/за- (плач-у́, пла́т-ишь, -ят)
    Pay the cashier. - Плати́те в ка́ссу.
pension - пе́нсия
    on pension (retired) - на пе́нсии
pepper - пе́р(е)ц
person - челове́к (*pl.* лю́ди)
philological (*relating to the study of language and literature*) - филологи́ческий
philology (*study of language and literature*) - филоло́гия
philosophy - филосо́фия
phonograph record - грамаласти́нка
photo - фотогра́фия (на)
physician - врач (*all endings stressed*)
physics - фи́зика
pizza - пи́цца
place of work - ме́сто рабо́ты
please - пожа́луйста; бу́дьте добры́
    Please bring a menu. - Принеси́те, пожа́луйста, меню́.
    Please give (us, me) the check. - Рассчита́йте (нас, меня́)!

pleased - (*dative* +) прия́тно
    Pleased to meet you. - Очень прия́тно (с ва́ми, с тобо́й) (познако́миться).
pleasure: with pleasure - с удово́льствием
political - полити́ческий
political science - полити́ческие нау́ки
poorly - пло́хо
portion - по́рция
possible: it's possible - мо́жно: *dative* + на́до + *infinitive* (*for someone to do something; see 8.6*)
potato - карто́фель (always singular); (*conversational*) карто́шка (*always singular*)
practice - пра́ктика
precisely - то́чно
prepare - гото́вить/при- (гото́в-лю, -ишь, -ят)
prepared - гото́вый
pretty - краси́вый
pretty good - неплохо́й
pretty well - непло́хо
previously - ра́ньше
printer - при́нтер
private (business, university, etc.) - ча́стный
    private practice - ча́стная пра́ктика
probably - наве́рное
profession - профе́ссия
    What's your profession? - Кто вы по профе́ссии?
psychology - психоло́гия

Q, R

Quebec - Квебе́к
quickly - бы́стро
quite - дово́льно
radio - ра́дио (радиоприёмник)
rarely - ре́дко
read - чита́ть/про- (чита́-ю, -ешь, -ют)
real estate agency - бюро́ недви́жимости
Really? - (Indeed?) Пра́вда?; (Oh, so that's it!) Вот как?!
receipt - чек
recently - неда́вно
record (phonograph) - пласти́нка
recording - за́пись (*fem.*)
red - кра́сный
refrigerator - холоди́льник
relative - ро́дственник
relax - отдыха́ть (отдыха́-ю, -ешь, -ют)
resemble - похо́ж (-а, -и) (на + *accusative*) (*See 10.1*)
rest - отдыха́ть (отдыха́-ю, -ешь, -ют)
restaurant-cafeteria - кафете́рий
retired - на пе́нсии
rice - рис
roast beef - ро́стбиф
roll (bread) - бу́лка
roommate - сосе́д(ка) по ко́мнате; (male only) това́рищ по ко́мнате
ruble - рубль (masc.; 2-4 рубля́, пять рубле́й; *endings always stressed; see 9.2*)
rug - ков(ё)р (*ending always stressed*)
running shoes - кроссо́вки (*pl.*)
Russia - Росси́я
Russian - ру́сский/ру́сская; ру́сский; по-ру́сски (*See 3.5, 3.6*)
    Russian area studies - ру́сское странове́дение

Russian class (*lesson, not course*) - уро́к ру́сского языка́
Russian course - курс ру́сского языка́
Russian department - ка́федра ру́сского языка́
Russian language teacher (*in college*) - преподава́тель ру́сского языка́
Russian textbook - уче́бник ру́сского языка́

S

salad; lettuce - сала́т
    cucumber salad - сала́т из огурцо́в
salesperson - продав(е́)ц (*all endings stressed*) / продавщи́ца
salt - соль (*fem.*)
same kind of - тако́й же
sandwich (open-faced) - бутербро́д
Saturday - суббо́та
sauce - со́ус
sausage - колбаса́
say - сказа́ть (*perf.; see* говори́ть)
    They say that... - Говоря́т, что...
scholar - учёный (*declines like adjective; no feminine form*)
school (*primary or secondary; not post-secondary*) - шко́ла
school of international affairs - институ́т междунаро́дных отноше́ний
school teacher - учи́тель (*pl.* учителя́) / учи́тельница
science - нау́ка
political science - полити́ческие нау́ки
scientist - учёный (*declines like adjective; no feminine form*)
second - второ́й
secretary - секрета́рь (*masc. endings, applies to men and women; all endings stressed*)
selection - вы́бор
self - сам (сама́, са́ми)
self-serve grocery store - универса́м
serious - серьёзный
she - она́
shirt - руба́шка
shishkebab - шашлы́к
shoes - ту́фли (*pl.*)
athletic shoes - кроссо́вки (*pl.*)
short jacket - ку́ртка
show - пока́зывать (пока́зыва-ю, -ешь, -ют)/показа́ть (покаж-у́, пока́ж-ешь, -ут)
Show! - Покажи́(те)!
shower (*noun*) - душ; (*verb*) принима́ть душ
simply - про́сто
sister - сестра́ (*pl.* сёстры)
size - разме́р
skirt - ю́бка
slowly - ме́дленно
    Speak more slowly. - Говори́те ме́дленнее.
small - ма́ленький
smart - у́мный
so - тако́й (*adj.*); так (*adv.*)
    This course is so interesting! - Этот курс тако́й интере́сный.
    You speak Russian so well! - Вы говори́те по-ру́сски так хорошо́!
so... (*lit.* it means) - зна́чит...
sociology - социоло́гия
sock - нос(о́)к (*stress always on ending*)
soft drink - лимона́д

sometimes - иногда́
son - сын (*pl.* сыновья́)
soon - ско́ро
soup - суп
south - юг (на)
souvenir - сувени́р
Spanish - испа́н(е)ц/испа́нка; испа́нский; по-испа́нски (*See 3.5, 3.6*)
speak - говори́ть (говор-ю́, -и́шь, -я́т)/по- (*The other perfective form,* сказа́ть, *means to say*)
    Let's chat - Дава́йте поговори́м
sporting goods - спортто́вары
sports (*in general; not sport*) - спорт (*always singular*)
St. Petersburg - Санкт-Петербу́рг; (*adj.*) Санкт-Петербу́ргский
stadium - стадио́н (на)
stairway - ле́стница
stand - стоя́ть (стою́, -и́шь, -я́т)
state (of the U.S.)- штат
state (adj.: government-owned) - госуда́рственный
steak - бифште́кс; fried steak - ланге́т
still - ещё
stocking - чул(о́)к (*endings always stressed*)
store - магази́н
department store - универма́г
stove - плита́ (*pl.* пли́ты)
straighten up (house, apartment, room) - убира́ть (убира́ю, убира́ешь, убира́ют) (дом, кварти́ру, ко́мнату)
street - у́лица (на)
student (*university, college, institute; not pre-college*) - студе́нт/студе́нтка
    exchange student - стажёр (*stazher, student on special course not leading to degree; used for American graduate students doing work in Russia*)
study - занима́ться (занима́-юсь, -ешься, -ются) (*do homework*); изуча́ть (изуча́-ю, -ешь, -ют)(*take a subject in school or college; requires direct object*); -учи́ться (учу́сь, у́чишься, у́чатся)(*be a student; cannot have direct object*)(*See 4.3, 5.2*)
suburb - при́город
such (*used with noun*) - тако́й
suit - костю́м
suit jacket - пиджа́к
suitcase - чемода́н
Sunday - воскресе́нье
supper - у́жин
surprise - сюрпри́з
sweater - сви́тер (*pl.* свитера́)
swimming pool - бассе́йн
swimming trunks - пла́вки (*always plural*)

Т

table - стол (*ending always stressed*)
take - брать (бер-у́, -ёшь, -у́т; брала́, бра́ли)/взять (возьм-у́, -ёшь, -у́т; взяла́, взя́ли)
Take it! (*Said when paying at a store, in a restaurant, etc.*) - Получи́те!
take (a shower) - принима́ть (душ) (приним-а́ю, -ешь, -ют)
tape recorder - магнитофо́н
tasty - вку́сный
tea - чай

teach - преподава́ть (препода-ю́, -ёшь, -ю́т)
teacher (*in college*) - преподава́тель
technology - те́хника
tee shirt - ма́йка
television - телеви́зор
television station - телеста́нция (на)
tell - (narrate) расска́зывать (расска́зыва-ю, -ешь, -ют)/рассказа́ть (расскаж-у́, расска́ж-ешь, -ут); Tell (me)... (*request for narrative, not just a piece of factual information*) - Расскажи́(те) (мне)...
terribly - стра́шно
textbook - уче́бник
    Russian textbook - уче́бник ру́сского языка́
time: What time is it? - Ско́лько сейча́с вре́мени?
thank you - спаси́бо
    Thank you very much - большо́е спаси́бо; огро́мное спаси́бо
that (*as opposed to* э́тот *refers to things very far away*) - тот (то, та, те)
theater - теа́тр
their(s) - их
then (*at that time; in that case*) - тогда́; (later) пото́м
there - (*answers* где) там; (*answers* куда́) - туда́
there is - есть (+ *nominative; see 6.3*)
there is not - нет (+ *genitive; see 6.4*)
they - они́
thing - вещь (*fem.*)
think - ду́мать/по- (ду́ма-ю, -ешь, -ют)
third - тре́тий (тре́тья, тре́тье, тре́тьи)
this - э́тот (э́та, э́то, э́ти) (*See 2.7*)
this is (that is; those are; these are)- э́то
three (children) - тро́е (дете́й; *collective number; see 7.4*)
Thursday - четве́рг
tie - га́лстук
time: for a long time - давно́ (+ *present tense verb*); до́лго (+ *past tense verb*)
tip - чаевы́е (*adj. decl. - plural*)
to - в (+ *accusative case for direction*); на (+ *accusative for direction*) (*See 5.4*)
to the left - нале́во
to the right - напра́во
today - сего́дня
together - вме́сте
tomato - помидо́р; (*adj.*) - тома́тный
    tomato salad - сала́т из помидо́ров
    tomato sauce - тома́тный со́ус
tomorrow - за́втра
too - то́же
tourist (*adj.*) - туристи́ческий
toy - игру́шка
trade office; business office - комме́рческая фи́рма
tradition - тради́ция
travel (*adj.*) - туристи́ческий
    travel agency - туристи́ческое бюро́
truth - пра́вда
Tuesday - вто́рник
two (children) - дво́е (дете́й; *collective number; see 7.4*)

U, V, W

ugly - некраси́вый
Ukrainian - украи́н(е)ц/украи́нка; украи́нский; по-украи́нски (See 3.5, 3.6)
uncle - дя́дя
understand - понима́ть (понима́-ю, -ешь, -ют); Understood (Got it). - Поня́тно.
university - университе́т
unusual - необыкнове́нный
usually - обы́чно
vegetable - о́вощ; (adj.) - овощно́й
very - о́чень
video cassette - видеокассе́та
video cassette recorder - видеомагнитофо́н
visa - ви́за
voice - го́лос (pl. голоса́)
wall - стена́ (pl. сте́ны)
want - хоте́ть (хочу́, хо́чешь, хо́чет, хоти́м, хоти́те, хотя́т) (See 6.1)
watch - смотре́ть/по- (смотр-ю́, смо́тр-ишь, -ят)
watch (wristwatch) - часы́ (pl.)
water - вода́ (pl. во́ды)
we - мы
We like Russian cuisine. - Мы лю́бим ру́сскую ку́хню. - cuisine
We opened the door - Мы откры́ли дверь. - open
Wednesday - среда́
week - неде́ля (2-4 неде́ли, пять неде́ль)
Welcome! (To someone from out of town) - С прие́здом!; You're welcome - пожа́луйста
Well done! (Used with both genders; pl. молодцы́) - Молод(е́)ц!
well... - (intructory word) ну...
well - хорошо́
pretty well - неплохо
west - за́пад (на)
what - что; (adj.: which one) како́й (See 2.7, 4.5)
   What day is it? - Како́й сего́дня день?
   What did you say? - (formal) Как вы сказа́ли?; (familiar) Как ты сказа́л/а
   What do you advise (us, me) to order? - - Что вы (нам, мне) посове́туете взять?
   What else? - - Что ещё?
   What is (are) ... called? (said of things, not people) - Как называ́ется (называ́ются)...?
   What is ...'s name? - Как зову́т (+ accusative)? (See 7.7)
   What is ...'s nationality? - Кто по национа́льности (+ nominative)?
   What is ...'s profession? - Кто по профе́ссии (+ nominative)?
   What is that? - - Что э́то тако́е?
   What language - на како́м языке́ (вы говори́те, чита́ете, пи́шете) (do you speak, read, write; see 3.5)
   What languages - на каки́х языка́х (вы говори́те, чита́ете, пи́шете) (do you speak, read, write; see 3.5)
   What time is it? - Ско́лько сейча́с вре́мени?
   What's your name? - Как вас (тебя́) зову́т?
   What's your patronymic? - Как ва́ше о́тчество?
which - како́й (кака́я, како́е, каки́е)
when - когда́ (See 4.5)
where (at) - где; (to) - куда́ (See 5.4)

where from - отку́да
white - бе́лый
who - кто
whose - чей (чья, чьё, чьи) (See 2.4)
why - почему́
wife - жена́ (pl. жёны)
window - окно́ (pl. о́кна)
with pleasure - с удово́льствием
without - без (+ genitive)
woman (young) - де́вушка
women's; feminine - же́нксий
women's (men's, children's) merchandise - това́ры для же́нщин (мужчи́н, дете́й)
word - сло́во (pl. слова́)
work - (noun) - рабо́та (на); (verb) рабо́тать (рабо́та-ю, -ешь, -ют)
place of work - ме́сто рабо́ты
write - писа́ть/на- (пиш-у́, пи́ш-ешь, -ут) Write! (I'm awaiting your letter) - Жду письма́.
writer - писа́тель
written - пи́сьменный
written exercise - пи́сьменноеное упражне́ние

Y

year - год (2-4 го́да, 5 лет) (See 7.4)
   year(s) [old] (See 7.4) - 2-4 го́да; 5-20 лет with dative)
   last year - в про́шлом году́
yellow - жёлтый
Yerevan (city in Armenia) - Ерева́н
yes - да
you (formal and plural) - вы; (informal) ты (See 1.1)
You can't be serious! response to compliment - Что́ вы (ты)!
young - молодо́й
   young man (also used as a form of address) - молодо́й челове́к; young woman (also used as a form of address) - де́вушка
younger - мла́дший
younger (than someone by x years) - моло́же (+ genitive + на ... лет)(See 10.1)
your (formal or plural) - ваш (ва́ша, ва́ше, ва́ши); (informal) - твой (твоя́, твоё, твой)

INDEX

Accent. *See* Stress.

Accusative case

Forms

Plural modifiers and nouns *Book 1*: 111-13, 288

Pronouns and question words *Book 1*: 204

Singular modifiers and nouns *Book 1*: 111-113, 205-207

Uses

Direct object *Book 1*: 111, 205

On day of week - **в** *Book 1*: 126

Resemblance **похож на** *Book 1*: 298

Time expressions *Book 1*: 126, 304

With **звать** *Book 1*: 205

With prepositions

With **в, на** to express direction *Book 1*: 140-41, 301

With **через** and **назад** *Book 1*: 304

Adjectives *Book 1*: 47 - Ex. D, 59-61, 191

Declension tables *Book 1*: 319

Short *Book 1*: 126, 142

Soft-stem *Book 1*: 153; *Workbook 1*: Unit 2

Adverbs *Book 1*: 81, 130 - Ex. B

Word order *Book 1*: 81, 123

Age, expressing *Book 1*: 201

Agreement, grammatical *Book 1*: 60, 61, 78, 234

Alphabet *Book 1*: 4-9,

And Book 1: 86

Animate vs. inanimate nouns *Book 1*: 111, 205-207

Aspect. *See* Verbs, Aspect

Assimilation of consonants *Book 1*: 17; *Workbook 1*: Unit 5

Brother with numbers *Book 1*: 202

But Book 1: 86

Calendar, Russian *Book 1*: 124

Capitalization. *See* Punctuation.

Cases *Book 1*: 36; *See also* Accusative case; Dative case; Genitive case; Instrumental case; Nominative case; Prepositional case; Environments, grammatical

Children with numbers *Book 1*: 203

Clothing

Items of *Book 1*: 44-45,

Metric sizes *Book 1*: 220

Colors, names of *Book 1*: 153

Commas. *See* Punctuation.

Compliments, making and responding to *Book 1*: 73

Conjugation. *See* Verbs, Conjugation

Conjunctions

а, и, но *Book 1*: 86

где *Book 1*: Unit 3, 114

как *Book 1*: 114

когда *Book 1*: Unit 3

потому что *Book 1*: 114

что *Book 1*: Unit 3, 114

Consonants

Assimilation *Book 1*: 17; *Workbook 1*: Unit 5

Devoicing at end of words *Book 1*: 16; *Workbook 1*: Unit 5

Hard vs. soft *See* Palatalization.

Mutation *Book 1*: 198

Voiced vs. voiceless *Book 1*: 16-17

Currency, Russian *Book 1*: 269

Customs, passing through *Book 1*: 47-48

Dative case

Forms

Modifiers and nouns *Book 1*: 240-241

Pronouns and question words *Book 1*: 201

Uses

Age *Book 1*: 201, 242

Indirect object *Book 1*: 242

Subjectless constructions *Book 1*: 244, 270

With prepositions

по *Book 1*: 243

Day with numerals *Book 1*: 304

Days of the week *Book 1*: 126

Declension. *See* Cases.

Direct objects *Book 1*: 111

Educational system in Russia *Book 1*: 99, 104, 125, 286, 287

Endings *Book 1*: 36, 55, 61, 78-80

Environments, grammatical *Book 1*: 64, 81, 298, 301

Languages *Book 1*: 81-82

Families in Russia *Book 1*: 186, 187, 188

Family, members of *Book 1*: 180-181

Feminine. *See* Gender.

Fleeting vowels *Book 1*: 57 - note 3

Food, names of *Book 1*: 252-253, 259, 278-279

Formal vs. informal speech forms *Book 1*: 32, 155

Furniture, names of *Book 1*: 153

Future tense *Book 1*: 271-274; *See also* Verbs, Aspect.

Of *to be Book 1*: 271